THE APPROVED MENTAL HEALTH PROFESSIONAL PRACTICE HANDBOOK

Kevin Stone, Sarah Vicary and Tim Spencer-Lane

First published in Great Britain in 2020 by

Policy Press
University of Bristol
1-9 Old Park Hill
Bristol
BS2 8BB
UK
t: +44 (0)117 954 5940
pp-info@bristol.ac.uk
www.policypress.co.uk

British Library Cataloguing in Publication Data
A catalogue record for this book is available from the British Library

ISBN 978-1-4473-5152-8 paperback
ISBN 978-1-4473-5155-9 ePdf
ISBN 978-1-4473-5153-5 ePub

Cover design by Andrew Corbett
Front cover image: www.alamy.com

Printed and bound by CPI Group (UK) Ltd, Croydon, CR0 4YY

Contents

About the authors

Dr Kevin Stone is an Associate Head of the Department of Law at the University of the West of England (UWE), Bristol. He is a qualified and practising social worker and Approved Mental Health Professional (AMHP) within the South West region of the United Kingdom, and has been a social worker since 2003. He currently teaches law and practice on the AMHP programme at UWE, and was formerly the programme leader. His research agenda focuses on the AMHP role and the application of the Mental Health Act 1983. More recently his research has explored the experiences of Nearest Relatives undertaking the role, and what the barriers are for nurses becoming AMHPs. Kevin has published widely (see www.drkevinstone.com) and is the co-author of *The Best Interests Assessor Practice Handbook* (Policy Press, 2018).

Kevin2.stone@uwe.ac.uk
On Twitter: @AmhpResearch @KevinStoneUWE

Dr Sarah Vicary is Associate Head of School, Nations, in the School of Health, Wellbeing and Social Care, Faculty of Wellbeing, Education and Language Studies of The Open University. Sarah is a qualified registered social worker (registered as Sarah Matthews), having graduated with a Master's degree in Social Work in 1987. She has worked primarily in mental health services, including as a frontline practitioner, an Approved Social Worker, manager of a multidisciplinary mental health crisis service and a senior manager for inner city emergency mental health services. Sarah was for nine years a Mental Health Act Commissioner. She completed her PhD at the University of Manchester in which she explored the role and experiences of AMHPs. Sarah is widely published in social work and mental health. Her latest publications include Vicary, S., Young, A. and Hicks, S. (2019) '"Role over" or roll over? Dirty work, shift, and Mental Health Act assessments', *British Journal of Social Work*, 49(8), pp 2187–206, and Wiles, F. and Vicary, S. (2019) 'Picturing social work, puzzles and passion: exploring and developing transnational professional identities', *Social Work Education*, 38(1), pp 47–62.

Sarah.vicary@open.ac.uk
On Twitter: @sao_sarah

Tim Spencer-Lane is a lawyer who specialises in mental health, mental capacity and social care law. He led the Law Commission's review of the Deprivation of Liberty Safeguards, which reported in 2017. Tim was also in charge of the Law Commission's review of the regulation of health and social care professionals, and the review of adult social care which formed the basis of the Care Act 2014. He is currently on secondment to the Government Legal Department (Department of Health and Social Care), where he advises on mental health and capacity law. Tim is the author of the *Care Act Manual* (3rd edn, 2019, Sweet & Maxwell), a general editor of the *Encyclopedia of Social Services and Child Care Law*, a contributor to *Cross on Local Government Law*, and legal editor of *Community Care Inform*. He is also a senior lecturer at Kingston University, where he teaches on the Best Interests Assessor and Adult Safeguarding courses, and a long-standing Associate Lecturer at The Open University, where he teaches on Social Work Law.

t.spencer-lane@open.ac.uk

On LinkedIn: www.linkedin.com/in/tim-spencer-lane-90a01638/

Acknowledgements

To all the AMHPs who practise tirelessly in their duties, and
gain little or no acknowledgement for the role they undertake
in upholding people's human rights on a daily basis.

As authors, we would like to express our thanks specifically to Rachel Hubbard, Robert Lomax and Gill Ince, who were the original co-authors of this book. For Rachel and Robert, their love of writing took them in a different direction to commence doctoral study.

The authors would like to thank Andy Brammer, Derek Boothby, Sheena Morgan, David Chandler and Lou Winston for being critical friends to the book, as well as colleague AMHPs from across professions who shared their views and stories with us.

Kevin Stone would like once again to thank his wife, Helen Stone, for the understanding she has shown while he took the time to write another book, and also dedicates it in loving memory of his parents Gordon Stone (21 September 1934–7 August 2015) and Mavis Stone (4 May 1940–12 January 2020).

Sarah Vicary would like to acknowledge AMHP colleagues past and present, and especially Helen Taylor and Sue Heston with whom she trained all those years ago.

Tim Spencer-Lane would like to thank his family for their love and support.

Commonly used acronyms and abbreviations

Patient/Service User/Lived Experience = Person

★★★

ADASS	Association of Directors of Adult Social Services
AMCP (or AMCaP)	Approved Mental Capacity Professional (the new role under the Liberty Protection Safeguards which will replace the Best Interests Assessor under the Deprivation of Liberty Safeguards)
AMHP	Approved Mental Health Professional
ASW	Approved Social Worker
BASW	British Association of Social Workers
BBR	British Bill of Rights (proposed replacement for Human Rights Act 1998)
BIA	Best Interests Assessor
BOAT/COT	British Association and College of Occupational Therapists
CA	Care Act 2014
CAT	Care and Treatment
CCG	Clinical Commissioning Group
CMHT	Community Mental Health Team
CoP	Code of Practice (could be MCA, DoLS or MHA)
COP	Court of Protection
CPA	Care Programme Approach
CPD	continuing (or continual) professional development
CQC	Care Quality Commission
CRPD	(United Nations) Convention on the Rights of Persons with Disabilities
CSSIW	Care and Social Services Inspectorate Wales
CTO	Community Treatment Order
DH	Department of Health
DHSC	Department of Health and Social Care
DoLS	Deprivation of Liberty Safeguards
DOL	deprivation of liberty
EA	Equality Act 2010
ECHR	European Convention on Human Rights
ECtHR	European Court of Human Rights
EPA	Enduring Power of Attorney
EU	European Union
FTT	First Tier Tribunal

HCPC	Health and Care Professions Council
HIW	Healthcare Inspectorate Wales
HRA	Human Rights Act 1998
HSCIC	Health and Social Care Information Centre
IMCA	Independent Mental Capacity Advocate
IMHA	Independent Mental Health Advocate
LA	local authority
LPA	Lasting Power of Attorney
LPS	Liberty Protection Safeguards (proposed replacement for the Deprivation of Liberty Safeguards)
LSSA	Local Social Services Authority
MCA	Mental Capacity Act 2005
MHA	Mental Health Act 1983
MHRT	Mental Health Review Tribunal
MHRT1	First-Tier Mental Health Review Tribunal
MoJ	Ministry of Justice
NHS	National Health Service
NMC	Nursing and Midwifery Council
NR	Nearest Relative
OPG	Office of the Public Guardian
OT	Occupational Therapist
PACE	Police and Criminal Evidence Act 1984
PSRB	Professional Statutory and Regulatory Body
RCN	Royal College of Nursing
SOAD	Second Opinion Approved Doctor
SW	social worker
SWE	Social Work England (which has recently replaced the Health and Care Professions Council as the regulator of social workers in England)
UDHR	Universal Declaration of Human Rights

1

Introduction

Welcome to *The Approved Mental Health Professional Practice Handbook*. This book has been written to acknowledge the complexities of being an Approved Mental Health Professional (AMHP) and the decisions to be taken under the Mental Health Act 1983 (MHA). The book focuses on the practice of undertaking the role, as well as on training and continuing professional development (CPD). Engaging in MHA work is much broader than simply applying and interpreting mental health and other legislation correctly. This work requires an AMHP to focus on the practicalities, the ethical dilemmas involved and to engage in critical reflection to enable the outcomes for the person concerned to be at the forefront of the AMHP's thinking. This handbook has been written in consultation with practitioners and those who can be subject to the provisions of the Act (persons being assessed, carers, Nearest Relatives [NRs]) to include as many perspectives as possible. Where relevant, these narratives are included in the chapters.

This handbook is designed for those who have already been approved as AMHPs, trainees and those who manage and educate both. It aims to be both a practical and reflective guide as well as a resource to apply and critique the complexities of the role. It will draw on relevant legislation, case law, Codes of Practice and Reference Guides but is not intended to be a law text. We recommend reading it alongside one of a number of law texts that exist, such as Richard Jones' *Mental Health Act Manual* (Jones, 2019) or Brenda Hale's *Mental Health Law* (Hale, 2017). It is designed to complement these by offering a resource to explore the ethical and practical challenges of applying the law in practice as an AMHP. It offers tools and ideas based on the authors' and contributors' experiences of teaching, advising, working and researching as AMHPs.

At the time of writing mental health legislation is progressing through a process of change and, some might say, modernisation. We will draw your attention to the areas of change which have already been enacted and those which are still on the horizon. Where further change is still possible we have added a graphic to point you towards our online resources (to be found at https://policy. bristoluniversitypress.co.uk/the-approved-mental-health-professional-practice-handbook/online-resources) and you will see:

 Please see online resources for update

This is to indicate that if the law or policy changes during the lifetime of this first edition you will be able to find updates on the web page, which will be included in the next edition.

Undertaking an approved programme of educational study is the first stage in becoming a competent and effective AMHP. What then follows are the continuing approval meetings within the local authority (LA) (at least every five years), and the annual CPD, as well as the actual MHA work which stretches you as a professional and challenges your skills. We argue that no job description about the AMHP role will ever sufficiently detail the nature of the role nor cover the scenarios that AMHPs face. It is also very encouraging to report much contemporary research being undertaken by and for AMHPs, on topics such as: the sociological concept of dirty work (Morriss, 2015); reasons for becoming an AMHP (Watson, 2016); exploring differences and similarities between nurse and social work AMHPs (Stone, 2018); experiences of nurse AMHPs (Stone, 2019); shift and 'role over' (Vicary et al, 2019) and hybrid roles (Leah, 2019). Our aim is to include all of these current studies where appropriate to illustrate that AMHPs are vibrant, highly skilled individuals.

Throughout the book we will be highlighting relevant AMHP Key Competences from the English and Welsh AMHP Regulations.[1] Distinction will be drawn where there is divergence between the two countries (as they do differ). Although Social Work England (SWE) and Social Care Wales set criteria that AMHP trainees must meet to pass their programme of education, and standards that educational programmes must meet, the Key Competences within the Regulations are the standards which AMHP practice should adhere to. Therefore, we highlight the Key Competences at the beginning of each chapter as an indicative guide to what the chapter content will focus on. Regulation of AMHP education in England has moved from the Health and Care Professions Council (HCPC) to SWE which will continue to approve and monitor AMHP courses against the HCPC standards until they are reviewed by SWE. For Wales, AMHP regulation remains with Social Care Wales. A national AMHP workforce plan was published by the Office of the Chief Social Worker for Adults in November 2019 (Department of Health and Social Care, 2019) and, where appropriate, this report will be highlighted. Meanwhile, an All-Party Parliamentary Group has suggested that there needs to be a minimum number of AMHPs to tackle workforce shortages and ensure compliance with the legislation, and that AMHPs have been spending too much time sourcing hospital beds (APPG, 2019). The actual implementation of section 140 of the MHA, making provisions to secure appropriate resources where this is of 'special urgency' and for those 'who have not attained the age of 18 years', has been found wanting and attracted debate. Some areas have agreements between Clinical Commissioning Groups (CCGs) and Local Authorities, but largely implementation is patchy at best. It is hoped guidance will be forthcoming that builds on the recommendations of the Independent Review of the Mental Health Act (DH, 2018, p 120). These are examples of the topics covered in this text.

Terminology

We have already started using acronyms and abbreviations as we have explained the focus of this book. This is inevitable when discussing complex issues and systems. Hereafter, when we use key terms they will be given in full at the first mention in each chapter followed by the abbreviation in brackets – for example, Approved Mental Health Professional (AMHP) and the Mental Health Act 1983 (MHA) – and thereafter we use the abbreviations – AMHP and MHA – respectively. A list of abbreviations used commonly in AMHP practice appears at the start of the book for ease of reference.

Various terms used to identify the person who is being assessed under, or is subject to, the MHA can be identified in the wider mental health literature, such as 'service user', 'assessed person', 'survivor' and 'patient' (as used in the MHA). The authors recognise the importance of getting such terminology right and have opted to use the neutral term *person* in this book as offering the most non-stigmatising means to identify the person subject to the provisions of the MHA, and we apologise if the use of this term falls short of people's expectations. This view was reinforced when a person with lived experience reminded us:

> "… 'patient' … what I am trying to convey is the fact that any person subject to any mental health intervention is a person."

We will refer to family members as *relatives*, as defined by section 26(1) of the MHA, and those not so contained within section 26(1) as *wider family*. Those who are identified as a *carer* or *Nearest Relative* (NR) will be described as such.

This book does not cover any detail relating to medical diagnosis that might be found in the International Classification of Diseases (ICD10) or Diagnostic and Statistical Manual of Mental Disorders (DSM-5). This is because the AMHP needs to operate from a broader framework of mental disorder, as defined by section 1(2) of the MHA:

> 'mental disorder' means any disorder or disability of the mind; and 'mentally disordered' shall be construed accordingly.

Mental disorder is a legal concept, albeit based on a medical model of illness. However, in practice, the term should not be reduced to a purely medical paradigm of understanding and can and does include multiple perspectives as to how the phenomenon of mental ill health is expressed, understood and assessed. The concept of mental disorder under the MHA also has synergy with the concept of 'unsoundness of mind' in Article 5 of the European Convention on Human Rights (ECHR), although it is debatable whether they are an exact match. Article 5 requires that any deprivation of liberty must be based on 'objective medical expertise', thus reinforcing the medical model of illness in this sphere (*Winterwerp v Netherlands* 6301/73 [1979] ECHR 4). Where a diagnosis is stated, it will be referring to a medical diagnosis, while recognising that this is not the domain of the AMHP. Therefore, this book does not discuss medical treatment options for mental health that will be available to people as inpatients or when in the community.

The book also does not claim to offer easy answers to the ethical and practical dilemmas and difficulties that arise in everyday practice as an AMHP as a result of resourcing and structural challenges. Practice wisdom will inevitably need to be drawn on from more experienced colleagues and tested in court when the law does not cover all the scenarios that an AMHP may face.

We also do not cover Part III of the MHA, which encompasses 'Patients Concerned in Criminal Proceedings or Under Sentence', other than in relation to conditional discharge, which is discussed in Chapter 9. (Part III of the Act is going to be the focus of a future book.)

Guiding Principles

The Guiding Principles of the MHA in England and Wales should be the foundation of and the lens through which AMHPs work. Therefore, we have added them here at the beginning of this book to represent this importance. However, as they are located in the Codes of Practice for England and Wales, they do not have full weight of statute law or statutory instrument, but they should be followed, and departed from only if there are cogent reasons to do so. These Guiding Principles are set out in the box which follows, showing how they differ for England and Wales. These principles are discussed in more detail in Chapter 3.

ESSENTIAL KNOWLEDGE: LAW

Guiding Principles

England
- Least restrictive option and maximising independence
- Empowerment and involvement
- Respect and dignity
- Purpose and effectiveness
- Efficiency and equity

Wales
- Least restrictive option and maximising independence
- Empowerment and involvement
- Dignity and respect
- Effectiveness and efficiency

- Fairness, equality and equity
- Keeping people safe

These principles are expanded further within the respective Codes of Practice for each country which are available at:

England: https://assets.publishing.service.gov.uk/government/uploads/system/uploads/attachment_data/file/435512/MHA_Code_of_Practice.PDF

Wales: www.wales.nhs.uk/sites3/documents/816/Mental%20Health%20Act%201983%20Code%20of%20Practice%20for%20Wales.pdf

Structure of the book

This book is divided into three main parts, with chapters exploring key elements of the AMHP role relating to context, practice and theory. Each chapter will follow a similar format:

- Aims in relation to professional standards
- Main body of chapter, with boxes contained within for additional content including: case studies with discussion questions; commentaries or summaries on key topics; legislation and reflective activities
- A conclusion with a summary of the key messages, knowledge review activities and suggestions for further reading.

We have included at the end of the book a list of the case-law references that we have cited throughout the book, in alphabetical order. We would recommend that you familiarise yourself with this case law by reading the judgments for yourself, noting the legal arguments contained and the reasons the judges gave for the decisions they reached.

The remainder of the book is divided into three parts as we consider the AMHP in context, the AMHP in practice and, finally, AMHP theory. We have included research findings where evidence exists and have also highlighted where greater understanding is needed. To assist you in navigating the book we now include a short summary of each chapter.

Part 1: The AMHP in context

Chapter 2: Practice context

This chapter aims to consider the AMHP in context, and to explore issues and themes that arise. As probably one of the most powerful roles within England and Wales, the AMHP role is for good reason independent and autonomous.

On the one hand, an AMHP can be directed to consider a referral for an MHA assessment, yet on the other hand, an AMHP makes decisions independently and cannot be directed to use their powers. The AMHP is central to coordinating professionals and resources for the purpose of assessing need and risk and deciding if it is proportionate for a person to lose their liberty, even if temporarily. This chapter explores the historical background to the role, its interprofessional nature, and the process of becoming and remaining as an AMHP, along with issues relating to the lack of a national register and the unique contribution made by the AMHP role.

Chapter 3: Ethical context

Being aware of, applying and critically reflecting on ethics is fundamental to the AMHP role. In this chapter the ethical considerations which are fundamental to AMHP practice are discussed, including the ongoing debate about their impact, including questioning whether such work can ever be ethical. In addition, this chapter explores the values to be considered in relation to the balance and tension involved in AMHP practice, concepts that apply equally to those from all of the eligible professions who undertake the role and who, we suggest, need to be morally active practitioners. We also explore the concept of vicarious liability. The Guiding Principles as laid down in the legislation are fundamental to AMHP practice. However, in any given situation, one or more of the principles may have more importance than another and there will also be a tension between them. It will be shown therefore that the principles, while designed to inform decisions, do not determine them.

Chapter 4: Social perspectives in mental health

The causes, manifestations, maintenance and recovery from mental health distress are not clear cut, and there are different perspectives about mental disorder, primarily the binary of either the medical or the social model. An AMHP is required to have a critical understanding of both models but in particular is required to bring in the social perspective as a balance to the medical perspective and independence. For this reason, this chapter will explore these differing models to better understand their meaning for AMHP practice. It will explore the social perspective in relation to the medical and will also debate whether AMHP professionals from different backgrounds can bring this same perspective. Areas of practice such as the Equality Act 2010 and cultural competence will be examined, including the impact of urban and rural boundaries.

Chapter 5: The multi-professional context

This chapter explores the multi-professional AMHP examining who can now be approved to undertake the role. It will detail the regulations that apply and provide a brief analysis of the strengths and weaknesses of the diversification of professional background including whether there is a difference in the way these different professionals undertake the role and the attitude towards it by them and by others. The chapter will also include verbatim accounts by a sample of AMHPs in relation to this.

Part 2: The AMHP in practice

Chapter 6: Completing an MHA assessment

This chapter considers the differing stages of the MHA work, from taking the referral to making a decision to detain or negotiating least restrictive alternatives when considering detention and involvement in Community Treatment Orders (CTOs). Coordinating MHA assessments can be a complex piece of work to undertake. This chapter will consider all the relevant stages that need to be considered and arranged when setting up an MHA assessment, the MHA interview and the options to be considered when concluding the assessment. It also looks at the involvement of the Nearest Relative. This chapter should be read with Chapter 7, which considers the risks and challenges in MHA assessments.

Chapter 7: Risks and challenges in MHA assessments

MHA work inherently contains risks and challenges that an AMHP needs to manage as part of the MHA assessment. This chapter considers most of these as they are known at the time of writing. This chapter focuses on AMHP personal safety, what can be done when a person goes 'absent without leave', responding to safeguarding concerns and scrutinising detention papers, as well as some other niche areas. The reality is that new risks and challenges for MHA work are always emerging as society changes and modernises, so undoubtedly this chapter will need to be updated over time.

Chapter 8: Applying the interface between the MHA and the Mental Capacity Act

This chapter considers the relationship between the MHA and the Mental Capacity Act (MCA) 2005. There is considerable overlap between the two Acts, and the relationship can be extremely complex. This chapter sets out how the MCA enables care and treatment to be delivered when a person lacks capacity to consent, focusing in particular on the legal cover for decision-makers conferred by section 5 of the MCA. It then explores the three primary interfaces between the two Acts: first, inpatient care and treatment and the circumstances in which detention under the MHA will 'trump' the provisions of the MCA; secondly, deprivation of liberty in hospital for the purposes of care or treatment; and thirdly, community MHA powers (such as a Community Treatment Order) and how the MCA applies in such cases. The chapter also contemplates the Mental Capacity

(Amendment) Act 2019, which replaces the Deprivation of Liberty Safeguards with the Liberty Protection Safeguards, due to be introduced on 1 October 2020.

Chapter 9: The AMHP and community provisions

This chapter explores the occasions where AMHPs engage in community provisions, under the MHA other than through MHA assessments, and under other legislation. To enable people to remain in the community, the MHA permits a person's freedom to be restricted to enable community living, for example through CTOs, guardianship and conditional discharge. The chapter also considers the duty to provide aftercare services under section 117 of the MHA, as well as services under health and social legislation such as the Care Act 2014 and the Social Services and Well-being (Wales) Act 2014. It also considers the use of the inherent jurisdiction of the High Court to safeguard vulnerable adults and in some cases to deprive a person of their liberty.

Part 3: AMHP theory

Chapter 10: Upholding rights and anti-oppressive practice

This chapter explores the importance of upholding a person's rights as they interface with the mental health system and with ourselves as professionals. AMHPs are powerful professionals who can, when needed, and in the right circumstances, deprive a person of their liberty. Therefore, AMHPs have a need to be reflective and understand the frameworks that they work within. These frameworks can include upholding the rights of those who use mental health services not to be discriminated against, and to be protected from unequal and equitable approaches. Discrimination within mental services can manifest itself in many ways, through direct and indirect means, intentionally and unintentionally.

Chapter 11: Resilience as an AMHP

This chapter will consider what is needed to survive as an AMHP, both in training and in practice. First, it will focus on the practicalities and implications of an experienced member of staff returning to full-time study as an AMHP trainee, perhaps managing feelings of being de-skilled and frustrated by returning to education and having to undertake a placement within their own organisation. The chapter will go on to explore the value of becoming an AMHP, how this fits into continuing professional development, engagement with research and the maintenance of learning in this specialist role. All this is highly relevant; the AMHP role can be challenging, both physically and psychologically. There is then a need for AMHPs to reflect on how they maintain their resilience and self-esteem in diverse and complex situations, including conflict management, and acknowledging the emotional aspects of the role. Finally, there will be an emphasis on reflective practice as an AMHP and ensuring that practitioners know what sources of support are available.

Chapter 12: AMHP decision-making

This chapter considers the nature of the AMHP role in terms of its unique features and key decision-making responsibilities. AMHPs have to make significant decisions as part of their role, most obviously whether they apply for a person to be compulsorily admitted to hospital or not. However, AMHPs have to make a host of other practice decisions before and after the decision whether to detain under the Act, including involvement of the nearest relative and family, the correct form of transport, whether to use 14 days to decide to detain or not, protection of property, caring responsibilities, pets and so on. This chapter will support AMHPs to reflect on the factors that impact on their decision-making, introduce frameworks to support ethical decision-making and consider the role of interprofessional working in the AMHP context. It will also link to the discussions on risk and AMHPs understanding their own risk thresholds and the implications of this for practice.

Closing remarks: Looking forward

Mental health legislation in recent times has seen significant change, and we predict will continue to do so. We are anticipating a Bill to amend the MHA arising from the recommendations from the independent review of the MHA (DH, 2018), as well as changes to the MHA Codes of Practice. These closing remarks will consider what changes we can predict in the next few years and argue for what changes may still need to be made.

We hope that you will find this book beneficial as we draw as widely as possible from the existing resources.

Note

1   The relevant regulations are: the Mental Health (Approved Mental Health Professionals) (Approval) (England) Regulations 2008, SI 2008/1206; and the Mental Health (Approval of Persons to be Approved Mental Health Professionals) (Wales) Regulations 2008, SI 2008/2436.

Part 1
The AMHP in context

2

AMHP practice context

Chapter aim

This chapter will enable you to meet the following AMHP key competence themes:

- Articulating the role of the AMHP

- Working effectively in partnership

- Application of AMHP skills

- Professional decision-making

- Managing and communicating informed decisions

Schedule 2 of the Mental Health (Approved Mental Health Professionals) (Approval) (England) Regulations 2008 Key Competences 4(a)–(k), 5(a)–(i)

Schedule 2 of the Mental Health (Approval of Persons to be Approved Mental Health Professionals) (Wales) Regulations 2008 Key Competences 4.1–4.11, 5.1–5.6

Introduction

AMHPs are employed in varied employment contexts throughout England and Wales: working within dedicated AMHP teams in local authorities (LAs); embedded in National Health Service (NHS) trusts, including mental health community teams; or working sessionally on a rota. Such diversity means that service delivery can be different from area to area and these differences may be reflected in practice. Alongside this, AMHPs are working within a legislative and policy context which can be interpreted differently across geographical regions. Therefore, it is necessary for the AMHP to understand their working context, to recognise these differences and to reflect on how this impacts on their work. This chapter aims to consider the AMHP in context, and explores the issues and themes that arise.

The AMHP role is probably one of the most powerful within England and Wales, and therefore for good reason is independent and autonomous. On the one hand an AMHP can be directed to consider a referral for an MHA assessment, yet on the other hand an AMHP makes decisions independently and cannot be directed to use their powers. The AMHP is central to coordinating professionals and resources for the purpose of assessing need and risk, and deciding if it is proportionate for a person to lose their liberty, even temporarily. We return to the issues of independence and proportionality in Chapter 3.

Through the making of an application for detention founded on medical recommendation(s), an AMHP can remove a person's liberty: for up to 28 days (under MHA, s 2) or for up to six months, initially (under MHA, s 3). They can also restrict a person's movement through making a recommendation for a Community Treatment Order (CTO) or making an application for guardianship under section 7 of the MHA. All of these actions are interfering with the freedom of the person concerned to a greater or lesser degree, and where the interference amounts to a deprivation of liberty, the European Convention on Human Rights (ECHR) provides that the AMHP must act 'in accordance with a procedure prescribed by law' (ECHR, Art 5(1)). This procedure is set out in the MHA 1983 (as amended on several occasions, including by the MHA 2007), as explained by the accompanying Codes of Practice for England and Wales. The AMHP, when intervening in the life of the person being assessed, should also justify how this meets the requirements of Article 8(2) of the ECHR.

 ESSENTIAL KNOWLEDGE: LAW

Article 8 ECHR – Right to respect for private and family life

1. Everyone has the right to respect for his private and family life, his home and his correspondence.
2. There shall be no interference by a public authority with the exercise of this right except such as is in accordance with the law and is necessary in a democratic society in the interests of national security, public safety or the economic well-being of the country, for the prevention of disorder or crime, for the protection of health or morals, or for the protection of the rights and freedoms of others.

Therefore, an AMHP should always ask themselves what legal authority (statute, case law, guidance or practice codes) supports their actions and decision-making from referral through to admission, if that is required.

Historical background

The policy drivers for the creation of the AMHP role are complex. AMHPs have their roots in the Poor Laws, later enshrined in the Mental Health Acts of 1930 and 1959. Mental Welfare Officers (MWOs), as they were termed under the Mental Health Act 1959, and Duly Authorised Officers (DAOs), as they later became known, oversaw admissions to hospital. Meanwhile, the emergence of Psychiatric Social Workers (PSWs), a separate role, had its origins in nineteenth-century philanthropy. PSWs were predominantly female and undertook what they deemed to be therapeutic work. This distinction was blurred with the creation of unified local authority social services departments in 1971 which in effect brought together the procedural and therapeutic aspects. The MHA 1983 created the Approved Social Worker (ASW) and, it is suggested, a fillip for social work in mental health. However, continued uncertainty about the status and a lack of resources are said to have contributed to the reported stress experienced in the role (Hudson and Webber, 2012), leading, in turn, to declining numbers (McNicoll, 2016). The AMHP role was opened up to other non-medical professionals in part to mitigate that the ASW workforce was seen as being in decline and ageing, with most members near to retirement (Evans et al, 2005; Huxley et al, 2005a), the first narrative underpinning the policy changes. A second narrative focuses on new roles within mental health crossing traditional professional boundaries under the New Ways of Working policy, which was underpinned by competence, not profession, and the drive to share knowledge and skills across professional and practitioner boundaries (DH, 2007, p 10). Considering both narratives, it can be extrapolated that there was an intention to enable other professionals to undertake the 'approved' role and, by doing so, overcome any perceived predicted shortages while diversifying the role beyond social work towards development of an interprofessional workforce.

There are two studies which have had a fundamental influence on opening up the ASW role to other non-medical professions, and the aim of both was to explore the contribution of ASWs to mental health services. In the first of these studies (Huxley and Kerfoot, 1994) it was suggested that the role be opened up to probation officers, while in the second (Huxley et al, 2005b) it was suggested that the numbers of ASWs were in decline. The first formal recommendation to open up the ASW role to other allied health professionals was made by the Richardson Committee, the expert panel appointed to review the MHA (DH, 1999, p 46), arising from a desire to reflect the contemporaneous concern of integration as well as the supposed decline in numbers of social workers. The proposal was met with varied responses, based on perceptions about which profession was best suited to fulfil the role, not least fundamental aspects of it such as independence and emphasis on the social perspective. On the one hand, both of these aspects were said to fit with social work, which 'naturally' brings a social perspective (BASW, 2005) and independence of medical influence (Davidson and Campbell, 2010) (both are discussed in more detail in Chapter 4). On the other hand, it was suggested that other professionals are equally capable of holding these perspectives (DH, 2005; Hurley and Linsley, 2007).

Interprofessional nature

The interprofessional nature of the AMHP role occurs on two fronts: within the role and profession; and when working with other professionals and the public. Within the role, evidence has suggested that nurse and social work decision-making can be similar (Stone, 2018), and this echoes that AMHPs, regardless of their professional background, leave AMHP education with a very similar depth of knowledge, despite starting the AMHP educational programmes with differing levels of understanding of the AMHP role and function (Bressington et al, 2011). This is encouraging, as it potentially means that a diverse AMHP workforce can successfully exist if there is structural and political will to enable it to do so (Stone, 2018), although to date this is difficult to evidence due to low take-up of AMHPs who are not social workers (Bogg, 2011; ADASS, 2018).

AMHPs do not act or work alone but contribute to broader mental health services in England and Wales. An AMHP is required to effectively engage with the person, NRs, carers and wider family, alongside the interprofessional work undertaken with doctors, nurses and allied health professionals within LAs and NHS trusts.

When the AMHP agrees to accept a referral for an MHA assessment and coordinate both it and the MHA interview, there are legal and good practice requirements that will need to be considered. Depending on whether the person being assessed is known to mental health services or not, the local NHS Mental Health Trust and LA will have information that is needed to inform decisions. Unhelpfully, this may not all be stored or recorded in the same place and an AMHP may need to rely on others to access it. Some people who are assessed under the MHA may already be supported, for example through the Care Programme Approach (CPA) in England. Others may not be in receipt of services at all (see Chapter 9). The AMHP will need to liaise with secondary mental health services to establish when is the 'best' time to undertake the assessment and who should attend. Legal requirements such as gaining, and evidencing attempts to gain, doctors with prior acquaintance (although often the responsibility of the doctor to accept that they have had prior acquaintance), all require an AMHP to work interprofessionally and to be effective in doing so.

Becoming an AMHP

One of the contextual challenges for AMHPs is how they become AMHPs in the first place, and in turn how that professional status is gained and maintained. Although there is currently work under way on developing an AMHP workforce plan for England, there is no such work being undertaken for Wales. How the national workforce plan for England (Department of Health and Social Care, 2018) will be implemented and enforced is unknown at this stage. Therefore, at the time of writing there is currently a lack of evidence to support arguments that there is consistency across England and Wales as to how AMHPs are developed and retained. The inconsistency can be articulated in several areas:

- Routes into AMHP education and subsequent practice differ; local authorities and NHS services from where AMHP trainees are recruited are not standardised.
- Approved educational programmes to educate and train AMHPs differ (although all need to meet the Health and Care Professions Council (HCPC) approval criteria in England, which have now been transferred to Social Work England, and the criteria for Wales as provided by Social Care Wales).
- Processes for gaining approval to practise once the programme of study has been successfully completed differ.
- There are differing CPD requirements for re-approval to practise in the role each year (see later under 'Continuing professional development').
- There is no national register of AMHPs in England and Wales; it is each local authority's responsibility to keep a record of each AMHP it approves and not the responsibility of a central government agency.

To train as an AMHP you need sufficient experience in mental health practice to be able to be effective in your role and to understand the context in which you will be working. What can be offered as experience will differ as to whether the applicant for training is currently working in an NHS mental health team as a social worker and care coordinator, say, as compared to a social worker working with a generic adults team within an LA, or a child protection social worker who has worked with parents with mental health difficulties. All may have valid experience but this will need to be articulated differently. People who make decisions on who to accept onto training programmes will need to be mindful of these transferable skills and not just look for traditional applicants, or rely on traditional routes into AMHP training.

REFLECTIVE ACTIVITY

Case studies: Alison and Jacob

1. **Alison** has worked for the majority of her career as a children and families social worker. During her career she has worked with numerous families where the parents have had mental health difficulties, and some have been detained. Although her primary focus is the children, she has worked alongside mental health services when assessing parenting capacity. Alison has become aware that the local AMHP service are looking for trainees, and are particularly looking for applicants with children and families

backgrounds as they are seeing more children and young people requiring assessments in the place of safety suite or in the community and want to develop capability in this area.

    – Does Alison have enough experience in mental health practice to apply to become an AMHP, and why?

2.   **Jacob** has worked as an inpatient mental health nurse on an acute ward and wants to train to become an AMHP. He has never worked in the community as he graduated to the ward, but is very familiar with working with people when they are most distressed and has been involved in MHA processes on the ward.

    – Does Jacob have enough experience in mental health to apply to become an AMHP, and why?

Currently there are 19 HCPC-approved AMHP educational training programmes across England (HCPC website, 2019, accessed July 2019) and one Care Council for Wales-approved programme for Wales. Each programme is different, but higher education institutions must demonstrate that they meet the HCPC/Care Council for Wales criteria before they can accept trainees onto their programmes. The reason that we raise this is because these criteria differ from the AMHP Regulations that are in the statutory instruments under the MHA. Although the two documents relate to each other, they are different, as the HCPC criteria set out what a trainee must do to prove their competence to pass the approved programme of study, and the regulations detail the expectation of AMHP competency for those practising in the role. As an AMHP it is advisable to keep your eye tuned to the competences in the MHA Regulations.

Gaining approval

Another area of variable AMHP workforce policy is the process by which an AMHP progresses to become approved by their LA following their initial AMHP education. This process is not centralised, partly due to a lack of evidence or framework to suggest, or regulate, a system that every LA should follow, or even to indicate from whom that authority arises.

Continuing professional development

For an AMHP to maintain currency of practice and knowledge, ongoing training is required by the AMHP Regulations 2008. For AMHPs approved within England, the relevant regulation states:

in each year the AMHP is approved, the AMHP shall complete at least 18 hours of training agreed with the approving LSSA [local social services authority] as being relevant to their role as an AMHP. (Mental Health (Approved Mental Health Professionals) (Approval) (England) Regulations 2008, reg 5(a))

However, this differs for Welsh-approved AMHPs, where there is even greater onus placed on the local authority to decide not only what that training should be but the number of hours to be demonstrated annually:

> the AMHP must complete whilst he or she remains approved such training as required by the approving LSSA, at such intervals as determined by the LSSA as being necessary. (Mental Health (Approval of Persons to be Approved Mental Health Professionals) (Wales) Regulations 2008, reg 7(a))

The challenge is that what constitutes such approved local authority training is not standardised either nationally or within England and Wales but delegated to each local authority to decide. For example, could child protection training be considered appropriate training? Some may argue that it could, but others that this training lies within the substantive professional role (ie nursing or social work) and so cannot be counted as agreed AMHP training. Also, as MHA, section 114ZA(3) (for England) and MHA, section 114A(4) (for Wales) state:

> The functions of an approved mental health professional shall not be considered to be 'relevant social work' for the purposes of Part 4 of the Care Standards Act 2000 (in England), and Parts 3 to 8 of the Regulation and Inspection of Social Care (Wales) Act 2016.

Therefore, a view needs to be taken as to whether training hours can be double-counted: once for the AMHP's substantive role as a professional for the purposes of professional registration, and then as an approved AMHP seeking re-approval.

The lack of a national register

Just as there is no national standard for continuing training, at the time of writing there is no national registration for AMHPs to record who they are or where they are located. One of the implications of this is that it is not known with any certainty how many AMHPs are approved at any given time, or in turn actually undertaking the role, either within England or Wales. These statistics are held locally by each approving authority, but there is no requirement as yet for these to be collected on a national level. The All-Party Parliamentary Group on Social Work and the British Association of Social Workers (APPG, 2019) are recommending that the AMHP workforce be strengthened by making the number of AMHPs per capita a statutory matter within any revisions to the MHA. While this would be welcomed by most, geographical and local needs should also shape how workforce threshold levels are set as clearly rural and urban needs will differ. The lack of a national register has also potentially hampered the ability to establish quantitatively rather than anecdotally if the workforce is in decline (Huxley et al, 2005a; Hudson and Webber, 2012; McNicoll, 2016).

Although the provision of a national register may change with the introduction of the forthcoming regulatory body Social Work England, there is no certainty at this stage, and of course different regulations apply in the devolved nations of the United Kingdom. Also, although any registration may improve the current gap in knowledge, it may not be welcomed by other professionals who may then have also to register with Social Work England in addition to their own professional body (such as the Nursing Midwifery Council (NMC) or HCPC) and be subject to further fees. The lack of a central registration process has also hindered research in this field, as there is a lack of ability to establish a reliable national sampling frame. The 'problem' is not a new one: Huxley and Kerfoot (1994) reported that calculating the numbers of ASWs or distribution of them was a complicated issue, either to explore or explain.

MHA law specialists

AMHPs are often seen by some as experts on mental health law, particularly on the process for compulsory admission to hospital, and they are seen to make a unique contribution to community mental health teams (Bailey and Liyanage, 2010). However, care should be taken; an AMHP is not giving legal advice, nor is an AMHP's view an appropriate substitute for gaining independent advice via local authority legal services. The fact that AMHPs are frequently asked for a legal opinion perhaps suggests the high regard in which they are held, and, moreover, reinforces the unique position they hold in the mental health system. It is also a role that some commentators report AMHPs perceive in sociological terms as both dirty and prestigious (Morriss, 2015), involving attempts to shift responsibility from others, usually medics (Vicary et al, 2019).

Articulating the AMHP role

The AMHP will need to be able to explain their role in an MHA assessment to a wide audience to enable them to understand it, for instance, to the person themselves, to the person's family and also to professionals, who may demand more technical representations of what the AMHP is responsible for. The skills required in order to do so should not be understated and could differ whether explaining to carers, NRs, families or professionals. In all cases it needs to be made clear that:

- undertaking an MHA assessment is not a procedural matter which has a determined outcome;
- a decision to detain must be proportionate to the risks and needs presented; and

- a decision should not be one led by resources, although availability or lack of such will impact on any assessment.

The AMHP should make it clear that they are always undertaking their work on behalf of the local authority (MHA, s 114(10)(a) for England, and s 114(10(b) for Wales) and not, for instance, for the hospital managers or the NHS trust. But, importantly, the AHMP acts as an independent decision-maker, who cannot be directed by the LA to make a particular decision, and nor can their decisions be overturned by the LA.

▶ KEY MESSAGES

- The development of the AMHP role has a complex contextual background fuelled by policies to integrate the workforce.

- AMHPs now hail from four non-medical professional backgrounds.

- While approval programmes are regulated nationally in England and Wales, the mandatory requirement for continuing professional development is not, and nor is there a national register of AMHPs.

KNOWLEDGE REVIEW

- The AMHP is an interprofessional role which can be undertaken by registered mental health and learning disability nurses, occupational therapists, social workers and chartered psychologists.

- The AMHP is an advanced role working in differing work contexts within social care and health teams.

- During the period of approval and re-approval AMHPs must complete continuing professional development as agreed by the approving local authority.

FURTHER READING

- Department of Health (2005) *Reform of the Mental Health Act: Summary of consultation responses,* London: Department of Health.

- Huxley, P. and Kerfoot, M. (1994) 'A survey of Approved Social Work in England and Wales', *British Journal of Social Work,* 24(3), pp 311–24.

- Huxley, P., Evans, S., Webber, M. and Gately, C. (2005) 'Staff shortages in the mental health workforce: the case of the disappearing Approved Social Worker', *Health and Social Care in the Community*, 13(6), pp 504–13.

- Matthews, S. (2014) 'Underpinning themes, theories and research', in S. Matthews, P. O'Hare and J. Hemmington (eds) *Approved mental health practice: Essential themes for students and practitioners*, Basingstoke: Palgrave Macmillan.

3

The ethical context

This chapter will include exploration of ethical issues for AMHP practice including:

- proportionality;
- types of ethics;
- the ethical nature of the existence of mental health legislation and how this is reflected in reviews of it;
- vicarious liability;
- Guiding Principles; and
- the concepts of good faith and reasonable care, including the *Bolam* test.

Introduction

Robert Johns' opening chapter in his book exploring ethics and law for social workers (Johns, 2016) is titled 'But I want to be a social worker, not a philosopher!' This exclamation captures the ultimate challenge faced by all social workers, which is perhaps brought into sharp relief for AMHPs, who must practise within a legal and ethical context, especially when dealing with the accompanying dilemmas that can arise. Ethics, a subdivision of philosophy, is concerned with moral issues, including the concepts of right and wrong. AMHPs make decisions, taking into consideration all the circumstances of the situation, which means that they must know how to weigh up ethical dilemmas proportionally when applying the law while also ensuring that they can account for their decisions. In doing so, AMHPs must follow their relevant professional codes of conduct or standards. These include:

- the Health and Care Professions Council's *Standards of Conduct, Performance and Ethics* (HCPC, 2016), which apply to registered social workers, occupational therapists and psychologists;
- the Nursing and Midwifery Council's *The Code* (NMC, 2018);
- the *Mental Health Act 1983: Code of Practice for Wales* (Welsh Assembly Government, 2016), which applies to social workers in Wales;
- the College of Occupational Therapists' (2015) *Codes of Ethics and Professional Conduct*;
- the British Association of Social Workers' *Code of Ethics for Social Work* (BASW, 2018); and
- the British Psychological Society's (2018) *Codes of Ethics and Conduct*.

What are ethics?

Being aware of, applying and critically reflecting on ethics are fundamental to the AMHP role. Some view the relationship between law and ethics as an uneasy marriage (Dickens, 2013), while others question whether roles such as that of the AMHP can ever be ethical, balancing, as it does, the need for intervention with the possible removal of a person against their wishes (Kinney, 2009). Applying ethics to social work, Dickens (2013, pp 46–55) has identified four ethical approaches, which are paraphrased below:

- **Kantian ethics, or deontology**: holds that a person must be treated as a rational being capable of choice. In social work terms, this is developed into respect for the person and self-determination. It supports the belief that the law should allow intervention only when necessary to protect the person and others.
- **utilitarian ethics**: holds that the law does not justify disregarding a person's rights but may justify overruling them provided proper safeguards and processes are followed based on the belief that the right action is that which promotes the greatest good of the greatest number.

- **virtue ethics**: holds that the role of law is to create the conditions for a person to act virtuously.
- **care ethics**: emphasises the centrality of caring human relationships as the foundation for moral behaviour.

For the AMHP role in particular, Bogg (2014, pp 92–3) identifies two ethical approaches:

- **teleology**: where the management of risk to the individual or to other people becomes the primary concern; and
- **deontology**: where the action is of equal importance to the outcome.

That mental health legislation exists is an ongoing ethical debate in itself, justified by several notions ranging from benevolence, whereby the state wishes to ensure the health of its members, through to therapeutic justifications, whereby the state is deemed to have the right to protect itself to ensure the collective wellbeing. The rationale for mental health legislation is often captured in reviews of the legislation. In England and Wales, one such early review, undertaken by a Royal Commission set up in 1954 known as the Percy Commission after its chair, made recommendations that still characterise the ethical basis of the MHA today. Several statements which appear in its summary are listed below (Percy Commission, 1957, pp 1–20):

- In our view, individual people who need care because of mental disorder should be able to receive it as far as possible with no more restriction of liberty or legal formality than is applied to people who need care because of other types of illness.
- Mental disorder makes many patients incapable of protecting themselves or their interests, so that if they are neglected or exploited it may be necessary to have authority to insist on providing them with proper care.
- [Mental disorder] affects the patient's behaviour in such a way that it is necessary in the interests of other people or of society to insist on removing him for treatment even if he is unwilling.

While the language may now seem a little dated, the ethical approach resonates with contemporary thinking. The concept of proportionality as reflected, for instance, in Article 8 of the European Convention on Human Rights (ECHR) is the principle that the state and its officers should intervene only as much as necessary to achieve a legitimate goal, perhaps best captured for AMHPs under the principle of least restriction, or of seeking the least restrictive alternative.

Are ethics the same as values?

Banks (2001) defines values as a set of fundamental moral or ethical principles to which social workers are committed. Echoing Dickens (2013), Banks too suggests that these principles are a combination drawn from Kantian and utilitarian traditions. As referred to above, social work values are contained in Codes produced by regulatory bodies and professional associations as a means of regulating the power of social workers and providing protection for the person. However, just as with the law, these Codes do not give answers to problems that arise in practice. Banks (2001) points out that, aside from the general ethical issues, there are those that involve two conflicting ethical principles. Although not exhaustive, the following list outlines the values and also hints at the balance and tension involved in social work and AMHP practice:

- Rights and responsibilities
- Empowerment and anti-oppressive practice
- Respecting diversity and responding appropriately to difference
- Partnership
- Accountability and vicarious responsibility

The morally active practitioner

Banks (2001) coins the term 'morally active practitioner': one who uses their own reflection, advice through supervision, and research evidence to consider carefully any decisions that have to be made. We will explore the use of supervision later in Chapter 7.

REFLECTIVE ACTIVITY

Reflection on morally active practice

– Take a few moments to consider how your personal and professional values impact on your decision-making. What are the consequences?

– How has your professional training and membership of a professional body influenced your view of mental disorder and the interventions that may be needed when working with a person or their carer in a mental health scenario?

Decision-making by an AMHP demands working as a morally active practitioner, whereby questions are asked of one's own, and also of commonly accepted, practices in the light of the core ethical dilemmas and tensions that arise. Is it possible to detain a person against their will in an *empowering* manner?

Vicarious liability

The doctrine of vicarious liability refers to the legal responsibility of a person for the actions of another party who was under their control which caused injury to a third party. It most commonly arises in the employment context. In essence, employers are responsible for the actions or omissions of their employees committed during the course of employment. However, in some cases employers can be absolved of this responsibility, for instance if the employee is acting in a personal capacity. For AMHPs the situation is more profound. AMHPs must be independent of the detaining or responsible authority and are approved to act by an LA even when they are working within the NHS. The AMHP acts 'on behalf' of the local authority, and therefore the authority will be vicariously liable for any lack of care or bad faith (*TTM v Hackney LB* [2010] EWHC 1349 (Admin) at [35]).

Guiding Principles for the MHA and the MCA 2005

MHA Guiding Principles

The amendments made to the MHA in 2007 included a requirement for the Codes of Practice for England and Wales to include a statement of principles and a list of matters that the principles should address. These principles are used to support best practice and provide a framework which AMHPs should always have regard to. In short, the Act tells us what to do, the Codes tell us how and the principles give guidance as to how to apply both. While this may seem a simplistic explanation, decisions that have to be made can be complex and always concern unique circumstances according to the individual. The Guiding Principles are fundamental to AMHP practice but, in any given situation, one or more of these principles may have more importance than others, and there will also be a tension between them. These principles, therefore, while designed to inform decisions do not determine them. The responsibility for decision-making rests with the AMHP, whose practice may be questioned if the law, its principles and guidance are not seen to be applied.

 **ESSENTIAL KNOWLEDGE: LAW**

Force of the Guiding Principles

While section 118 of the MHA underpins this approach, the Guiding Principles are set out in the Codes of Practice for England and Wales rather than on the face of statute. Case law has confirmed that MHA decision-makers should always consider the guidance in the Codes with great care, and should depart from it only if they have cogent reasons for doing so (*R (Munjaz) v Mersey Care NHS Trust* [2005] UKHL 58; [2006] 2 AC 148 at [21]). However, even statutory principles (such as those in section 1 of the Mental Capacity Act [MCA] 2005) are normally worded in such a way as to give the decision-maker a degree of flexibility in how to apply them. Therefore, in practice, the force of the principles in the MHA Codes is not dissimilar to the force of those contained in the MCA 2005.

It is important to note that 'persons', as referred to in section 118, covers roles other than just AMHPs. Also included are: approved clinicians, and managers and staff of hospitals, independent hospitals and care homes. However, the Codes of Practice do not apply to all professionals who are involved in MHA work. Those not covered include:

- commissioners of health services;
- the police;
- ambulance services; and
- others in health and social services (including in the independent and voluntary sectors) involved in commissioning or providing services to people who are, or may become, subject to compulsory measures under the Act.

For the groups identified above, the Codes are not statutory guidance, but as they are still beneficial to these persons in carrying out their duties, it is recommended they receive training on the Codes and ensure that they are familiar with the requirements (DH, 2015a; Welsh Assembly Government, 2016).

Just as with our consideration of ethical differences, principles or values can mean different things to different people.

 ESSENTIAL INFORMATION: LAW

The Mental Health Act 1983 Guiding Principles as a framework

The Guiding Principles are found in the Code of Practice for England, paragraphs 1.2–1.24 and in paragraphs 1.1–1.31 of the Welsh Code.

In the following table, the summaries for each principle are taken mainly from the English Code of Practice for convenience.

Principle title	Narrative*
Purpose (in Wales this is referred to as 'the keeping people safe principle')	Decisions under the Act must be taken with a view to minimising the undesirable effects of mental disorder, by maximising the safety and wellbeing (mental and physical) of patients, promoting their recovery and protecting other people from harm.
Least restriction (in Wales this is referred to as 'the least restrictive option and maximising independence principle')	People taking action without a person's consent must attempt to keep to a minimum the restrictions they impose on a person's liberty, having regard to the purpose for which the restrictions are imposed.
Respect (in Wales this is referred to as 'the dignity and respect principle')	People taking decisions under the Act must recognise and respect the diverse needs, values and circumstances of each patient, including their race, gender, age, sexual orientation and any disability. They must consider the patient's views, wishes and feelings (whether expressed at the time or in advance), so far as they are reasonably ascertainable, and follow these wishes wherever practicable and consistent with the purpose of the decision. There must be no unlawful discrimination.
Participation (in Wales this is referred to as 'the empowerment and involvement principle')	Patients must be given the opportunity to be involved, as far as is practicable in the circumstances, in planning, developing and reviewing their own treatment and care to help ensure that it is delivered in a way that is as appropriate and effective for them as possible. The involvement of carers, family members and other people who have an interest in the patient's welfare should be encouraged (unless there are particular reasons to the contrary) and their views taken seriously.
Effectiveness, efficiency and equity (in Wales this is referred to as 'the effectiveness and efficiency principle')	People taking decisions under the Act must seek to use the resources available to them and to patients in the most effective, efficient and equitable way, to meet the needs of patients and achieve the purpose for which the decision was taken.
Fairness, equality and equity (Wales only)	This involves recognising diverse needs, avoiding unlawful discrimination, making reasonable adjustments and ensuring effective communication (including by offering the use of the Welsh language).

* The narrative is paraphrased from Care Services Improvement Partnership/ National Institute for Mental Health in England (2007).

MCA 2005 principles

The principles to be followed under the MCA 2005 are embedded within the Act itself in section 1, and not contained within Codes of Practice as for the MHA. See earlier box, 'Force of the Guiding Principles', for further discussion of this point.

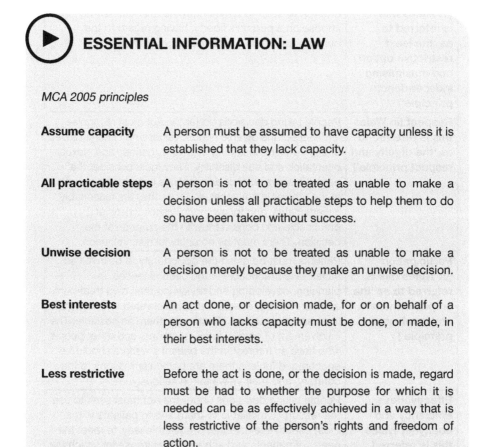

ESSENTIAL INFORMATION: LAW

MCA 2005 principles

Assume capacity	A person must be assumed to have capacity unless it is established that they lack capacity.
All practicable steps	A person is not to be treated as unable to make a decision unless all practicable steps to help them to do so have been taken without success.
Unwise decision	A person is not to be treated as unable to make a decision merely because they make an unwise decision.
Best interests	An act done, or decision made, for or on behalf of a person who lacks capacity must be done, or made, in their best interests.
Less restrictive	Before the act is done, or the decision is made, regard must be had to whether the purpose for which it is needed can be as effectively achieved in a way that is less restrictive of the person's rights and freedom of action.

It is worth noting at this stage that the fifth principle of the MCA uses the word 'less' in relation to the restrictive option, and the MHA principles use the term 'least'. However, the MHA Code in England makes clear in the description that it is referring to less restrictive options rather than only the least.

Application of the Guiding Principles

REFLECTIVE ACTIVITY

Case study: Jimmy

Jimmy has a long-standing medical diagnosis of bipolar disorder but has also recently been diagnosed with having a cancerous growth on his neck which needs attention. He is, however, refusing to accept any treatment for his physical illness.

Questions
- What should be taken into account for this person's overall well-being?
- Consider the purpose principle. How might it apply in this situation?

Purpose principle
When considering detention of a person under the MHA, all aspects of their care have to be considered. Therefore, the person's physical health as well as overall wellbeing needs to be addressed. However, the purpose of the use of the Act is the assessment of mental disorder. It cannot be used to enforce treatment for physical illness, although AMHPs have a responsibility to consider how this may interact with mental welfare. Risk assessment and the management of risk is a paramount importance of this principle.

REFLECTIVE ACTIVITY

Case study: Javid

Javid, who is from an ethnic minority community, is living alone. He has a history of drug use, but also has periods of abstinence. Javid's behaviour changed recently, becoming more irritable and impulsive. His relatives are becoming concerned, as although they have seen this behaviour before, he has lost a lot of weight, and some of his belongings appear to be missing. His sister has been staying with him, and she has noticed he is not sleeping, as he believes neighbours are wanting to harm him and he has taken to carrying a knife to protect himself. He has also been seen muttering. His sister has additionally noted that he is getting a lot of visitors. Javid's sister contacts his GP for advice.

Questions
- Does Javid require an MHA assessment?
- Does the referral suggest hospital admission may be needed?
- Consider the least restriction and respect principles.

Application of least restriction principle
All assumptions should be suspended in order to provide a service that is fair, equitable and offers the least restriction for the person, as you consider all the options.

Application of respect principle
Diversity has to be acknowledged. This will be especially the case for patients such as those from ethnic minorities who are disproportionately over-represented in applications for detention. The wishes and feelings of the person must be taken into account. There must be a respect for diversity.

REFLECTIVE ACTIVITY

Case study: John

John is an older person, who, up to recently, had lived with his wife of 40 years until she died three months ago. His children currently live away, having moved away due to work. John has recently been calling his children in a distressed state, commenting that he cannot see any point in living. The family are concerned as John is a retired chemist and is familiar with toxins. One of his children has taken him to the GP, and now he is being offered support by the local community mental health team, but John refuses to engage effectively, as he says he is not listened to, and does not need any help. John has started just sitting in his armchair surrounding himself with photographs.

Questions
- What are appropriate services for John?
- What does his refusal to engage mean?
- Consider the participation principle.

Application of participation principle

Where practicable, people should be involved in planning and developing their own care. This should also include carers and family members, all of whose views should be taken seriously unless there are particular reasons why this should not happen.

REFLECTIVE ACTIVITY

Case study: Emily

Emily is a 15-year-old child who has been taken to a place of safety after having been found walking next to a train line. Police were called by a member of the public. Emily told the police that she was following the fairies to the flower bed. She was very cooperative with the police but became sexually disinhibited, requiring female police officers to attend. Emily had no sense of danger and at one point was seen sitting on the rails. Emily has recently been preparing for exams in school. Her parents have informed the police that Emily has been very stressed. Staff at the place of safety are concerned that she has become psychotic, and would prefer she was moved to the children's hospital but the hospital has refused to accept Emily.

Questions
–   What resources are appropriate for Emily?
–   Consider the effectiveness, efficiency and equity principle.

Application of effectiveness, efficiency and equity principle

Where practicable, Emily should be admitted to a resource that is appropriate to her age that gives an equal focus to her physical and mental health. As she is a child, children and young people's services should be informed and work together to develop a plan, moving forwards.

In short, these Guiding Principles should be used to inform decision-making. No one principle carries more weight than another. What might be guided by principle is not always possible in practice, however.

Good faith and reasonable care

The nature of an ethical dilemma is that all outcomes may have an actual or perceived negative outcome for someone, to some degree. It is in these circumstances, and where there is no clear answer, that AMHPs can find themselves feeling stressed, under pressure and vulnerable. Couple this with the need to act quickly, balance priorities, and with limited or sometimes no resources, and it is no surprise that the impact of decision-making can be negative. Nonetheless, AMHPs will find themselves in situations where decisions need to be made and cannot be delayed. The MHA offers to those who undertake 'any act purporting to be done in pursuance of this Act' (such as an AMHP) protection under section 139(1) as long as that act was undertaken in 'good faith' and with 'reasonable care'. The issues that surround decision-making are examined further in Chapter 12.

 ESSENTIAL KNOWLEDGE: LAW

MHA, section 139(1)

No person shall be liable, whether on the ground of want of jurisdiction or on any other ground, to any civil or criminal proceedings to which he would have been liable apart from this section in respect of any act purporting to be done in pursuance of this Act or any regulations or rules made under this Act unless the act was done in bad faith or without reasonable care.

It is always important for an AMHP to document clearly the reasons for any decisions made. If there is time, it is also important to discuss the decision with others (including other AMHPs), and record that you have done so. It is suggested that a useful way of framing such discussion could be through the so-called '*Bolam* test' to establish if the course of action is accepted as being in 'accordance with a practice accepted as proper by a responsible body'. The *Bolam* test applies to, and arises from, clinical negligence legal cases, but can also be adapted for AMHP purposes. The test provides that:

> [A doctor] is not guilty of negligence if he has acted in accordance with a practice accepted as proper by a responsible body of medical men skilled in that particular art … Putting it the other way round, a man is not negligent, if he is acting in accordance with such a practice, merely because there is a body of opinion who would take a contrary view. (*Bolam v Frien Hospital Management Committee* [1957] 1 WLR 583, 587)

This specific case concerned a man who suffered from serious injury as a result of electroconvulsive therapy. He sued the hospital body for negligence for not giving him a muscle relaxant, not restraining him, and not warning him about the risks involved. However, the court accepted that there was a firm body of medical opinion which supported this practice, and moreover that not warning the patient of the 'remote risks' was justified as it would have led to the patient refusing the treatment.

The implication for the AMHP role is that a '*Bolam* discussion' offers a means of demonstrating clearly that your decision has been fully considered and is reasonable, and represents a course of action that is accepted as proper by a body of professional opinion. In particular, by ascertaining and having regard to the views of other AMHPs, you are more likely to be able to show that your final decision is professionally defensible and has been undertaken in good faith.

As a matter of law, the *Bolam* test has been developed subsequently by the courts. In *Bolitho v City and Hackney Health Authority* [1997] 4 All ER 771, for example, it was acknowledged that in rare cases a judge is entitled to conclude that the body of opinion is not reasonable or responsible and therefore cannot provide the standard by which the doctor's conduct will be assessed. Moreover, the Supreme Court in *Montgomery v Lanarkshire Health Board* [2015] UKSC 11 confirmed that when it comes to informed consent, the *Bolam* test no longer applies; instead, the test is whether a reasonable person in the patient's position would be likely to attach significance to the risk, or the doctor is (or should be) reasonably aware that the particular patient would be likely to attach significance to it. Nevertheless, considering the *Bolam* test may still be a useful tool for AMHPs in demonstrating that they have followed best practice.

▶ KEY MESSAGES

- Ethical considerations are fundamental to AMHP practice. There is an ongoing debate about their impact, including questioning whether such work can ever be ethical.

- In addition, the values which need to be considered also hint at the balance and tension involved in AMHP practice and apply equally to all members of the eligible professions, who need to be morally active practitioners and understand the concept of vicarious liability.

- The Guiding Principles contained within the Code of Practice are fundamental to AMHP practice but in any given situation, one (or more) of the principles may have more importance than another and there will also be a tension between them. These principles, therefore, while designed to inform decisions do not determine them.

 KNOWLEDGE REVIEW

- Different types of ethical approaches underpin AMHP practice and have also influenced review of mental health legislation, including the very existence of such legislation.

- The Guiding Principles contained within the Code of Practice should be adhered to, when undertaking MHA work.

 FURTHER READING

- Bogg, D. (2014) 'Ethics and values', in S. Matthews, P. O'Hare and J. Hemmington (eds) *Approved mental health practice: Essential themes for students and practitioners*, Basingstoke: Palgrave Macmillan, pp 86–98.

- Kinney, M. (2009) 'Being assessed under the 1983 Mental Health Act: Can it ever be ethical?', *Ethics and Social Welfare*, 3, pp 329–39.

4

Social perspectives in mental health

Chapter aim

This chapter will enable you to meet the following AMHP key competence themes:

- Articulating and demonstrating in practice a social perspective on mental health

- Application of knowledge of mental disorder

- Application of skills for working in partnership

- Application of skills: making and communicating informed decisions

Schedule 2 of the Mental Health (Approved Mental Health Professionals) (Approval) (England) Regulations 2008
Key Competences 3(a)–(d), 4(a), (f), (g), (h), 5(a), (g), (h)

Schedule 2 of the Mental Health (Approval of Persons to be Approved Mental Health Professionals) (Wales) Regulations 2008
Key Competences 3.1–3.5, 4.1, 4.6, 4.7, 4.8, 5.1, 5.6

The chapter includes:

- an exploration of social and medical perspectives;
- a discussion of independence and where this overlaps with the social perspective;
- a discussion of the social perspective and whether it fits naturally with a particular profession;
- the Equality Act 2010; and
- cultural competence, including working with diverse communities and in different geographical contexts.

Introduction

The causes, manifestations, maintenance and recovery from mental health distress are not clear. Even the meaning attributed to each of those words can differ between professions. Despite this, professionals can, and do, assert that their particular paradigm of knowledge of mental disorder offers a better understanding than others, and you may have heard of differentiating perspectives, such as the social model, the medical model and social perspectives. For this reason, this chapter will explore these differing models to better understand their meaning for AMHP practice.

One of the aspects deemed important and adopted by, or imposed on, AMHPs is that of assessing social issues, or of bringing in the social perspective, as required by the AMHP Regulations (see the Chapter aim box at the beginning of the chapter). An AMHP is required to have a critical understanding of the social perspective of mental disorder and mental health needs and to apply this to their practice. However, questions arise as to what a social perspective is, what it is challenging, and whether a single definition can be uniformly applied to all situations or be adopted by one profession only.

Perspectives

Defining the social perspective and the medical perspective

In one edited collection exploring social perspectives in mental health, the authors write that understanding of 'mental distress' and 'problems of living' has appeared on many agendas, including sociology, psychology and social work, but despite this, there is a lack of clarity as to what exactly the social perspective is (Tew, 2005, p 13). An attempt to provide some clarity contained within that book is paraphrased here. The **social perspective** is:

- an end to 'them' and 'us' thinking. Mental distress is situated within a continuum of everyday lived experience.
- a commitment to a holistic approach. An integrated understanding of people in their social contexts includes the need to engage with the contradictory elements that may constitute a person's experience and social relationships.
- a commitment to hear and take seriously what people have to say about their mental distress.

It is contended that since a person's life does not follow a simple or consistent pattern, there is a need to move away from a conventional medical paradigm and diagnostic categories, and instead a partnership approach is suggested, working together in a way that enables people to recover a meaningful degree of control over their lives (Tew, 2005, pp 13–16).

The traditional medical paradigm or **medical perspective** is perhaps easier to define. It views mental disorder in terms of pathological disorder classified through diagnosis according to symptoms. The medical perspective is a discourse that has for some decades dominated in mental health services, albeit challenges to it are not new. For an AMHP the social perspective works at least alongside this perspective, but also challenges it based on various viewpoints.

Early commentators argue that the medical model places too much emphasis on the individual as being the cause of the problem (Mechanic, 1959), and suggest instead that a mental disorder is a pattern of conduct induced by the response of significant others (Szasz, 1961). Basing his formulation upon primary and secondary deviation theory, Scheff (1963) proposes that most psychiatric symptoms are either ignored or denied and hence terminate or else are responded to, regarded as instances of illness, and a self-fulfilling process is initiated which culminates in the individual capitulating to pressures and rewards to accept the role of the mentally ill. Other exponents include Laing (1959), who believes that mental illnesses, rather than being disease entities, are in fact names given by society to the reactions of normal human beings to abnormal circumstances.

For our purposes, the social perspective can be summed up as knowledge of the social construction of problems, the nature of social context and the possible impact of both. In one study exploring the early days of the operation of the MHA 1983, the characteristics of the population subject to assessment and applications for detention suggested a close relationship between psychiatric severity and social disadvantage (Hatfield, 2008). This same author suggested that since this social perspective was clearly indicated, social workers, being trained in the social sciences, in theory at least understand the issues.

Social model of disability?

The social model of disability is a critique of the medical model and how disablement actually occurs. It rejects that disability arises from biological determinism, ie from a biological cause, but rather argues that disability is created by how societies and communities are structured and organised in the way that they respond to individual uniqueness and diversity. Therefore, it seeks to remove barriers that cause a person to feel disabled. It challenges negative, discriminating and stigmatising attitudes that reduce self-worth and which prevent a person from participating fully in their society or community (Payne, 2014).

The social perspective and social work

There is a long-standing debate whether the social perspective is synonymous with social work. This was the view of the professional association in its evidence to the Joint Committee on the draft Mental Health Bill (British Association of Social Work, 2005) and is echoed by other commentators. Walton (2000), in her study of Approved Social Workers, suggests that the social perspective is that of a social worker. Earlier studies conclude that a referral for an assessment under the MHA was an opportunity to offer a social work service (Fisher et al, 1984). Meanwhile, others suggest that the knowledge and skills of undertaking AMHP work when taken together are recognisably and distinctively those of social work, and that the role should develop a social risk orientation rather than a mental health one (Sheppard, 1990). Sheppard went on to develop a conceptual framework based on social rather than medical risk referred to as a Compulsory Assessment Schedule, which was tested (Sheppard, 1993), but never adopted. Others contend that to undertake AMHP work implies using a set of procedures, approaches and attitudes discrete and separate from social work (Myers, 1999).

In a book collating 28 homicide and other inquiries about people known to mental health services published between 1988 and 1997, the complexity of the social work role in mental health services is highlighted (Reith, 1998), and they were also summed up by one inquiry chair as 'competing functions' (Blom-Cooper, 1996, p 166). Such competing functions are perhaps best embodied in the AMHP, whereby the need to bring a social perspective occurs in the context of the dominance of the medical model of mental health and also needs to be independent of it.

REFLECTIVE ACTIVITY

Case study: Nadine

Nadine is currently being supported by mental health crisis services to take her medication and to avoid a hospital admission. Three weeks ago, Nadine had a bereavement of a very close uncle who had supported her both emotionally and financially when she was out of work two years previously. Because of this they had become really close and saw each other regularly. In the last week Nadine has been feeling very stressed at work as the team she works in is reducing in size due to public sector cuts. This stress has had an effect on Nadine's sleep and she had begun to withdraw from going out with friends, resulting in Nadine becoming psychotic and hearing derogatory voices, which she has found very distressing. This triggered the GP referring Nadine to the crisis team. In the past when Nadine has become psychotic, she has found that regaining the structure in her life is really important, something which her mother had lacked when she had also experienced the extremes of a mood disorder. Nadine is reluctant to take the medication that is offered as she strongly dislikes the side effects and recalls her mother taking medication in the past which left her sedated and confused.

Question
–   Consider this case study from a medical and social model, and a social perspective. How does this assist or hinder you in your understanding of what has caused Nadine to feel this way, and what may Nadine find useful in her recovery?

Independence

A fundamental aspect of being an AMHP is that the role should be enacted independently. As Matthews (2014, p 12) suggests, there are two elements to independence:

- independence from the influence of the employer – that is, independence of and accountability for decision-making;
- independence from the influence of the medical perspective.

Previously, Brown (2002) suggested a third: independent training.

We discussed the relationship between the AMHP and their employer in Chapter 3, and we have also noted that AMHPs do receive training, independently of doctors. We will therefore focus here on independence from the medical perspective.

Independence from the medical perspective

Described variously as a creative tension (Brown, 2002) and a voice outside the medical hegemony (Manktelow et al, 2002), the requirement for the independence of the AMHP role in this respect clearly echoes the debates and recognises the different perspectives discussed earlier in this chapter. However, the notion that AMHPs do make decisions independently of doctors is a difficult one to ascertain according to the literature. One regulatory report published in 2001 stated that disputes were rare (Social Services Inspectorate, 2001), while Roberts et al (2002) undertook a national survey and reported that agreement rather than conflict was the norm. More recently, Peay (2003) found inconsistency in the decision-making among Approved Social Workers and section 12(2) psychiatrists (doctors appointed under the MHA to undertake medical assessments) and observed changes in decision-making when consultation between these professionals took place, thus challenging the premise of independent decision-making.

This is not to say, of course, that every decision accords, but it is to suggest, rather, that there is a gap in the evidence. One possible counter-example is provided by Walton (2000, p 406), who reported that, in the five years prior to her study of Approved Social Workers, in one geographical location, even where there were medical recommendations, alternative approaches were found in 18 per cent of instances.

AMHPs need to make accountable decisions throughout their role; however, some will be founded on the decisions of others. Two examples of this might be: accepting a referral from a crisis team who have decided they cannot meet the needs and manage the risks of an individual in the community; and making an application for detention founded on the decision of an assessing doctor to make a medical recommendation. In the first example, the AMHP can challenge the view of the crisis team that further attempts should not be made to keep the person in the community, but may be forced to accept the referral if they continue to decline further involvement and the needs and risks are sufficient to warrant it. In the latter case, as an AMHP cannot make an application for detention without at least one medical recommendation, the AMHP will need to decide whether all the circumstances of the case warrant using their independent decision.

Social perspective, independence and professional background

The social perspective and independence are often conflated when discussing the AMHP role. Within the regulations, the ability to assert a social perspective in decision-making and to make properly informed, independent decisions is required (see 'Essential knowledge' box below), while the explanatory notes to the MHA state that AMHPs should provide an independent social perspective.

 ESSENTIAL KNOWLEDGE: LAW

AMHP Regulations

English
Key Competence Area 5: Application of Skills: Making and Communicating Informed Decisions
(a) [the ability to] assert a social perspective and to make properly informed independent decisions.

Welsh
Key Competence Area 5: Application of Skills: Professional Decision Making
5.1 The ability to assert a social perspective in decision making and to make properly informed, independent decisions.

One of the reservations about broadening the AMHP role to other professionals was partly the belief that these other professionals would not be able to uphold the social perspective, but this has been questioned. For example, a literature review exploring the relationship between social work and occupational therapy concluded that the two professions shared values, in particular the aspiration to address a person's whole situation (Knott and Bannigan, 2013). More recently, research also found that the professional background had little impact on the effective accomplishment of the role (Vicary, 2017). AMHPs can train from a range of diverse professional backgrounds, but all need to ensure that in practice the social perspective is represented and reflected in their approach and work. Combining the value base of the social perspective with the principle of independence is the fundamental moral framework for AMHP practice, irrespective of professional background. Stone (2018) found when using a case study vignette that there was little difference between social workers' and mental health nurses' decision outcomes when deciding whether to make an application for detention or not. This challenged the perceived notion that nurses would make a higher number of applications for detention than social workers, due to the close relationship nurses were perceived to have with their medical colleagues.

The Equality Act and protected characteristics

In this next section we will consider the importance of ensuring that AMHP work is focused on working in a diverse world and why this is needed.

The Equality Act 2010

The Equality Act 2010 (EA) protects people in the United Kingdom from discrimination, harassment and victimisation. Section 4 lists nine protected characteristics:

- **Age** (a person belonging to a particular age group, for example 50-year-olds, or range of ages, for example 18- to 30-year-olds);
- **Disability** (a person who has a physical or mental impairment which has a substantial and long-term adverse effect on that person's ability to carry out normal day-to-day activities);
- **Gender reassignment** (the process of transitioning from one gender to another);
- **Marriage and civil partnership** (marriage as a union between a man and a woman or between a same-sex couple, and in addition both same-sex and opposite-sex couples can now also have their relationships legally recognised as civil partnerships);
- **Pregnancy and maternity** (a person expecting a baby, with maternity referring to the period after the birth);
- **Race** (a group of people defined by their race, colour, nationality [including citizenship], ethnic or national origins);
- **Religion or belief** (religion refers to any religion, including a lack of religion, and belief refers to any religious or philosophical belief, and includes a lack of belief);
- **Sex** (male or female); and
- **Sexual orientation** (a person's sexual attraction towards their own sex, the opposite sex or both sexes).

The EA protects people from discrimination:

- when at work;
- when using public services or education;
- when using business and other organisations that provide services and goods (such as shops, restaurants);

- when using transport, joining a club or association; and
- when coming into contact with public bodies.

There are four main types of discrimination:

- **Direct discrimination**: this means treating a person worse than another person because of a protected characteristic (for example, an employer does not employ someone with mental health problems because they believe that such people will not be able to cope with the stress of the job).
- **Indirect discrimination**: this can occur when an organisation puts in place a policy or rule which has a worse impact on someone with a protected characteristic (for example, a local authority is proposing to change its charging policy for social care services and decides to hold consultation events in the evening, but female service users complain that they cannot attend due to child care responsibilities).
- **Harassment**: this is where an individual is treated in a way that violates their dignity or creates a hostile, humiliating or offensive environment (for example, if a man with learning disabilities visits a pub and is subject to derogatory and offensive comments from staff).
- **Victimisation**: where a person is treated unfairly because they are taking action under the EA (for example, making a complaint of discrimination) or supporting someone else to do so.

The EA requires service providers and those exercising public functions, including social care and health services, to make reasonable adjustments for people with an impairment (including mental impairment) that constitutes a disability. Providers must take reasonable steps to avoid putting a person with a disability at a substantial disadvantage compared with those who are not disabled. Reasonable adjustments can mean making alterations to buildings by providing lifts, wide doors, ramps and tactile signage, but may also mean changes to policies, procedures and staff training to ensure that services work equally well for people with mental health problems.

Carers and relatives of people with a mental health condition are protected from direct discrimination by the EA under the rule of 'discrimination by association'; where somebody has been treated less favourably than others because of their association with a disabled person. Of course, carers are also protected in their own right against discrimination on the grounds of any protected characteristic.

Cultural competence

Working in diverse communities

It is well established statistically that there is an over-representation of black and ethnic minority people who are detained under the MHA, but the reasons behind this are not clear and the causality not easy to establish beyond the belief that mental health services are institutionally racist. Indeed, the disproportionate numbers form one of the reasons given in the recent independent review of MHA for undertaking the review (DH, 2018). The reasons for this prevalence may be twofold: first, the impact that prejudice has on an individual, and second, the way in which society is structured. As we noted earlier, studies make clear the links between disadvantage and admissions to mental hospital (Hatfield, 2008). However, as we shall see, prejudice and structural issues apply in different contexts.

Section 149 of the EA also requires public bodies (such as hospitals and local authorities) to have due regard to the need to:

- eliminate discrimination, harassment, victimisation and any other conduct that is prohibited by or under this Act;
- advance equality of opportunity between persons who share a relevant protected characteristic and persons who do not share it;
- foster good relations between persons who share a relevant protected characteristic and persons who do not share it.

This is known as the 'public sector equality duty' and, in the context of mental health care, has featured heavily in legal cases relating to commissioning decisions and cuts to funding.

Despite the widespread provisions of the EA's protected characteristics, it does not cover every eventuality. Hair colour and body characteristics that are seen as being in contradiction to society's norms are not so protected, and therefore in the absence of law and policy, best practice and professional guidance need to fill that void.

REFLECTIVE ACTIVITY

AMHPs will need to respond to assessments for diverse people in diverse communities.

Questions
- How sound is your cultural competence?
- Have you had an assessment where you weren't culturally prepared?
- Where can you gain advice on cultures you are not familiar with to enhance your cultural competence?
- How is your knowledge of the world's religions?
- What could be the impact on an MHA assessment if the person being assessed feels culturally and/or religiously isolated?

Urban and rural communities and boundaries

In many respects, the literature that discusses mental disorder, and in turn AMHP practice, has the urban environment as its default. In their chapter discussing just this, Murr and Waterhouse (2014) explore whether such a clear binary exists and conclude that there is as much difference within rural communities as there is a comparison between rural and urban. Despite this, they suggest that training AMHPs to work in rural areas requires knowledge about what is meant by rural, its communities and cultures.

 ESSENTIAL KNOWLEDGE: PRACTICE GUIDANCE

The MHA in rural settings

Issues for consideration when working as an AMHP in a rural setting include:

- *Practicalities*: finding a remote location where there are no road names; poor reception for mobile phones; distance involved for conveyance.
- *Particular risk factors*: to self (fatigue, managing delay and isolation); to others (availability of guns and drugs and familiarity with death).
- *Ethical dilemmas*: maintaining confidentiality; the likelihood that if you live in the area the person may be known to you personally.

Murr and Waterhouse, 2014, pp 120–4

In terms of the social perspective, the vulnerability that can manifest itself in rural communities is core. While social disadvantage can be a result of economic difficulties it may also be exacerbated by issues such as isolation. Some questions might be: are there fewer places for people to meet, and what impact does geographical distance have?

It is also the case that AMHP work concerns geographical boundaries that sometimes need to be traversed. The most obvious instance of this for the MHA is the border between England and Wales. While it is basically the same MHA that applies (although some parts of the MHA only apply in one country or the other), each country has its own Code of Practice, statutory forms and regulations. In addition, the devolved Welsh Assembly Government places additional expectations on AMHPs through the Mental Health (Wales) Measure (Welsh Assembly Government, 2010). Also, the MHA enables movement of patients between other countries and islands. Although different legislation applies in Scotland, that legislation will also apply for AMHPs facing issues when dealing with a person who lives in Scotland but who may be temporarily placed in England.

Person and carer perspective

Terminology can cause tensions and, despite our best attempts to be inclusive in our use of language, we will often fail to achieve that aim. The 'public' includes both us and them, and so will be adopted here, and we apologise if you feel this is incorrect. The importance of involving the public in the education, development and practice of AMHPs is well documented. It will be for the professional standards required of the professions who can become AMHPs.

REFLECTIVE ACTIVITY

Case study: Sam

An AMHP attends a training day where a person who self-defines as a mental survivor called **Sam** recalls her experiences of being assessed under the MHA and being subsequently detained. Sam explains that the AMHP did not seem to listen to her, or take on board her point of view. Sam also felt like her home had been invaded by people she did not know and who did not treat her in a dignified way. She particularly recalls that no one would sit next to her and sat in an oppositional manner. Professionals asked her questions in an uncoordinated manner which she found confusing. She recalls that being detained was like being in prison, with the noise of the ward and overall environment being very frightening and that she wanted to leave as soon as she arrived. She was immediately required to take medication that she did not want or feel she needed, which left her feeling drowsy and out of control.

Questions
Reflect on what Sam has shared with you about her experience of being detained.

–   What can you learn about being assessed under the MHA?
–   What can be learnt about the implication of the AMHP's decision to make an application?
–   What mechanism or arrangements do you have in place to discuss the MHA assessment with the person who you assessed to get feedback after the event?

(▶) KEY MESSAGES

- The importance of AMHPs understanding the context in which they work is fundamental to the role and, arguably, engagement within the community makes for effective intervention.

- In rural areas, for example, where physical resources may be sparse, an AMHP will need to understand where support may be sought in less 'usual' ways.

- In other circumstances, AMHPs need to be aware of individual and societal matters that cause mental distress to determine the understanding of it and the way in which it should be assessed.

KNOWLEDGE REVIEW

- The AMHP has a duty to ensure that the social perspective is evident in the MHA process and in the decision-making as a balance to the medical perspective.

- The EA needs to underpin all MHA work and engagement with those assessed under the MHA, the nearest relative and wider family.

- AMHPs need to ensure that they are culturally competent and know where they can gain knowledge on cultures with which they are not familiar.

FURTHER READING

- Murr, A. and Waterhouse, T. (2014) 'The impact of space and place', in S. Matthews, P. O'Hare and J. Hemmington (eds) *Approved mental health practice: Essential themes for students and practitioners*, Basingstoke: Palgrave Macmillan.

- Tew, J. (ed) (2005) *Social perspectives in mental health: Developing social models to understand and work with mental distress*, London: Jessica Kingsley.

- Walton, P. (2000) 'Reforming the Mental Health Act 1983: an Approved Social Worker perspective', *Journal of Social Welfare and Family Law*, 22(4), pp 401–14.

5

The multi-professional AMHP role

Chapter aim

This chapter will enable you to meet the following AMHP key competence themes:

- Application of knowledge of mental disorder

- Application of skills for working in partnership

  Schedule 2 of the Mental Health (Approved Mental Health Professionals) (Approval) (England) Regulations 2008 Key Competences 3(a), 4(c)

  Schedule 2 of the Mental Health (Approval of Persons to be Approved Mental Health Professionals) (Wales) Regulations 2008 Key Competences 3.1, 4.3

This chapter explores the multi-professional role of the Approved Mental Health Professional (AMHP), examining who can now be approved as AMHPs, and whether there is a difference in the way practitioners from different professional groups undertake the role, and in their own and others' attitudes towards it.

The chapter includes:

- details of the regulations that apply;
- an analysis of the strengths and weaknesses of diversification of professional background;
- working in partnership;
- some verbatim accounts by AMHPs from the differing eligible professions as to their views of the role.

Introduction

The AMHP role has, since 3 November 2008, been available to four professional groups, as listed in Schedule 1 to the Mental Health (Approved Mental Health Professionals) (Approval) (England) Regulations (SI 2008/1206) and the Mental Health (Approved Mental Health Professionals) (Approval) (Wales) Regulations

(SI 2008/2436), thereby dissolving the exclusive domination by social work of the approved status. The Mental Health Act 2007 brought in this amendment (as well as others), with the aim of diversifying eligibility.

AMHP status is attributed to a professional who is approved by a local authority (LA) to act and undertake the role. It offers a unique identity which is aligned to an eligible qualified professional, registered with the appropriate body.

 ESSENTIAL KNOWLEDGE: LAW

Who is eligible: England

The professional requirements are as follows:

(a) a **social worker** [registered in Part 16 of the Register maintained under article 5 of the Health Professions Order 2001];

(b) a first level nurse, registered in Sub-Part 1 of the Nurses' Part of the Register maintained under article 5 of the Nursing and Midwifery Order 2001, with the inclusion of an entry indicating their field of practice is **mental health or learning disabilities nursing**;

(c) an **occupational therapist** registered in Part 6 of the Register maintained under article 5 of the Health Professions Order 2001; or

(d) a **chartered psychologist** who is listed in the British Psychological Society's Register of Chartered Psychologists and who holds a relevant practising certificate issued by that Society.

> Schedule 1, para 1 to the Mental Health (Approved Mental Health Professionals) (Approval) (England) Regulations 2008/1206
> (emphasis added)

Who is eligible: Wales

In order to fulfil the professional requirements, a person must be one of the following—

(a) a **social worker** registered with [Social Care Wales];

(b) a first level nurse, registered in Sub-Part 1 of the [register] maintained under article 5 of the Nurses and Midwifery Order 2001, with the inclusion of an entry indicating that his or her field of practice is **mental health or learning disabilities nursing**;

(c) an **occupational therapist** registered in Part 6 of the Register maintained under article 5 of the Health Professions Order 2001;

> (d) a **chartered psychologist** listed in the British Psychological Society's Register of Chartered Psychologists and who holds a relevant practising certificate issued by that Society.
>
> Schedule 1, para 1 to the Mental Health (Approval of Persons to be Approved Mental Health Professionals) (Wales) Regulations 2008/2436
>
> (emphasis added)

The departure from social work dominance of the AMHP role is crystallised in section 114ZA(2) of the MHA for England, and section 114A of the MHA for Wales, where it is stated that the functions of an AMHP are not to be considered to be 'relevant social work' for the purposes of Part 4 of the Care Standards Act 2000 (in England), and Parts 3 to 8 of the Regulation and Inspection of Social Care (Wales) Act 2016. This diversification also has an implication as to what is counted as continuing professional development and for maintaining AMHP knowledge.

Becoming an AMHP

To be approved as an AMHP the LA needs to be satisfied that a person has the appropriate competence in dealing with 'persons who are suffering from mental disorder'. This is usually a two-stage process:

- first, successful completion of an approved AMHP education programme approved by Social Work England or Social Care Wales; and
- secondly, the LA confirms it is satisfied, usually through an approval meeting, that a person is competent to practise.

The LA can authorise an AMHP to practise for a five-year period, and within each year that the AMHP is approved (in England) they will need to undertake at least 18 hours of training deemed by the LA as being relevant to the AMHP role. The nature and substance of this re-approval varies, but ultimately must be in a form and on a topic which is approved by the LA.

There is no definitive agreement as to why the AMHP role needed to be opened to a broader range of professionals. The potential to do so was first suggested in the early 1990s. Following a survey to elicit the characteristics of AMHPs' predecessors, Approved Social Workers (ASWs) (numbers, rates per head of population, location and workload), it was concluded that the ASW role stood out as one of the few stable features in mental health services (Huxley and Kerfoot, 1994). Despite this, the study's authors proposed that other professions such as community psychiatric nurses and probation officers could, with training, become specialist mental health workers, including Approved Social Workers, a proposal made to protect the specialist ASW role as it was feared at the time of the survey that the suggested redeployment of these other professions might actually diminish it (Huxley and Kerfoot, 1994). However, other than indicating that the role required training, no other suggestion about its peculiar character was made. Huxley and other colleagues undertook a similar survey ten years later (Huxley et al, 2005b) during the protracted period of debate surrounding reform of mental health legislation in England and Wales, and amid the growing trend to make appropriate use of relevant skills elsewhere in the mental health workforce under the New Ways of Working policy. In much the same way as contemporary commentaries, this study concluded that the numbers of ASWs were declining, at the same time as the workloads were increasing (Huxley et al, 2005b). Several reasons were put forward, the first of which was that numbers of ASWs in the first survey were inactive by the time of the second. Others, based on conjecture, included that social work training courses lacked specialist mental health elements, thereby not 'attracting' expertise. The authors also mused that the opportunity to seek employment in other roles with better pay and conditions was more attractive. Whatever the reasons, opening up the role was first formally included in the report of the Richardson Committee, which noted that other professions were equally capable of being ASWs (DH, 1999). The government of the time argued that the extension of the role would reflect modern mental health practice based on multidisciplinary community mental health teams, a relaxation of professional boundaries and shared responsibility for cases among team members. However, there were also pragmatic reasons behind the reform, including a desire to combat low morale, and to seek to address poor recruitment and problems with retention (see Matthews, 2014). This policy was subsequently mirrored by the regulations which established the Best Interests Assessor role under the MCA.

The design of AMHP services within England and Wales varies across the two countries. Indeed, there is no set structure or configuration laid out in guidance or statute. While this seeming lack of harmonisation might be seen to reflect the diverse communities and populations served, this variation can and does lead to difference in terms and conditions for AMHPs. This is brought into even sharper focus given the range of professionals that are now eligible, and in a context where there is a belief in some geographical areas that the workforce is in decline.

Benefits of different professions?

It is perhaps an undeniable argument that diversifying the role beyond social work to nursing, occupational therapy and psychology has theoretically added new skills to the AMHP service, and in turn that this diversification could respond to a variety of mental health assessments which may require the different skills that such professions bring. The research in this area is growing, but early indications suggest that professional background makes little difference to the capacity to understand or undertake the role but rather depends on personal attributes (Vicary, 2017; Stone, 2018). Despite the fact that eligibility to act as an AMHP is now diversified, social workers remain the dominant profession (ADASS, 2018). The reasons for this dominance have been explored, and it is proposed that these may include structural barriers as to why nurses struggle to become AMHPs (Watson, 2016; Stone, 2019), as well as there being a dominant social workforce who transitioned from being Approved Social Workers, and the functions of the AMHP being vicariously connected to the LA, where social workers are, in the main, employed.

In practice, one of the challenges to achieving a more interprofessionally diverse AMHP workforce is that, as AMHPs usually staff a rota, the LA does not have the capacity to pick and choose the person most suitable to be the coordinating AMHP for the assessment. It is, in any case, a difficult judgement to make as to why one AMHP would be more suitable than another. The emphasis on interviewing a person in a suitable manner places the responsibility on the AMHP to gain appropriate doctors and it is not for the LA to consider who might be the most appropriate AMHP. Nonetheless, AMHPs from varying backgrounds can bring different skills to the AMHP service.

The following narratives were captured when AMHPs from differing backgrounds offered their reflections on how their professional backgrounds assisted them in meeting the AMHP competences within the MHA.

PERSPECTIVE: OCCUPATIONAL THERAPIST AMHP

As an occupational therapist, I didn't know as much as the social workers on child and family law. However, as an occupational therapist I am trained to think client-centred, promote autonomy, what is meaningful to the service user. We are also trained to risk assess. That is essentially the role of an AMHP in an MHA assessment. Occupational therapists consider the medical and social models; they are dual trained to work in both mental and physical health. They tend to specialise in one field.

I worked in physical older people work before moving to forensics and I've been in mental health ever since. So occupational therapists are experienced in working in acute settings, community, social services, schools, etc ... I think the skills of a care coordinator are critical regardless of the profession. It's having a broader scope of the person's life and having awareness of local services and what options for support people have.

The occupational therapist code of practice contains loads of stuff in there that shows how our professional codes meet those of being an AMHP.

PERSPECTIVE: NURSE AMHP

Psychiatric wards are predominantly run under the medical model. Nurses are taught increasingly about the recovery model (thank you, social work), so the broad notion that nurses 'as doctors handmaidens' will follow blindly the 'medical model' is increasingly redundant. I'm making broad strokes here and generalising regarding our medical colleagues, but this is just to make a wide comment. For example, a nurse AMHP 'may' be less likely to detain a woman onto a mixed-sex admission ward as opposed to a woman-only crisis house (a voluntary option of course).

Nurses will have sound knowledge on issues that relate to poly-pharmacy or dosing that exceeds BNF guidelines, etc – important because of the research re black men being more likely to be in this bracket. In two to three applications, the nurse may have something to add specific to the treatments administered and if/how this is discriminatory.

Most nurses are well versed in, or have experience of, challenging patients who are intent on going AWOL, aka trying to leave despite being detained on the ward. The scenario of the patient recently admitted, eg at night, who then decides, "Actually I want to go, I've made a mistake coming here". This type of scene typically played out at the door of the ward is a sensitive impasse that nurses are skilled at dealing with. The de-escalation, the avoidance of coercive care but at the same time the assertiveness that "You need to stay here for now", type of thing. This is anchored in detailing rights eg informing patients of NR powers, tribunal applications, etc.

The social perspective of care may be assumed to be more a social work domain, but not necessarily. Nurses who have worked on ward may have had a much more immersed social experience with patients. If you consider the ward on a 12-hour shift – in essence, the patient is living there, side by side with 24-hour nursing staff. During inpatient care the nurse is there when patient eats, sleeps, wash, prays, etc – it's a 24-hour perspective. It may be a restricted environment but often the opportunity to witness, share and take part in social 'experiences' is greater than may be managed in a 'task-orientated' community or home visit.

PERSPECTIVE: SOCIAL WORK AMHP

For social work, working within a social model of disability and promoting a social perspective in mental health was ingrained in my practice as a mental health social worker before I trained to become an ASW and then as an AMHP. I think it helped that I graduated from university to a community team mental health, so engaging in community work was very familiar to me when I started working as an AMHP. My knowledge of mental health conditions developed whilst I was in my first mental health social work role. I don't recall having much mental health teaching during my university education. In the same way my knowledge of psychiatric medication has grown over the years, but it is has felt more of a mental health apprenticeship for me where I now feel confident in what I am doing as a mental health social worker.

I have always been very rights focused and I like how we are there as an AMHP to ensure that the service users' rights are being upheld, and this keeps me anchored to ensure that as an AMHP I act proportionally. I feel that the ethical expectations of me as an AMHP are very similar to those of social work.

At the time of writing we did not have a perspective from a chartered psychologist but if this changes we will add this to the companion website.

 Please see online resources for update

The five key competence areas

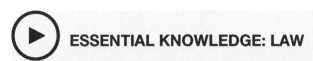

ESSENTIAL KNOWLEDGE: LAW

Key areas of competence

In England, all competent AMHPs must demonstrate competence in five areas in their discharge of their duties as an AMHP in practice.

1. Application of values to the AMHP role
2. Application of knowledge: the legal and policy framework
3. Application of knowledge: mental disorder
4. Application of skills: working in partnership
5. Application of skills: making and communicating informed decisions

> Schedule 2 to the Mental Health (Approved Mental Health Professionals) (Approval) (England) Regulations 2008

In contrast, the Welsh competences are:

1. Values-based practice
2. Application of knowledge: legislation and policy
3. Application of knowledge: mental disorder

4. Application of skills: effective partnership working

5. Application of skills: professional decision making

Schedule 2 to the Mental Health (Approval of Persons
to be Approved Mental Health Professionals) (Wales) Regulations 2008

In the competence areas that you find at the beginning of each chapter in this book, their importance to the practice of AMHPs is acknowledged. However, the requirement to meet these is additional to the competences that each eligible professional brings to their work as an AMHP by virtue of their own professional accreditation and subsequent registration. Although studies have established that variation between the practice of AMHPs from various backgrounds is not evidenced (Bressington et al, 2011; Vicary, 2017; Stone, 2019), perhaps the knowledge and skills acquired through their professional training are equally valuable to the AMHP. The requirement for the social perspective to be demonstrated can dominate and polarise professions, when in fact the evidence of one profession's ownership of a particular discourse is not as strong as some might claim. If the regulations above are to be applied to AMHP practice, perhaps what is needed is a recognition of the background skills that each professional eligible to become an AMHP can offer.

We continue with a brief discussion of these five key competence areas.

Values

The AMHP needs to demonstrate that they have the values required. This means applying anti-oppressive practice and a focus on equality. AMHP practice will bring you in contact with individuals from diverse backgrounds and cultures which will require you to have cultural competency, and to look for sources to gain guidance if needed to counter any discrimination that you observe. There are several instances within the role for you to uphold people's rights and explain their rights to appeal and advocacy. The MCA needs to be embedded in your practice as AMHPs need to ensure that an individual's self-determination, dignity and respect are upheld by valuing their expressed needs and wishes and supporting them wherever possible to make decisions that affect them. Due to the differing settings in which MHA assessments can occur, maintaining confidentiality, choice, dignity and privacy can be challenging but should be sensitively approached. These aspects of practice have been covered in more detail in Chapter 3.

The legal, policy and research framework

Knowledge of legal provisions, policy and research should be sound, in relation primarily to the MHA, so that the fundamental issues and principles that apply to a given set of circumstances involving adults, young people and children are understood. Codes of Practice and Guidelines, in addition to local and national guidance, are not separate entities. Moreover, published literature relating to AMHP practice is growing and attention should be given to research and new knowledge as to the role. The evidence also sets out the levels of accountabilities that exist in the role: to the person being assessed, the nearest relative (NR), families, the wider public and to your employer. As a 'public authority' within the meaning of section 6 of the Human Rights Act 1998 (HRA), the AMHP must understand the implications of the European Convention on Human Rights (ECHR) and apply the relevant Articles and case law in the work they undertake. (When considering the HRA, it would be useful to refer to Chapter 10.) Furthermore, AMHPs also need to be attuned to sensitivities around race and culture and to be open to learning from the experience of those who have been discriminated against because they have a mental disorder.

Broad knowledge base of mental disorder

The AMHP needs to draw on a broad knowledge base of mental disorder and have a sound understanding of the differing models that help understand the phenomenon of mental disorder. As we discussed in Chapter 4, this means seeing the distinction between the social model of disability and social perspective in mental health, while understanding the contribution of social, physical and development factors. Having a broad understanding of mental disorder acknowledges that we cannot easily categorise what is observed and need to work with persons with lived experience and other professionals to establish this, recognising the impact it is having on those persons, their relatives and carers. AMHPs also need to understand the implications of a range of treatments and interventions for people that are available. AMHPs will also require an understanding of the legal meaning of mental disorder. Under the MHA, this meaning is contained in section 1 of the MHA and is purposefully wide; it includes 'any disorder of disability of the mind'. The only caveats are:

- that dependency on alcohol or drugs is excluded; and
- in respect of longer–term detention, the definition only applies to a learning disability if it is associated with abnormally aggressive or seriously irresponsible behaviour.

A broad definition of mental disorder is intended to reduce unnecessary constraints on professionals and to focus attention away from unnecessary esoteric debate about the diagnosis of mental disorder.

Working in partnership

As discussed in Chapter 4, the social perspective of mental disorder must be represented through the work of the AMHP, and articulated when needed to all of those involved, alongside a broader understanding of mental health needs. This is important as an AMHP needs to communicate with a wide range of people, including the person and their relatives as well as other professionals when working together. Being able to build and maintain relationships therefore is a key function. If the AMHP is going to be able to weigh up least restrictive options, there needs to be understanding of the context in which they work and how to collaborate with and advocate for others to enhance the outcomes for people who are assessed and their carers. 'Risk' can often be a misconstrued word, as it can have different meanings depending on the person and profession using it. To this end, the AMHP will need to be able to articulate what they mean by risk, and contribute to discussion as to how it can be assessed and managed

As MHA work is, on occasion, work carried out in a crisis situation, it can elicit feelings of anxiety and fear. AMHPs are not invincible but should have skills in managing difficult situations where conflict may arise, and how this may impact on everyone involved, particularly the person, carers and wider family. AMHPs must ensure that empowerment is discharged in the AMHP role towards the person as far as practicable.

As discussed in Chapter 6, AMHPs must lead and coordinate the work involved in organising and undertaking the assessment. This includes the intricacies of negotiating and managing the process through to the compulsory admission of a person to hospital, or the arrangements for Community Treatment Orders. To fulfil any of these functions, there has to be a sound grasp of the relevant legal and practical processes that must or should be followed. This includes the involvement of other professionals involved, as well as the person, the role of the NR, wider family members and other carers.

The ability to balance competing demands is vital in order for the AMHP to be able to operate lawfully under section 6 of the HRA. In some cases, AMHPs will need to consider achieving a balance between different Articles of the ECHR, such as where lawful detention under Article 5 will result in the person being removed from their home with consequences for their employment and family life, thus engaging their Article 8 rights. Another example might be deciding whether information about the person should be shared to ensure that the NR is appropriately informed and consulted, in circumstances where the person is objecting to their information being shared, which requires the AMHP to balance the Article 8 right to private and family life with the need to protect the rights and freedoms of others.

Making and communicating informed decisions

The AMHP must demonstrate the ability to ensure that the social perspective is asserted in the independent decision-making process and informs those decisions. They will need to evidence those decisions in a clear, concise and sensitive way, both verbally and in writing, to demonstrate independent accountability of those decisions. As we discuss further in Chapter 12, this will be key to the completion of statutory documentation and local record-keeping, and ensuring that confidentiality is maintained when information is shared where appropriate. AMHPs will need to ensure that they are familiar with presenting a case at a court hearing, such as a First–Tier Mental Health Review Tribunal (MHRT1) including providing evidence and arguing a particular perspective. There can be no doubt that the role of the AMHP is one that requires independence, autonomy and authority, but equally needs to be reflective to enable their future work to be shaped through supervision and consultation with the person, the NR, carers and others, including the identification of needs that could not be met.

Leadership and commissioning of a diverse workforce

A diverse workforce not only encompasses practising AMHPs but also those who lead them in each LA area, including those who assess their competence, and determine whether trainees are approved. A further advantage of AMHPs coming from differing professions is that, as they gain promotion and move beyond frontline AMHP work, their knowledge and skills will be available to them when managing these services and also when making commissioning decisions. If the aim is truly to have a diverse AMHP workforce, then this needs to be reflected in the leadership of the AMHP workforce as well, including practice assessors and leads who also come from diverse professional backgrounds. The AMHP workforce plan (Department of Health and Social Care, 2019) discusses the development of the workforce, but it will be interesting to see if in 10 years' time the social work profession still dominates the role, particularly as the 'AMHP workforce in decline' narrative has endured from when the ASW workforce was also deemed to be in decline.

▶ KEY MESSAGES

- The LA approves AMHP to practise under MHA, section 114.

- The AMHP is a status which can be given to a social worker, mental health or learning disabilities nurse, occupational therapist or chartered psychologist.

- AMHPs must adhere to the competences of the role, and also their own professional competences and ethics.

- AMHPs can be approved for five years, and within each year must complete 18 hours of LA-approved professional development relevant to the AMHP role.

 KNOWLEDGE REVIEW

- The 'identity' of the AMHP as a unique professional includes acknowledging the range of professions able to practise and actually practising in the role, the purpose of the role, its values and organisational contexts in social and health care.

FURTHER READING

- Bailey, D. and Liyanage, L. (2012) 'The role of the mental health social worker: political pawns in the reconfiguration of adult health and social care', *British Journal of Social Work*, 42(6), pp 1113–31.

- Coffey, M. and Hannigan, B. (2013) 'New roles for nurses as approved mental health professionals in England and Wales: a discussion paper', *International Journal of Nursing Studies*, 50(10), pp 1423–30.

- Knott, G. (2016) 'The Approved Mental Health Role', in J. Clewes and R. Kirkwood (eds) *Diverse roles for occupational therapists*, Cumbria: M&K Publishing.

Part 2
The AMHP in practice

6

Completing a Mental Health Act assessment

Chapter aim

This chapter will enable you to meet the following AMHP key competence themes:

- Application of AMHP values

- Application of knowledge relating to the legal and policy framework

- Application of knowledge of mental disorder

- Application of skills for working in partnership

- Application of skills for making and communicating informed decisions

Schedule 2 of the Mental Health (Approved Mental Health Professionals)
(Approval) (England) Regulations 2008
Key Competences 1(a)–(d), 2(1)(a)–(e) 3(a)–(d), 4(a)–(k), 5(a)–(i)

Schedule 2 of the Mental Health (Approval of Persons to be Approved
Mental Health Professionals) (Wales) Regulations 2008
Key Competences 1.1–1.7, 2.1–2.5, 3.1–3.5, 4.1–4.11, 5.1–5.6

In this chapter we will consider the stages that are involved in progressing an MHA assessment from initial referral through to the differing outcomes that arise. These stages include an exploration of the information that an AMHP will need to seek, collect, analyse and weigh up before an MHA assessment is progressed, as well as establishing what risks are being communicated to the AMHP, and considering what outcomes others are seeking, to ensure that advancing an MHA referral is justifiable.

This chapter needs to be read alongside the MHA, the relevant case law, the MHA Codes of Practice and the Reference Guide, as it is not attempting primarily to be a 'law chapter' (although it does consider key legal provisions). Instead, this chapter seeks to map the process that an AMHP is likely to face and advise how to approach it, using practice wisdom gathered from wide sources.

Links will be made to Chapter 7 when considering the risks and challenges in MHA assessments.

Introduction

This chapter includes:

- taking the MHA assessment referral;
- the MHA assessment;
- resourcing the MHA assessment;
- the MHA assessment interview;
- the decision and outcome of the MHA assessment; and
- the post-assessment requirements.

The reason we have divided the chapter into these subsections is to reflect the differing, but interrelated moments of AMHP work. In a qualitative study exploring the work of the AMHP's predecessors, Approved Social Workers (ASWs), Quirk describes these subsections as: the build-up to the assessment, the assessment and the aftermath (Quirk, 2008). Each requires different skills and knowledge, but all are interlinked if robust practice is to be adhered to.

The MHA referral

The MHA is a powerful piece of legislation, the ultimate capability of which is to deprive a person of their liberty. Outcomes can involve removing that person, by force if necessary, to a psychiatric hospital, or restricting a person's freedom of movement in the community through the use of guardianship. The referral for an MHA assessment is a key stage in the MHA process. Such requests need to be considered carefully as to whether they should be accepted or not, and may involve remedying any conflicts of interest that present themselves.

Need for referral

Section 13(1) of the MHA (set out in full below) provides that an AMHP should consider the case if there is 'reason to think that an application ... may need to be made'. There is no guidance as to what constitutes 'a reason to think' in this context, and therefore practice in this respect will differ. What we do know is that an MHA assessment is an interference by a public authority (Human Rights Act 1998 [HRA], s 6(1)) in the private and family life (European Convention on Human Rights [ECHR], Art 8) of any person being assessed. In addition, anyone whom an AMHP contacts within the person's family or wider friends and neighbours may also be subject to this interference. Therefore, the act of contacting them needs to be considered carefully, and recorded appropriately to demonstrate that it is proportionate, and can be justified.

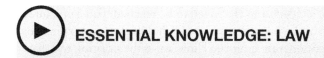

ESSENTIAL KNOWLEDGE: LAW

MHA, section 13(1)

If a local social services authority **have reason to think** that an application for admission to hospital or a guardianship application may need to be made in respect of a patient within their area, they shall make arrangements for an approved mental health professional to consider the patient's case on their behalf.

The 'reason to think' threshold is not an overly high threshold as a matter of law. It does not require certainty that an application is needed, only a belief that one *may* be needed. Section 13(1) does not necessarily require a formal referral or request to be made to trigger the duty, although in most cases these will supply enough information for the 'reason to think' test to be satisfied.

Nevertheless, the very act of gathering information in order to justify an assessment progressing, and agreeing to progress that assessment, needs to be balanced proportionally. It may be felt by the referrer that making a request for an MHA assessment is a procedural matter, as they feel they have done all they can to engage with the person in need of mental health services and therefore want to escalate this to an MHA assessment. In this sense, an AMHP has to apply the 'reason to think' test according to best practice and their own local authority's policy, as well as taking due consideration as to who is making the referral.

However, there are exceptions to this non-procedural stance to MHA referrals. The first and possibly the most common is where the referral concerns a person who is detained under section 136 of the MHA (that is, who has already been taken to a place of safety). However, even in this circumstance, the AMHP has to decide whether to:

- suggest the registered medical practitioner discharges the person if there is no mental disorder;
- proceed with asking one appropriate registered medical practitioner (approved under section 12(2) or with previous acquaintance of the patient) to accompany them;
- proceed with asking two appropriate registered medical practitioners to accompany them.

Another example is where a voluntary, or informal, patient is already in hospital and has been placed under section 5(2) of the MHA. In this circumstance, and under this section, the registered medical practitioner or approved clinician in charge of the treatment has determined that 'an application ought to be made'.

Even in this scenario there are decisions that need to be reached; you can request the person is reviewed again, before the section 5(2) holding power expires, by the registered medical practitioner or approved clinician, as the situation may have settled or changed. An AMHP may also find that the registered medical practitioner or approved clinician is a doctor with prior acquaintance and may want to make a medical recommendation in this respect. Even so, the AMHP must still reach a decision as to whether the MHA assessment referral needs to be progressed.

Another possible scenario is when a referral is received from a person appearing to be a Nearest Relative (NR), under section 13(4) of the MHA. In this instance an AMHP fulfils the local authority (LA) duty to consider and report upon the person's case. This does not mean an MHA assessment interview occurs. However, should no application be made, the AMHP is obliged to write to the NR with the reasons as to why not.

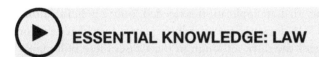

ESSENTIAL KNOWLEDGE: LAW

MHA, section 13(4)

It shall be the duty of a local social services authority, if so required by the nearest relative of a patient residing in their area, to make arrangements under subsection (1) above for an approved mental health professional to consider the patient's case with a view to making an application for his admission to hospital; and if in any such case that professional decides not to make an application he shall inform the nearest relative of his reasons in writing.

The key message is that engaging the powers of the MHA should not be simply a procedural matter, as to consider it as simply this diminishes the critical analysis that each an assessment by an AMHP requires.

When is a referral not a referral?

There are also a few other matters to consider at this stage, to say the least. First, there can often be a confusion between *taking* a referral and *accepting* a referral. Referral pathways between the LA and the NHS differ across England and Wales, but what is essential is that all parties understand their responsibilities at any given time in respect of that referral. Moreover, there is a danger that referrals are recorded only for those that are accepted. This fails to record the numbers of inappropriate referrals, or the referrals where an AMHP has been able to divert the need for an MHA assessment through challenging the referrer to try other (least restrictive) alternatives. The knowledge and skill base of AMHPs at this juncture should not be underestimated. If such non-assessments are not recorded in the statistical records of AMHP services, they will in turn not gain the recognition warranted for the work that has been diverted, and the time taken in doing so. A recent study has referred to such gaps as a limitation when making judgements about the worth of an AMHP (Wickersham et al, 2019).

One approach that can be taken by an AMHP is to discuss a referral but not to formally accept it until it has been assessed. This gatekeeping of the MHA pathway can be done by the AMHP either undertaking a solo or a joint visit to the person concerned to establish for themselves that the threshold for an assessment has been met, and that an MHA should go ahead. Section 115 of the MHA (discussed in Chapter 9) allows an AMHP to enter and inspect the property where a person resides (other than hospital). Although acknowledging that this is more resource-intensive, it does mean that the AMHP is not relying solely on another person's risk assessment. However, it may also mean that an AMHP, if only accompanied by one registered medical practitioner, may need to use section 4 of the MHA if the circumstances they find dictate that it is indeed an emergency situation.

Referrals for MHA assessments can arise from different people, such as the NR, other relatives, police officers, health professionals, or social workers. Most commonly those referred for an assessment are located in general or psychiatric hospitals, places of safety, accident and emergency departments, nursing homes, residential units or in their own homes. Therefore, in taking these referrals an AMHP needs to be tuned into the connotations and nuances arising as a consequence of the type of referrer or location. This might include consideration of what additional information and analysis is required.

REFLECTIVE ACTIVITY

Case study: John

John has recently been moved into a residential nursing home after his discharge from hospital following his recovery from psychosis, which impacted upon his autism considerably. The care home have called the AMHP service, having been given the number by the crisis team, stating that they cannot cope with John's night-time behaviour and are requesting an MHA assessment, which the GP is supporting. The residential nursing home have also informed the local authority that they intend to give John 28 days' notice to leave.

Questions
- What alternatives would you want the referrer to have considered before making the referral?

> – What factors do you need to consider when considering this referral for an MHA assessment?
> – What would be the impact of the assessment on John's wellbeing, and his accommodation?

AMHPs often have to achieve a fine balancing act between the needs and rights of the person being assessed, and the needs and rights of others. This includes listening to the differing views and wishes of the person's family, carers and the NR; while also giving diligent attention to any risks and the purpose of the intervention (see the Guiding Principles). At the same time the AMHP will need to balance the person's rights under Articles 5 and 8 of the ECHR, which may include considering the relationship between the person who appears to be the NR and the person being assessed. This will involve checking whether contacting them would cause harm to either the assessed person or the NR.

ESSENTIAL KNOWLEDGE: CODES OF PRACTICE

England

AMHPs should also consult wherever possible with other people who have been involved with the patient's care, including their care co-ordinator if they are supported on the care programme approach ... This could include people working for statutory, voluntary or independent services and other service providers who do not specialise in mental health services but have contact with the patient. For example, the patient may be known to services for older people or substance misuse services.

DH, 2015a, para 14.69

Wales

AMHPs should also consult wherever possible with other people who have been involved with the patient's care, including their care coordinator if they have one. This could include people working for statutory, voluntary or independent services and other service providers who do not specialise in mental health services but have contact with the patient.

Welsh Assembly Government, 2016, para 14.61

Good practice when taking referrals

 ESSENTIAL KNOWLEDGE: PRACTICE GUIDANCE

The referral requires the AMHP to consider numerous factors:

- The person's demographic details
- Are they a child, a young person or an adult?
- Are they already subject to powers under the MHA, such as on section 17 leave, on a Community Treatment Order (CTO), subject to section 37/41, or detained under section 136?
- The location of the person
- Have they been arrested under the Police and Criminal Evidence Act 1984 (PACE)?
    - Has a mental health diversion service been involved?
    - If a decision has been made to detain the person under PACE, section 2 or 3, will the custody sergeant release them to your custody? Or does the custody sergeant want the person to be put before a magistrate for the alleged criminal offence?
- Who is currently involved: the GP? Other mental health services?
- When was the person last seen, and by whom?
- Why is the assessment being requested now?
- What, if any, least restrictive approaches have been attempted?
- If attempted, why have any alternatives not been successful?
- What are the current risks: static, dynamic, contextual and relational?
- What are the current mental health needs?
- Are there any safeguarding concerns? If yes, has a referral been made?
- Are there any child in need or child protection concerns? If yes, has a referral been made?
- Is there any reason the AMHP should not be speaking to relatives, carers or the NR? (If a delay in contacting them is needed to enable the person to be spoken to first at the assessment, this should be recorded.)
- Are there any access requirements that need to be considered?
- Are there any reasonable adjustments that need to be considered?
- Is the person medically fit?
- Are the case notes up to date?
- Any other circumstances of the case that need consideration

These may seem like straightforward questions, but taking a detailed and informed referral is vital. Making an MHA referral to an AMHP can be seen as effective risk management by the professional making a referral; and at referral they may, wrongly, see their responsibilities towards the person ending. However, their referring involvement may still be required to offer support to the person and to source and allocate resources.

Again, it is as important to be clear whether you have *accepted* the referral or not, as it is to be clear on future roles and input. Do not make assumptions but record that conversation clearly. This is for a number of reasons:

- In believing that you have accepted the referral, a professional referrer may feel their concerns and risks have been adequately escalated and that they will avoid any criticism if undesired outcomes occur.
- If it is a referral from a member of the public, then reassurance should be given and they should not be passed from pillar to post in communicating their concerns. You should explain what the next steps are.
- If professionals use members of the public as proxy professional referrers, this should be challenged with the professional who has asked that person to call you, as they should have made the referral themselves.
- If called by a professional service, it is also good practice to ask the professional who last saw the person to make the referral to you, or to provide relevant information firsthand. A referral by someone who has not seen the person, or has not seen them shortly before making the referral, leaves little scope for asking questions to seek clarity and confirm contemporaneous information, which may be vital in deciding whether a referral should be accepted or not. Demonstrating how you have weighed up that undertaking an MHA assessment is proportionate and warranted is key to defensible decision-making. Although AMHPs do not practise in an ideal world, the drawback of receiving a second-stage referral can be problematic.

It is also beneficial, at each stage prior to liaising with relatives, to record whether the AMHP has been told of any reason why they should not contact any relatives. This is key, since the AMHP is required to determine who the NR appears to be and should exercise caution if that NR is a relative they have been advised should not be contacted, as the AMHP needs to balance Articles 5 and 8 of the ECHR in this regard. Recording discussions will also offer a defence as to why the AMHP made contact on those occasions when information relating to the NR and the dynamics of their relationship with the person was not known or available. Delays in speaking with the NR, and the reasons for such delays, should also be documented so these can be defended if necessary.

As an AMHP you need to be competent in documentary analysis; reviewing social and health care records is a key area of information to help guide your decisions, particularly around mental health history, family dynamics, risk, needs and safeguarding. Alongside this, it will be important to contact those involved in the care of the person being assessed which, in some circumstances, can involve the police and the Ministry of Justice (MoJ). Tips on recording are given at the end of the chapter.

REFLECTIVE ACTIVITY

Decision to accept a referral

– When taking a referral for an MHA assessment, what information do I need to enable me to decide if the referral should be accepted?
– How would I challenge the premise that an MHA assessment is required?
– How do my own risk thresholds interact with whether I accept a referral?
– How do I decide on the immediacy of the assessment?

Referrals for persons on section 17 leave, on a CTO (under section 17A) or subject to section 37/41

You may receive referrals for an MHA assessment where there is actually no direct role for an AMHP, but the referrer is nonetheless seeking guidance, at best, or at worst has not understood the law. These areas are commonly:

• where a person on section 17 leave fails to return to the ward when required to; or
• where a person who is on a CTO needs to be recalled to hospital and/or the CTO needs to be revoked; or
• where a person is on a section 37/41 restriction order and needs to be returned to the hospital.

 ESSENTIAL KNOWLEDGE: PRACTICE GUIDANCE

Consider these scenarios in turn:

Failure to return from section 17 leave/CTO recall

The person on either section 17 leave or on a CTO who has been recalled to hospital is 'liable to be detained' and therefore the responsible clinician needs to engage section 18 of the MHA to bring them back to hospital, organising a section 135(2) warrant if required, and arranging appropriate conveyance. Additionally, for the CTO the responsible clinician's notice in writing must be given to the person, as set out in Form CTO3 (in England) and Form CP 5 (in Wales), which must also be sent to the hospital managers. Your role as an AMHP will re-engage if the CTO needs to be revoked through the completion of part 2 of form CTO5 (in England) or part 2 of form CP 7 (in Wales).

Section 37/41 of the MHA

Although it is eminently possible and may be appropriate for a person subject to section 37/41 of the MHA to be admitted informally, or even under section 2 of the MHA, it is likely through consultation with the medical and social supervisors that the MoJ may seek to recall them to hospital using section 37/41 rather than using Part 2 of the MHA. In these circumstances the MoJ will issue a warrant for the police to use, and the NHS trust finds the appropriate forensic bed. As the AMHP it is likely that you will need to instigate the call to the Mental Health Casework Section of the MoJ, using the numbers available on their website.

Each of these three scenarios are examples of where, as the AMHP, you will need to advise the referrer that there is no role for the AMHP service or need for an MHA assessment, although you can signpost them to the appropriate people. However, these circumstances need to be known about at the referral stage, as information has a habit of emerging through the course of an MHA assessment; such as when a person is detained under section 136 of the MHA, and you later discover that they have absconded from a ward several counties away. Also – and this cannot be stressed enough – caution needs to be taken when being asked for 'legal advice' by other professionals, as other agencies should rely on their own legal advice arrangements. As you will have specialist knowledge of the MHA and Mental Capacity Act (MCA) 2005 it can feel professionally flattering to be asked, but you should guard against it as your local authority's insurance policy may not cover you to give legal advice, and therefore it is worth thinking about where their vicarious responsibility for you lies in this respect.

Exclusions

Despite the broad definition of mental disorder ('any disorder or disability of the mind'), there are limits to its application. First, section 1(3) states that 'dependence on alcohol or drugs is not considered to be a disorder or disability of the mind', and is therefore not a mental disorder. Paragraph 27 of the MHA 2007's explanatory notes further explains, however, that a person who is dependent on alcohol or drugs but also 'suffering' from another mental disorder or 'disorder which arises out of their dependence or use of alcohol and drugs or which is related to it' is not excluded. Practically, there will be people who are in a crisis who are dependent on alcohol or drugs and where it is not clear whether there is an associated mental disorder. In such cases, an MHA assessment should not be delayed (see 'Interviewing in a suitable manner' on p 83).

Secondly, under section 1(2A) and (2B) 'a "learning disability", mean[ing] a state of arrested or incomplete development of the mind (which includes significant impairment of intelligence and social functioning) shall not be considered to be a mental disorder requiring treatment in hospital (under sections 3, 7, 17A, 20A, 35 to 38, 45A, 47, 48, 51, or 72(1)(b)(c) and (4)) unless associated with 'abnormally aggressive or seriously irresponsible conduct' on the part of the person'. The effect is that such individuals cannot be made subject to certain provisions of the MHA solely for the treatment of their learning disabilities. This means that in such cases an AMHP can make an application under section 2 for assessment and under section 4 for assessment (in cases of emergency) without applying these additional criteria, but cannot make an application under section 3 of the MHA for treatment, or section 7 of the MHA for guardianship without the criteria being met. The Code of Practice for England, Chapter 20, and the Code of Practice for Wales, Chapter 20 should also be consulted.

This means that if a person needs hospital treatment solely for their learning disability and does not meet the additional criteria (and section 2 of the MHA cannot be used), and the admission would amount to a deprivation of liberty, the MHA will not be available and alternative legal authorisation will need to be considered, including the Deprivation of Liberty Safeguards (soon to be replaced by the Liberty Protection Safeguards) under the MCA.

In relation to autism, the Codes of Practice explain:

> The [MHA] definition of mental disorder includes the full range of autistic spectrum conditions, including those existing alongside a learning disability or any other kind of mental condition. It is possible for someone on the autistic spectrum to meet the criteria in the Act for detention without having any other form of mental disorder, even if the autism is not associated with abnormally aggressive or seriously irresponsible behaviour, but this will be very rare. (DH, 2015a, para 20.19 [England]; Welsh Assembly Government, 2016, para 34.15 [Wales])

Thirdly, the explanatory notes for the MHA 2007 explain that 'disorders or disabilities of the brain are not regarded as mental disorders unless (and only to the extent that) they give rise to a disability or disorder of the mind as well' (para 17). This is in contrast to the MCA, where the equivalent definition in section 2 refers to any impairment or disturbance in the functioning of the 'mind or the brain'.

The MHA assessment

As we have discussed, an MHA assessment starts from the moment an AMHP accepts the referral, based on their analysis of the referral information and any investigative work they have undertaken to justify an assessment progressing. The next stage is to coordinate the MHA assessment, which involves resourcing the assessment, establishing who appears to be the NR and undertaking the MHA interview, which is discussed later.

NR identification

When identifying who the NR appears to be, the following sections of the MHA apply:

- **section 26** – Definition of 'relative' and 'nearest relative';
- **section 27** – Children and young persons in care;
- **section 28** – Nearest relative of minor under guardianship [within the meaning of section 14 of the Children Act 1989];
- **section 33** – Special provisions as to wards of court.

The MHA Reference Guide (DH, 2015b) is also a useful resource, alongside the MHA Code of Practice.

The following is merely a high-level summary of the NR provisions. In many cases you will need to consider the relevant parts of the MHA, the Codes of Practice, a specialist textbook and other commentary (and in some cases take legal advice).

An NR is defined in section 26(1) of the MHA by reference to the following hierarchical list:

1. husband, wife or civil partner (including a person with whom the person being assessed has been living for not less than six months);
2. adult son or daughter;
3. father or mother;
4. adult brother or sister;
5. grandparent;
6. adult grandchild;
7. uncle or aunt;
8. adult niece or nephew;
9. any other.

A person only has one NR, determined by starting at the top of the list and working down (unless the person is a child subject to a care order, has had a guardian appointed, or is subject to a section 14A special guardianship order or subject to a child arrangement order under the Children Act 1989). Therefore, if there is no one in the first category, you go to the second, then the third and so on. If there is more than one person is one category, then various rules apply to determining which person is the NR (for instance, the oldest parent will be preferred). It is important to note that the NR is not necessarily the person's next of kin or the individual that the person would want to carry out this role. The identification rules are rooted in the 1950s and reflect many of the assumptions about the structure and role of the family that were prevalent in the immediate post-war period. As such, they fail to reflect the lives and circumstances of people in the 21st century and have attracted much criticism from practitioners and the public.

The NR identification rules fail to recognise non-traditional family structures, for example where relatives ordinarily reside abroad. Such relatives are normally excluded from the role (considered to be dead) unless the patient also ordinarily resides abroad. Similarly, the identification rules will normally exclude a long-term friend of the patient irrespective of how well they know the patient or whether they are best placed to act in the patient's interests (unless the two have ordinarily resided with each other for at least five years).

Where you are assessing a child who is subject to a care order (under section 31(11) or 38 of the Children Act 1989) the LA is the NR (the function is normally carried out by a delegated officer). This means that a LA can be both responsible at some level for the application for detention (AMHPs act on its behalf), and also the person acting as NR. Case law has not yet confirmed whether this particular conflict of interest could be resolved through regulation 24 of the Mental Health (Hospital) (England) Regulations 2008 (see 'Changing an NR' later), which enables a NR to delegate their functions to someone else. See also 'Assessing children and young people' in Chapter 7.

The NR rules also fail persons who have no identified relatives. This is particularly a problem in inner-city populations, where a large proportion of persons have lost contact with their families. Finally, the rules for identifying the NR when assessing a child are also outdated. For example, the father of a child cannot be the NR (at least solely by reason of the paternity) unless he is married to the child's mother or otherwise has parental responsibility (PR) for the child (PR being a power given by virtue of section 2 of the Children Act 1989 to the biological mother, the biological father if he was married to the mother at the time of their child's birth or has acquired it under provisions of the 1989 Act, and others who acquire it under the 1989 Act). It is therefore sensible for an AMHP to be well versed in the rules.

Identifying the NR can be straightforward in many instances, but in others it can be one of the most complex tasks in the MHA assessment and as a result mistakes are not uncommon. In some cases, these mistakes may invalidate the detention, meaning that the person is unlawfully detained. It can be particularly difficult to identify the NR in circumstances where a person has, or appears to be having, relationship problems, or is in the process of separating from their husband, wife or civil partner but it is uncertain how permanent this separation will be. In such circumstances, it is often unclear legally whether the partner is still the NR. Some of these difficulties will be exacerbated by the nature of the person's mental health problems, such as where they are delusional or paranoid about the nature of their relationship with the NR.

In order to establish the identity of an NR, AMHPs may be required to ask what will often appear to be inappropriate or intrusive questions of the person or their family, such as 'Who is your oldest grandparent?' or 'Were your parents married when you were born?'. These types of questions might provoke hostile reactions at the best of times, but even more so during the trauma of a mental health breakdown and alongside a full MHA assessment.

The NR has an important role under the MHA. Section 13(4) enables an NR to require an AMHP to consider a case. In addition, under section 11 the NR must, wherever practicable, be informed about an application for admission to hospital under section 2 and, in the case of section 3 and section 7 (guardianship) applications, they must be consulted, unless it is not reasonably practical or would involve delay, and they can block the admission.

NRs have the power to make an application for compulsory admission and guardianship, although this is rarely used in England or Wales. The Code of Practice states:

> An AMHP is usually a more appropriate applicant than a patient's nearest relative, given their professional training and knowledge of the legislation and local resources. This also removes the risk that an application by the nearest relative might have an adverse effect on their relationship with the patient. (DH, 2015a, para 14.30 [England]; Welsh Assembly Government, 2016, para 14.23 [Wales])

However, if the NR does make an application, section 14 requires an AMHP to also provide a report. The Code of Practice also states that:

> If the nearest relative is the applicant, any AMHP and other professionals involved in the assessment of the patient should give advice and assistance. However, they should not assist in a patient's detention unless they believe it is justified and lawful. (DH, 2015a, para 17.11 [England]; Welsh Assembly Government, 2016, para 17.16 [Wales])

Under sections 23 and 25, the NR can order the discharge of a patient who is detained in hospital under section 2 or 3, or who is subject to a CTO, by giving the hospital managers at least 72 hours' notice, in writing. The person must be discharged unless the responsible clinician certifies that in his or her opinion the person, if discharged, would be likely to present a danger to themselves or others. Where such a 'barring certificate' is issued, the NR may apply to the mental health tribunal, unless the person is detained under section 2 of the MHA. So far as guardianship is concerned, the NR can direct discharge of guardianship forthwith. Since there is no provision for barring by the responsible clinician, a discharge order of guardianship by an NR will be effective immediately it is given.

Changing an NR

The MHA allows the NR to be changed in certain circumstances. There are two ways that this can be done.

First, the NR may *delegate* their functions to any person (other than the person being assessed or a person disqualified under section 26(5)) who is willing to take on this role. Note that the person cannot prevent the delegation (whether or not they are subject to the MHA).

Secondly, under section 29(1) the county court may make an order directing that the functions of the NR be exercised by another person, including an LA. An application to the court can be made by the person being assessed, a relative, any person with whom the person being assessed resides or an AMHP.

An application can only rely upon the grounds set out under section 29(3), which are:

- the person being assessed has no NR, or it cannot reasonably be determined whether the patient has any NR, or who they are; or
- the existing NR is incapable of acting as such due to mental disorder or other illness; or
- the existing NR unreasonably objects to the application for the person to be admitted for treatment or to be placed under guardianship; or
- the existing NR has exercised their power to discharge the person or is likely to exercise their rights in such a way as does not give due regard to the person's welfare or to the interests of the public; or
- the existing NR is not a suitable person to act as such.

Under section 29 of the MHA, the county court can order that the functions of the NR shall be exercised by someone *else* regarded as suitable to act as such and who is willing to do so. The application may (but does not have to) nominate a person whom the applicant would like to be appointed as the acting NR.

Duties to inform and consult the NR

When contacting relatives and carers, the AMHP should consider under what authority this is being done, and whether it arises from a duty or power contained within the MHA (and explained in the Codes of Practice). This is important, for example, when considering the duties to consult and inform the NR under sections 11(3), 11(4) and 13(1A)(b), sections which refer to when an application is going to be made, and not the previous stage when the assessment is being set up.

 ESSENTIAL INFORMATION: LAW

Duties to inform and consult the NR

Under section 11 of the MHA

(3) Before or within a reasonable time after an application for the admission of a patient for assessment is made by an approved mental health professional, that professional shall take such steps as are practicable to inform the person (if any) appearing to be the

nearest relative of the patient that the application is to be or has been made and of the power of the nearest relative under section 23(2)(a) below.

(4) An approved mental health professional may not make an application for admission for treatment or a guardianship application in respect of a patient in either of the following cases—

(a) the nearest relative of the patient has notified that professional, or the local social services authority on whose behalf the professional is acting, that he objects to the application being made; or

(b) that professional has not consulted the person (if any) appearing to be the nearest relative of the patient, but the requirement to consult that person does not apply if it appears to the professional that in the circumstances such consultation is not reasonably practicable or would involve unreasonable delay.

Under section 13 of the MHA

(1A) If that professional is—

(a) satisfied that such an application ought to be made in respect of the patient; and

(b) of the opinion, having regard to any wishes expressed by relatives of the patient or any other relevant circumstances, that it is necessary or proper for the application to be made by him,

he shall make the application.

Therefore, under the duties to inform and consult with the NR contained in the MHA, the AMHP can, and in most cases should, liaise with other relatives and carers in order to carry out their statutory functions. This is explained further in the MHA Codes of Practice for England and Wales. As mentioned, caution should be exercised when doing so, as there may be occasions when the sharing of information needs to end as you detect potential harmful consequences to the person being assessed and/or the person you are having the conversation with, where you will need to opt to listen only.

It is also possible that an advance statement of wishes may exist stating who should be contacted and when. Such a statement is not legally binding but is something you should have regard to (if the person had capacity when they made the statement).

 Please see online resources for update

Resourcing the MHA assessment

The AMHP has the key role in the coordination of the MHA assessment. This includes not only coordination of the professionals that may accompany them but also the resources that are required to effectively and safely discharge their responsibilities. At times it can also mean creating resources to fit unique circumstances in order to achieve a safe and effective assessment environment.

The following parts of this chapter detail the resources that AMHPs will need and some that they may need to have thought about prior to the assessment taking place. All of these resources will involve balancing other requests that may have been received. Therefore, setting a time for the assessment can be challenging since access to all potential appropriate resources may not be possible. The order in which an AMHP is able to secure resources will largely be based on their own personal experience of their availability and their view as to what needs to be secured first. AMHPs often find that they will need to make follow-up calls in the organisation of an assessment and adjust the times to suit the availability of other resources that might be required.

ESSENTIAL KNOWLEDGE

MHA assessment – an adaptable checklist

Location/address of the assessment:

Access details (key safe, floor level, key needed, parking):

Nearest Relative's name, address and telephone number:

1st Doctor Section 12(2)/previous acquaintance – name and telephone number:

2nd Doctor Section 12(2)/previous acquaintance – name and telephone number:

GP details:

Crisis/Home treatment team details:

Conveyance details and reference number:

Police log number:

Inpatient bed (identified if needed) address and telephone number:

Presenting risks and needs which need to be highlighted to assessing team:

Doctors

For most MHA assessment interviews the AMHP will be taking two appropriate doctors, ideally a combination of one doctor with previous acquaintance and one section 12(2) doctor, or otherwise two section 12(2) doctors. The only exceptions to this are in an emergency situation under section 4 or under section 136 of the MHA, where a second doctor is not initially required. Sometimes doctors are determined to attend the assessment because they are on an organised rota, when there may be another doctor available who would be more suitable. Equally, a referring doctor may leave a medical recommendation but may not be available for when the MHA assessment interview is convened. In all cases, it remains the AMHP's responsibility to make the decision as to which doctors are the most suited to the person's circumstances from the broader group of those doctors available (see Chapter 7), and as to which medical recommendations to found their applications for detention on.

Beds

The need for an inpatient psychiatric bed arises as a consequence of an application being made. The responsibility to find a bed rests absolutely with the doctors, although this may have been delegated by the mental health NHS trust to a bed manager (see Chapter 7). Although the AMHP may have a view of what category of bed is required, the NHS should ultimately decide this, and the AMHP should not be put under pressure to make decisions regarding the appropriateness of particular beds (see Chapter 7).

Crisis services

The attendance of mental health home treatment teams or crisis teams accompanying the assessment team is now commonplace in most areas. Although these teams are not decision-makers as to whether a person should be detained, their opinion is of great importance as they represent potentially a less restrictive option, and they can be influential as to whether hospital admission may be avoided if the assessed person will engage with them. Therefore, trying to secure their attendance at an MHA assessment is often beneficial.

While crisis teams may often state that their role is to gatekeep beds, this does not give them the power to veto a decision among the assessing team to detain, and their attendance at the MHA assessment is at the discretion of the AMHP.

Equally, delaying an MHA assessment to enable a mental health home treatment team or crisis team to attend needs to be balanced against the urgency for the assessment.

Police involvement and section 135(1) or (2) warrants

Requests for warrants are becoming more commonplace as the police are challenging the legal framework underpinning their attendance at an MHA assessment without one. There are two types of warrant. The first is a section 135(1) warrant, where an AMHP may be required to seek a warrant from a Justice of the Peace within their jurisdiction to enable any constable to gain entry to a property (by force if necessary) for the purposes of removing them to a place of safety for an MHA assessment or make other arrangements for the person's treatment or care. The second is a section 135(2) warrant, which can be sought by a constable or other authorised person (not exclusively an AMHP) from a Justice of the Peace to enable any constable to retake a person who is liable to be detained. A common example under section 135(2) is where a person has absconded after an application for detention has been signed or where a person has been admitted and detained but has then failed to return from section 17 leave. To gain either warrant an AMHP must convince the Justice of the Peace (normally accompanied by a legal adviser) that there is reasonable cause to suspect that the person is believed to be suffering from mental disorder and needs to be assessed, and that it is a proportionate response in respect of the person's Article 8 ECHR right to a private and family life.

 ESSENTIAL KNOWLEDGE: LAW

MHA, section 135: Warrant to search for and remove patients

(1) If it appears to a justice of the peace, on information on oath laid by an approved mental health professional, that there is reasonable cause to suspect that a person believed to be suffering from mental disorder—

   (a) has been, or is being, ill-treated, neglected or kept otherwise than under proper control, in any place within the jurisdiction of the justice, or

   (b) being unable to care for himself, is living alone in any such place,

the justice may issue a warrant authorising any constable to enter, if need be by force, any premises specified in the warrant in which that person is believed to be, and, if thought fit, to remove him to a place of safety with a view to the making of an application in respect of him under Part II of this Act, or of other arrangements for his treatment or care.

(1A) If the premises specified in the warrant are a place of safety, the constable executing the warrant may, instead of removing the person to another place of safety, keep the person at those premises for the purpose mentioned in subsection (1).

(2) If it appears to a justice of the peace, on information on oath laid by any constable or other person who is authorised by or under this Act or under article 8 of the Mental Health (Care and Treatment) (Scotland) Act 2003 (Consequential Provisions) Order 2005 to take a patient to any place, or to take into custody or retake a patient who is liable under this Act or under the said article 8 to be so taken or retaken—

(a) that there is reasonable cause to believe that the patient is to be found on premises within the jurisdiction of the justice; and

(b) that admission to the premises has been refused or that a refusal of such admission is apprehended,

the justice may issue a warrant authorising any constable to enter the premises, if need be by force, and remove the patient.

Outside the framework of section 135, if you fear that there may be a need for police involvement at the assessment, it may be advisable to liaise with the police in advance, providing essential information to them so you can urgently seek their attendance via 999 knowing that there will be a pre-existing log on record containing that information. Requesting their attendance to prevent a breach of the peace is unlikely now to be sufficiently convincing. Depending upon the circumstances, section 17 of the Police and Criminal Evidence Act 1984 can be used by the police to enter and search a premises in order to save life and limb, or to prevent serious damage to property. It should be noted that the police often use the 'RAVE' criteria – Risk, Aggression, Violence and Escape – to determine if they should attend. Language is important here; the term 'urgent' to a police officer can mean utilising specialist resources such as helicopters, armed units and so on, which is not often the meaning the AMHP had in mind.

Locksmith

When using a section 135 warrant, a locksmith may affect a more proportionate entry into a property than the police forcing entry. A locksmith who is unfamiliar with MHA work may require clear direction, and also may need to be told to remain nearby to secure the property afterwards, thereby fulfilling the LA's responsibilities under section 47 of the Care Act 2014 (England) or section 58 of the Social Services and Well-being (Wales) Act 2014 by taking reasonable steps to protect a person's moveable property to prevent or mitigate the loss of or damage to that property. This is covered in greater detail in Chapter 7, along with AMHP responsibilities towards pets, property and children.

Requesting conveyance

This is probably one of the most difficult areas of AMHP practice. Planning how the person, if detained, will be conveyed to hospital needs to be considered during the setting up of the assessment. Not every geographical area has a dedicated transport service to take people to hospital following an MHA assessment. As with the police, if you use the ambulance service they will have an algorithm to decide priority, so quoting a 'psychiatric emergency' can be useful. If control and restraint is required, the AMHP will be needed in most circumstances to provide a risk assessment based on what is already known and decide who is going to be asked to use restraint. There should be a local agreement between police and ambulance service regarding conveyance and restraint, and when escalation to involve the police is justified.

The MHA assessment interview

Interviewing in a suitable manner

The MHA assessment interview can be undertaken in any environment, but the AMHP will need to try to ensure that the assessed person's privacy and dignity is upheld at every opportunity where possible, and that the person is interviewed in a suitable manner. Sufficient time should also be given to building a rapport, if possible, as you want the person to trust you and to be open.

 **ESSENTIAL KNOWLEDGE: LAW**

MHA, section 13(2)

Before making an application for the admission of a patient to hospital an approved mental health professional shall interview the patient in a suitable manner and satisfy himself that detention in a hospital is in all the circumstances of the case the most appropriate way of providing the care and medical treatment of which the patient stands in need.

There are occasions though when interviewing in a suitable manner may be challenging due to circumstances such as:

- the nature of the environment where the assessment must be undertaken;
- the behaviours exhibited by the person being assessed; or
- levels of intoxication from alcohol or drugs, or dependency on alcohol or drugs.

There may also be language difficulties, sensory impairments, translation needs, equality issues, reasonable adjustments and cultural needs that will need to be considered when undertaking the assessment interview to maximise the assessed person's participation and involvement in that interview. It is also sensible to clarify with other professionals whether the person is fit to be discharged if admitted to a general hospital and their view about the person's fitness to be interviewed.

The assessment interview

 ESSENTIAL KNOWLEDGE: PRACTICE GUIDANCE

The dynamics of an MHA assessment interview will vary due to the circumstances, including the location and the behaviour of the person being assessed. However, there are essential components:

- The MHA Codes of Practice state: 'At the start of an assessment, AMHPs should identify themselves to the person being assessed, members of the family, carers or friends, and the other professionals present. AMHPs should ensure that the purpose of the visit, their role and that of the other professionals is explained. They should carry documents with them at all times which identify them as AMHPs, and which specify both the LA which approved them and the LA on whose behalf they are acting.' (DH, 2015a, para 14.51 [England]; Welsh Assembly Government, 2016, para 2.33 [Wales])
- Structured questions need to be posed to gain the best information to help base a decision on. These should be planned with those attending the assessment prior to the start of the interview.
- There should be discussion of the identified risk with the person to gain their perspective.
- The person's views and wishes should be taken into account.
- There should be an opportunity for the person to ask questions.
- There is a need, where practicable, for the AMHP to see the person on their own.
- Mental capacity should be determined, in relation to specific care and treatment decisions.

(Where the person being assessed is a child or young person, see Chapter 7.)

This is what persons with lived experience told us.

ESSENTIAL KNOWLEDGE: VIEWS OF PERSONS WITH LIVED EXPERIENCE

Ensure that the person being assessed:

- has had adequate and reasonable opportunity and help to eat and has a drink of water before the assessment, and access to water during it;
- is not overtired and has had an opportunity to rest, as would be reasonable for anyone;
- understands the process, the assessment and why it has to happen (and that any friends and/or family members understand the process, the assessment and why it has to happen);
- is treated with dignity and respect;
- is asked what they want to happen.

Ensure that:

- professionals remember that an MHA assessment is stressful particularly for the person who is the subject of it;
- professionals recognise the need to include the person and their representatives at all times and that the way the assessment is structured should revolve around that person, for example if they need to take a break, if they need to have information repeated or explained in a different way, if their distress makes it unbearable to continue at that moment;
- the appropriate timescales have not been breached, and that the person is not hauled out of a custody suite and then expected to 'perform';
- the setting for the assessment is appropriate, even if rooms are few and far between; that there are enough chairs, space, light and air for all to be as comfortable as possible;
- the person/carer is asked whether they are comfortable and whether there is anyone else they need to help them;
- professionals/doctors/health care professionals bear in mind the nuances of, for example, domestic abuse, as signs can often be very subtle;
- the person is not too outnumbered by professionals and that they are properly introduced.
- the person is asked if name badges in these circumstances would be helpful, perhaps not ID badges but sticky labels or similar, as it is usually very stressful when people are being assessed.

The decision/outcome of the MHA assessment

ESSENTIAL KNOWLEDGE: PRACTICE GUIDANCE

The decisions that flow from an MHA assessment and the MHA interview fall within six broad areas:

- no further action or involvement from mental health services;
- engagement of community mental health services as more appropriate or as a least restrictive alternative;
- informal admission to a psychiatric ward, as recognised by section 131 of the MHA, assuming that the person has given valid consent or is not being deprived of their liberty;
- an application for detention under section 4, section 2 or section 3 of the MHA;
- an application for guardianship under section 7 of the MHA;
- a Nearest Relative application for detention in hospital or guardianship (this is extremely rare in practice but is a possibility, albeit a remote and arguably inappropriate one).

Within each option, consideration needs to be given to the NR, carers and relatives, and their involvement in a care and treatment plan.

The person and the NR need to be made aware of their rights. It is the hospital manager's duty to ensure that the person, once they are subject to the MHA, understands their rights to a tribunal, and to give information to the NR (see MHA, section 132).

See Chapter 7 for scrutinising detention paperwork prior to admission.

ESSENTIAL KNOWLEDGE: PRACTICE GUIDANCE

Vulnerability on admission

Special attention should be given to communicating vulnerability or special needs to the inpatient ward, the bed finders and also the LA concerning the welfare of certain hospital patients. This is because within section 13(2) of the

MHA the AMHP must 'satisfy [themselves] that detention in a hospital is in all the circumstances of the case the most appropriate way of providing the care and medical treatment of which the [person] stands in need'. Although this does not place a duty on the AMHP to investigate the proposed ward where they are going to be detained (*DD v Durham County Council* [2012] EWHC 1503 QB), the AMHP will be asked for a risk assessment, and has duties under 'Safeguarding' to highlight, record and refer safeguarding concerns. Such concerns may relate to sexual vulnerability, for instance, where a gender/sexuality appropriate or otherwise specific ward is needed.

Also, section 116 of the MHA places a duty on the LA to arrange for a child or young person who is in the care of the local authority by virtue of a care order, a person who is subject to Guardianship under the MHA, or a person for whom the NR has been transferred to the local authority, to be visited in hospital by the LA. Section 131A also requires that mentally disordered children who are admitted should be placed in child-friendly environments.

Important and relevant information should also be included in your brief outline and full reports which are sent to the ward on admission. (See also Chapter 7.)

How the outcomes above are realised depends on the views and perspectives of those present at the assessment, together with the AMHP's independent view. Crisis services, where they exist, can provide a possible least restrictive alternative to admission but cannot (yet) veto any application for detention.

Receiving medical recommendations

When presented with medical recommendations by the assessing doctors, an AMHP must scrutinise these to check for errors. Thereafter, the AMHP has 14 days in which to decide, independently, if they ought to make an application for detention. Utilising these 14 days if you are on duty as part of a set rota or if you are a nurse, occupational therapist, psychology or social work AMHP who does not work for the LA full time can be challenging and therefore there may be a disincentive to use this time. Thus, if you intend to take some or all of the 14 days to reach a decision, there needs to be a clear plan in place with the AMHP service, and another AMHP may need to re-interview the person if an application is needed later when you are not on duty.

NR power to make an application

The NR (as they appear to be) for a person has the same power as an AMHP to make application for detention of their relative or for guardianship. Applications, whether made by the AMHP or the NR, still need to be founded on medical recommendations. The MHA Code of Practice states:

> An application for detention may be made by an AMHP or the patient's nearest relative ... An AMHP is usually a more appropriate applicant than a patient's nearest relative, given their professional training and knowledge of the legislation and local resources. This also reduces the risk that an application by the nearest relative might have an adverse effect on their relationship with the patient. (DH, 2015a, para 14.30 [England]; Welsh Assembly Government, 2016, para 14.23 [Wales])

Informing or consulting the NR

If the decision of the AMHP is to make an application, they must adhere to MHA, section 13(3) and (4), which requires them to either inform or consult the NR unless it appears to the AMHP that in the circumstances such consultation is not reasonably practicable or would involve unreasonable delay. If in doing so, the AMHP feels that a decision relating to changing the NR needs to be made, it may be appropriate as outlined above for them to discuss with the NR authorising someone else to perform their functions or making an application to the county court for displacement.

Conveyance

When organising conveyance (see Chapter 7), the AMHP needs to decide whether any pre-organised method remains appropriate. The AMHP, and anyone authorised by them to convey the person, has the powers of a constable.

If an application is made for admission to hospital, the person becomes 'liable to be detained'. Section 6 provides that the application is sufficient authority to take and convey the person to hospital. Section 137 provides that the person is deemed to be in legal custody and the person required or authorised to convey the person (eg the AMHP) is granted the powers of a constable when doing so (see Chapter 7). This means, for example, that they may use reasonable force to stop the person escaping, to secure the conveyance or to arrest the person. In practice, difficulties can arise where there is a delay in the transport and the AMHP has to ensure that the person does not escape during this time. It is important to plan for such eventualities beforehand and seek assistance from others, including the police if necessary.

When conveyance begins, the AMHP needs to be clear with the authorised person (whether a police officer, or specialist transport or general ambulance staff) that they are happy to accept the power, know the limits of these powers and carry the medical recommendations and application for detention with the person, and that they cannot delegate the powers themselves to others. There is a general principle of public law that if legislation confers power on a specified individual or authority, it is that individual or authority that must exercise the power, and the power must not be given away to another person or authority unless express provision is made. The Codes of Practice state:

> People authorised by the applicant to transport patients act in their own right and not as the agent of the applicant. They may act on their own initiative to restrain patients and prevent them absconding, if absolutely necessary. When they are the applicant, AMHPs retain a professional responsibility to ensure that the patient is transported in a lawful and humane manner and should give guidance to those asked to assist. (DH, 2015a, para 17.18 [England])

> The task of conveying the patient may be delegated, for example, to ambulance staff, and help may be sought from the police. The AMHP (or other authorised person) is ultimately responsible for ensuring the patient is transported in a lawful and humane way and should give guidance to those asked to help (Welsh Assembly Government, 2016, para 9.10 [Wales])

It is the professional responsibility of the AMHP as applicant to ensure the patient arrives at the designated hospital. It is therefore advisable for the AMHP to contact the admitting ward to check their arrival and, in addition, that the detention papers have been accepted within the meaning of section 6(3) of the MHA.

Recording

Good recording is required of all professional roles, and AMHP work is no different. Typically, in the course of their work an AMHP (in addition to the official MHA forms) should keep case notes. Latterly, the AMHP is required to write an initial brief outline report (DH, 2015a, para 14.93 [England]; Welsh Assembly Government, 2016, para 14.89 [Wales]), followed by a full report (DH, 2015a, para 14.95 [England]; Welsh Assembly Government, 2016, para 14.87 [Wales]) as part of the admissions process, or record the outcome of the assessment where no admission under the MHA has been required. There may also be the requirement to write to the NR, if they made a request for an MHA assessment under section 13(4), and no application is made. Lastly, as an AMHP you may be required to write to the local authority to request that an NR is displaced or appointed. The format for this recording will vary nationally, as there are no regulated formats.

ESSENTIAL KNOWLEDGE: PRACTICE GUIDANCE

Recording

When recording either case notes, or writing the outline report and full report (if different), you should consider:

- Who is the intended audience?
- Is the purpose of the report clear?
- Will the person reading it be able to understand how you reached your decision?
- Is it defensible if you are called to account for your decision?
- Is it 'court worthy'?
- Will it demonstrate your AMHP key competence when seeking re-approval as an AMHP?
- Does it inform the reader of the source of information/evidence and would it be enough to remind you if you were called to account several years later?
- Have you identified sensitive third-party information that should not be shared?
- Has the report been proofread for errors?
- Has the report been signed and dated?

When writing your report you should also consider good practice in recording; the person who is the subject of the report may make a future request to see their social and health care records, or a freedom of information request may be made under the Freedom of Information Act 2000.

Chapter 7 will consider safeguarding, police involvement, scrutinising papers to avoid errors, pets and property issues, children in the household, personal safety, working with other professionals, managing persons who are AWOL or absent, and working with a lack of resources.

▶ KEY MESSAGES

- Taking a detailed and well-considered, balanced referral is key to whether the assessment progresses or not, and ensuring that all the pertinent factors have been included in the planning.

- The person who is being assessed under the MHA must be at the centre of the planning and decision-making.

- Recording all the different decisions that are made during the MHA referral and their rationale is essential to defensible decision-making.

KNOWLEDGE REVIEW

- The 'reason to think' threshold for a referral is not an overly high threshold as a matter of law. It does not require certainty that an application is needed, only a belief that one *may* be needed. Section 13(1) does not necessarily require a formal referral or request to be made to trigger the duty, although in most cases these will supply enough information for the 'reason to think' test to be satisfied.

- The MHA assessment interview can be undertaken in any environment, but the AMHP will need to try to ensure that, at every opportunity where possible, the assessed person's privacy and dignity is upheld, and that the person is interviewed in a suitable manner.

FURTHER READING

- Hale, B. (2017) *Mental health law,* London: Sweet & Maxwell.

- Jones, R. (2018) *Mental Health Act manual,* London: Sweet & Maxwell.

7

Risks and challenges in Mental Health Act assessments

Chapter aim

This chapter will enable you to meet the following AMHP key competence themes:

- Working in partnership

- Considering the feasibility of and contributing effectively to planning and implementing options for care such as alternatives to compulsory admission, discharge and aftercare

- Assessing and managing risk

- Effectively managing difficult situations of anxiety, risk and conflict

- Using appropriate independence, authority and autonomy

Schedule 2 of the Mental Health (Approved Mental Health Professionals) (Approval) (England) Regulations 2008
Key Competences 4(c), (e)–(k), 5(d), (f)

Schedule 2 of the Mental Health (Approval of Persons to be Approved Mental Health Professionals) (Wales) Regulations 2008
Key Competences 4.3, 4.5–4.11, 5.3, 5.5

In this chapter we will consider the unpredictability of MHA assessments, and some of the scenarios that can occur when assessing people under the MHA. This will include:

- assessing children and young people;
- those who abscond following an assessment interview;
- assessing those who are already liable to be detained, such as those already subject to section 37/41, section 17 or section 17A;
- managing confidentiality;

- safeguarding adults and children from harm; and
- the impact of inadequate resources.

There will also be an exploration of working with other professionals and the tensions that can arise through joint work. This chapter will cover the practicalities that an AMHP needs to consider when being involved in a community assessment and maintaining their own safety.

Introduction

Despite an AMHP's best attempts to predict and pre-empt the connotations, needs and risks within an MHA assessment, events and outcomes may occur which have not occurred previously and could not be predicted. Therefore, what is required is to think ahead about the possible scenarios that may unfold when undertaking MHA work and how to manage and resolve these. Also, the response to a challenge or difficulty will differ according to the legal status of the person at the centre of the MHA assessment; for example, whether they:

- are at liberty, with the same privileges that we all have as members of the public;
- are liable to be detained (in legal custody or at large) but not yet detained, for example on the basis that an application for admission to hospital has been made;
- are actually being detained in hospital; and/or
- have been arrested by the police and are therefore subject to the Police and Criminal Evidence Act 1984 (PACE).

The personal skills, knowledge and resourcefulness needed to solve complex difficulties and challenges should not be underestimated, and you may need to involve others in making decisions (see *Bolam* discussions in Chapter 3).

 ESSENTIAL KNOWLEDGE: CODES OF PRACTICE

England

Before making an application, AMHPs should ensure that appropriate arrangements are in place for the immediate care of any dependent children the patient may have and any adults who rely on the patient for care. Their needs should already have been considered as part of the assessment. Where relevant, AMHPs should also ensure that practical arrangements are made for the care of any pets and for the local authority to carry out its other duties under the Care Act 2014 to secure the patient's home and protect their property.

DH, 2015a, para 14.88

Wales

Before making an application, AMHPs should ensure that appropriate arrangements are in place for the immediate care of any dependent children the patient may have and any adults who rely on the patient for care. Their needs should already have been considered as part of the assessment. Where relevant, AMHPs should also ensure that practical arrangements are made for the care of any pets and for the local authority to carry out its other duties under the Social Services and Well-being (Wales) Act 2014 to secure the patient's home and protect their property.

Welsh Assembly Government, 2016, paras 14.80 and 14.81

Lack of resources

A significant challenge for MHA work arises when there is a lack of appropriate resources. Ask any AMHP about what they feel is the most challenging part of the role and they are sure to say a lack of bed availability, issues with transport and the inadequate alternatives for least restrictive options. A common scenario is where assessing doctors are able to make medical recommendations, but the AMHP cannot make an application for detention or utilise the least restrictive options as these are unavailable, an issue that is commonly reported, most recently in the All-Party Parliamentary Group report (APPG, 2019).

The lack of available beds is a common concern and is ultimately the responsibility of the doctor (DH, 2015a, para 14.77 [England]; Welsh Assembly Government, 2016, para 14.69 [Wales]). A decision to delay an MHA assessment due to lack of a bed needs to be weighed up carefully, as an assessment should proceed unless by doing so the risk to the person increases, for example if it causes the person distress and harm could occur, or if the person is likely to become aggressive. The delay, therefore, in these two scenarios could be justified as it would be unsafe to undertake an assessment without the means to manage that risk effectively. Typically, the delay only arises in respect of community assessments where the lack of a bed may increase the risk to the person who is going to be assessed for a variety of reasons. It is eminently sensible to confirm the bed directly with the ward (or via the bed manager) to gain some reassurance that the bed is available, and avoid a ward turning a patient away from being admitted. This is also a good opportunity to confirm the address of the ward.

Another common resource issue (discussed later in this chapter) is the availability and timeliness of an appropriate conveyance, on occasion leaving the AMHP waiting several hours in the community, possibly in a vulnerable, if not awkward, situation if they remain with the person.

Since the enactment of the Police and Crime Act 2017 the use of a place of safety for the purposes of sections 135 and 136 has been reduced to 24 hours, with a possibility of a 12-hour extension only if it is necessary because the person's condition means it would not be practical for the assessment to be carried out within 24 hours (section 136A of the MHA). The intention behind these reforms is in part to ensure that people are not being detained in inappropriate accommodation because a bed or transport cannot be made available. Whether underresourced services can achieve this aim remains to be seen.

Assessing children and young people

There is no minimum age limit for detention in hospital under the MHA. When it comes to assessing children (those aged under 16) and young people (those aged 16 and 17), special considerations will apply. The MHA never operates in isolation and when it comes to children and young people it is necessary to bear in mind other legislation such as the Mental Capacity Act (MCA) 2005 (for 16- and 17-year-olds), the Children Acts 1989 and 2004, the Children and Families Act 2014, the Social Services and Well-being (Wales) Act 2014, the Family Law Reform Act 1969, and the United Nations Convention on the Rights of the Child, as well as relevant case law, common law principles and the relevant codes of practice. The MHA Codes of Practice discuss the position of children and young people in chapter 19; this should always be your starting point.

Assessments will need to consider the issue of parental responsibility. Parental responsibility refers to all the 'rights, duties, powers, responsibilities and authority' which in law a parent has in relation to their child (section 3 of the Children Act 1989), and usually lies with the parents – but not always. When taking decisions under the MHA, it is essential to be certain where parental responsibility lies, especially if the child is subject, for example, to a care order under section 31 of the Children Act 1989. The concept of the scope of parental responsibility may also be relevant. This concept derives mainly from human rights case law and sets limits on the extent to which a person with parental responsibility may consent on behalf of a child or young person. The boundaries are not clearly defined, but it involves considering if this is a decision a parent should reasonably be expected to make and if there are any other factors that might undermine the validity of parental consent.

The issue of parent responsibility will normally be relevant when trying to work out who is the Nearest Relative (NR) of the child or young person. In relation to persons under 18, if the parents are not married, then the father is to be disregarded unless he has parental responsibility, which might have been obtained, for instance, through a court order or if an agreement had been made with the child or young person's mother. This can be a controversial area for AMHPs where the father may feel excluded from decisions concerning his child. For further discussion on the NR provisions, see Chapter 6.

MHA assessments will need to consider the child or young person's ability to consent to the proposed admission and assessment/treatment. This will depend on their capacity or competence to do so. The concepts of capacity and competence have similarities but are in legal terms distinct. The MCA 2005 will determine if a young person has *capacity* to consent. This Act applies to anyone aged 16 or over, and on the basis that the inability to make the decision in question is because of an impairment of, or a disturbance in the functioning of, the mind or brain. The 2005 Act does not apply if the person aged 16 or 17 is unable to consent to the assessment for some other reason, for example because they are overwhelmed by the implications. The *competence* of the child to consent to the assessment will be determined by the principles set out in *Gillick v West Norfolk and Wisbech Area Health Authority* [1986] AC 112. This case provided that if a child is of sufficient age and understanding, they can give valid consent to contraceptive advice and treatment, without the consent of the parents. The principles elucidated in *Gillick* will normally apply where a child is aged under 16.

When it comes to an MHA assessment, at least one of the people involved in the assessment of a person who is under 18 years old – that is, one of the two medical practitioners or the AMHP – should be a child and adolescent mental health services specialist (DH, 2015a, para 19.73 [England]; Welsh Assembly Government, 2016, para 20.18 [Wales]). When this is not possible, such professionals should be consulted as soon as possible. Children and young people admitted to hospital for treatment of mental disorder must be accommodated in an age-appropriate environment subject to any limitations imposed by their mental health or other needs (MHA, section 131A).

'The absent patient'

When considering the AMHP role in respect of 'the absent patient', it is important to understand the differing terminology used and when each term is applicable. The two terms to be discussed are 'absconding' and 'absent without leave' (AWOL).

'Absconding'

The term 'absconding' refers to a situation where an application has been made for a person's detention in hospital under Part 2 of the MHA, but the person escapes before they reach hospital. This situation is addressed by sections 137 and 138 of the MHA. Any person who under the MHA is required or authorised to be conveyed to any place, kept in custody or detained in a place of safety or any other place (under a direction by the Secretary of State for the purposes of a restriction order under section 42(6)) is deemed to be in legal custody. Further to this, the individual who is required or authorised to take the person into custody has the powers, authorities, protection and privileges of a police constable. For instance, they may use reasonable force to stop the person escaping. However, section 137 does not include powers to use force to enter premises and remove the person. As the applicant for the admission of the person under the MHA, the AMHP (or a person authorised by the AMHP) has authority to take and convey the person to the hospital named in the application. At this point the patient is considered to be 'liable to detention'.

 ESSENTIAL KNOWLEDGE: LAW

Escaping lawful custody

If the person escapes from legal custody, before being admitted to hospital, MHA, section 138 provides that they can be retaken by:

- the person who had custody immediately prior to the escape;
- any police constable or AMHP; or
- if the person is liable for detention under Part 2 of the MHA (or subject to guardianship or recall of a community treatment order [CTO]), any other person who could take them into custody under section 18 of the MHA (this would include hospital staff or any person authorised in writing by the hospital managers).

It is important to remind ourselves that the power to retake the absconding patient is, however, time limited, subject to the timescales set out in section 18(4) of the MHA.

 ESSENTIAL KNOWLEDGE: LAW

Time limits relating to an absconding patient

MHA, section 18(4) states:

A person shall not be taken into custody under this section after the later of—

(a) the end of the period of six months beginning with the first day of his absence without leave; and

(b) the end of the period for which ... he is liable to be detained or subject to guardianship, or in the case of the community patient, the community treatment order is in force.

Further to this, under section 18(5), a person cannot be taken into custody 'if the period for which he is liable to be detained is that specified in section 2(4), 4(4), 5(2) or 5(4) and that period has expired'.

So, what do these statutory provisions mean in practice and how should an AMHP demonstrate best practice in situations where a patient has absconded? It is useful to remember that, difficult and distressing as it may be when a patient who is liable to detention and for whom you, as AMHP, have custody absconds, these situations are rare. However, it is important that you are prepared and are familiar with the relevant chapter of the MHA Code of Practice (chapter 18 in England and chapter 17 in Wales), as well as with your local protocol and policy, to ensure that the appropriate steps are taken in a timely manner.

 ESSENTIAL KNOWLEDGE: PRACTICE GUIDANCE

Reporting an absconded patient

Key steps are:

1. The AMHP contacts the police to advise them of an absconding person, providing relevant information:

   (a) name, date of birth and legal status of the person;
   (b) the last known whereabouts of the patient, whether that is where they were being detained or if they had been seen elsewhere;
   (c) a description of the person including clothing and distinctive features;
   (d) any known health issues;
   (e) any risks to self and others.

2. The AMHP takes the completed paperwork to the admitting hospital and passes this and all other relevant information over to the nurse in charge, including the police log number.

3. The AMHP informs the duty AMHP manager, the NR and any other relevant person, while remaining mindful of the person's right to privacy.

'Absent without leave' (AWOL)

The definition of a person who is AWOL is contained in section 18 of the MHA. In summary, a person subject to formal detention is considered AWOL if they:

1. absent themselves from the hospital without leave granted under section 17 of the Act;
2. fail to return to the hospital at the expiration of any period of leave or on being recalled from leave;
3. absent themselves without permission from any place where they are required to reside in accordance with the conditions imposed on any grant of leave;
4. are subject to a Community Treatment Order (CTO) and have failed to return to the hospital when recalled, or subsequently abscond;
5. are subject to guardianship and are absent without permission from the place they are required by their guardian to live.

The AMHP role in circumstances where a person is AWOL is often limited, particularly in respect of those who are currently receiving treatment in hospital. In these circumstances the responsibility for assessing risk and alerting the relevant people and organisations, such as the police, is the responsibility of the hospital in which they are detained. However, section 18(1) of the MHA details those who may take the person and return them to hospital or another place as:

1. any AMHP
2. any officer on the staff of the hospital
3. any constable
4. any person authorised in writing by the managers of the hospital.

For those persons subject to a CTO all the above apply, with the addition of:

5. Any person authorised in writing by the responsible clinician.

For those patients subject to section 7 guardianship, the Act specifies:

1. any officer on the staff of a local social services authority;
2. any constable; or
3. any person authorised in writing by the guardian or local social services authority.

As with the absconding person, the timescales in which any person may be taken and returned as defined in section 18(4) apply (see 'Essential knowledge: law' box on pp 98-9).

It is unusual for an AMHP to be involved in the retaking and returning of an absconding person. However, in such circumstances, it is worth noting some key points:

- the responsibility for arranging transport for the person to hospital is held by the hospital from which they are absent, and
- where a person's whereabouts are known and the police are contacted, they may request the support of a suitably qualified and experienced mental health professional where possible, which may be an AMHP.

Working with other professionals

AMHP work is rarely solitary or focused on a singular professional perspective. Rather it is rooted in philosophies of collaborative practice, cooperation and shared decision-making. Such working with other professionals does not detract from the legal requirement for an AMHP to make an independent judgement during the assessment process but is a recognition of the AMHP's role of coordinating the process of assessment. However, working with colleagues who may have different perspectives and professional values can prove challenging to even the most experienced AMHP at times. Some of these challenges and tensions will be considered and explored here.

NHS mental health colleagues – roles and responsibilities

Working effectively alongside your mental health NHS colleagues is an essential part of undertaking an MHA assessment, as the majority of care and support for those with mental disorder arises from NHS resources, as it does similarly for inpatient care. There needs to be a clear understanding of roles within the LA and the NHS, of how urgency is understood, and of the implications when resources that an AMHP needs to effectively undertake their role are not available. One example of this is where a bed is not available when an AMHP ought to make an application for detention. Section 140 of the MHA requires clinical commissioning groups (CCGs) and Local Health Boards to notify local social services authorities of arrangements that are in place for the reception of patients in cases of special urgency or that are appropriate for children, but sometimes this is not well understood.

 **ESSENTIAL KNOWLEDGE: LAW**

MHA, section 140 – Notification of hospitals having arrangements for special cases

It shall be the duty of every clinical commissioning group and of every Local Health Board to give notice to every local social services authority for an area wholly or partly comprised within the area of the clinical commissioning group or Local Health Board specifying the hospital or hospitals administered by or otherwise available to the clinical commissioning group or Local Health Board in which arrangements are from time to time in force

(a) for the reception of patients in cases of special urgency;

(b) for the provision of accommodation or facilities designed so as to be specially suitable for patients who have not attained the age of 18 years.

Crisis services are increasingly attending assessments to act as gatekeepers to beds, and this needs to be managed. Crisis team workers are not part of the formal requirement for the person to be interviewed, usually by two registered medical practitioners and an AMHP, to decide if that person should be detained or not. If the assessing registered medical practitioners and AMHP all determine, through the completion of medical recommendations and an application for detention, that a person should be detained, the relevant NHS trust cannot refuse to provide a bed on the basis that the NHS team worker disagrees. In many cases, though, the NHS workers who attend may be arguing in favour of the less restrictive alternative, which is contained within the principles of the MHA Code. It is important that the AMHP has considered carefully all options before making an application, and, in particular, whether some form of community support is suitable and will proportionately manage the risk compared with a hospital admission.

Section 12 doctors/doctors with previous acquaintance – choosing the right doctors

Lack of availability of appropriate doctors for MHA assessments can be challenging. Some NHS trusts have doctors available on a rota system or have designated doctors available in certain settings such as health–based places of safety. However, this is not always the case, and those same designated doctors may already be engaged in other MHA work, as the geographical coverage of NHS trusts may include more than one local authority AMHP service placing demands on their time. Rotas and NHS arrangement should not, however, dictate which doctors are chosen for the assessment as the final choice needs to meet the criteria set out in section 12, and be appropriate for the person needing to be assessed.

Having 'previous acquaintance with the patient' as a registered medical practitioner is rather a low threshold; it does not require previous personal acquaintance, but rather previous knowledge of the case, although this does not extend to having reviewed the person's medical notes in advance of the assessment (*AR v Broglais Hospital* [2001] EWHC Admin 793). Doctors may fail to realise that they qualify as having previous acquaintance and therefore not highlight this on their medical recommendation, which may result in the AMHP having to explain on their application for detention why a doctor with prior acquaintance was not available, when in reality there was one present.

Delaying an assessment to enable a doctor with previous acquaintance to attend creates a dilemma. Waiting for an appropriate doctor to be available needs to be balanced against the delay of leaving a risky situation or an untreated or unsupported person longer than would be deemed acceptable.

A further issue arises if, as the AMHP, you believe that the registered medical practitioner has possibly acted perversely by not making a medical recommendation, leaving you with a decision as to whether you will ask the doctor to reconsider or seek the attendance of a further registered medical practitioner to assess, and how far you may take this to gain a medical recommendation. It would be very rarely justified to seek a different medical practitioner to undertake a reassessment, and you should seek legal advice first. The Code of Practice emphasises that where differences of opinion occur between professionals involved in the assessment, these should be discussed with each other (as well as consulting others), but ultimately professionals retain for themselves the final responsibility for their decision (DH, 2015a, para 14.109 [England]; Welsh Assembly Government, 2016, para 2.66 [Wales]).

The police – when is their involvement justified?

There are several occasions when police can become involved in MHA work. The most frequent occur when a person is detained under section 136 of the MHA and taken to a place of safety, or when a section 135(1) or section 135(2) warrant is required (these are covered in Chapter 6). Attendance at an MHA assessment by the police without a warrant is becoming increasingly unlikely due to police challenging the legality of their attendance and prioritising non-mental health work. This has clear implications if violence is anticipated at an assessment, or experienced while undertaking an assessment. The former may mean that an AMHP has to request a section 135(1) warrant to undertake the assessment safely, while if violence or aggression is experienced during the assessment (that cannot be de-escalated) the assessing team will need to retreat, and call the police.

None of which is particularly welcome, but it does mean that AMHPs need to consider how dignity and risk are managed proportionately. Finally, when engaging with the police it is worth remembering that police constables can be dispatched from differing disciplines (uniformed, plain-clothed, armed officers and so on) and recognising how each can have a differing impact on the assessment by virtue of their presence. Radios, which make noise, or the presence of the personal protection equipment (pepper spray, visible taser or firearms) can have an adverse effect on a mentally disordered person who is anxious or paranoid, for instance. Therefore, explaining the nuances to the police dispatcher and to the police who attend can enhance the experience of the assessment for the person being assessed and the outcomes that are achieved. It would also be beneficial to explain to the police dispatcher and those who attend the relevant law you are seeking to rely on (for example, which sections of the MHA will be relevant).

Conveyance – powers of a constable and who has these powers

An AMHP can authorise others to convey a person liable to be detained under section 6 of the MHA. Such individuals will also have the power of a constable to convey under section 137 of the MHA (see Chapter 6). The authorisation is usually given to ambulance crews (whether NHS or private transport) or to the police. The Code of Practice states: 'People authorised by the applicant to transport patients act in their own right and not as the agent of the applicant. They may act on their own initiative to restrain patients and prevent them absconding, if absolutely necessary' (DH, 2015a, para 17.18 [England]). (Conveying to hospital is discussed in the Welsh Code (Welsh Assembly Government, 2016) at paras 9.6 to 9.19.)

Under section 135(1) or section 135(2) the police are given powers to convey and can informally ask assistance of others, but this is not a delegation or authorisation. It is also worth noting that under section 135(2), a Justice of the Peace can authorise someone else to take the patient to the hospital or LA as directed.

Conveyance providers – choosing the correct means of conveyance

Choosing the correct means of conveyance is an important consideration for the AMHP when coordinating an MHA assessment. The MHA Codes of Practice state that the AMHP has a professional responsibility to ensure all necessary arrangements are made for the person to be transported to hospital (DH, 2015a, para 17.9 [England]; Welsh Assembly Government, 2016, para 9.7 [Wales]). As an AMHP your choice of conveyance maybe limited, depending upon who your local NHS trust has commissioned. This may also mean that waiting times for this transport to arrive can vary. If your NHS provides a dedicated conveyance service, you are fortunate in that you may be able to reduce waiting times between the completion of an MHA assessment and arriving at hospital. AMHPs have shared stories of having to wait in excess of four hours for conveyance to arrive, and if using NHS trust ambulances, the wait can be longer due to the prioritisation of acute physical life-threatening conditions. It is not advisable to transport people yourself, especially given that bed availability is often limited, which means that sometimes the person may need to be conveyed for a long distance to what may be the only available bed in the country. The Code of Practice advises that a private vehicle should be used only if the AMHP is satisfied that the person and others will be safe from harm and it is the most appropriate way of transporting the person. In such cases there should be a medical escort for the person other than the driver (DH, 2015a, para 17.17 [England]; see also para 9.10 of the Welsh Code [Welsh Assembly Government, 2016]).

 **ESSENTIAL KNOWLEDGE: LAW**

MHA, section 6 – Effect of application for admission

(1) An application for the admission of a patient to a hospital under this Part of this Act, duly completed in accordance with the provisions of this Part of this Act, shall be sufficient authority for the applicant, or any person authorised by the applicant, to take the patient and convey him to the hospital at any time within the following period, that is to say—

    (a) in the case of an application other than an emergency application, the period of 14 days beginning with the date on which the patient was last examined by a registered medical practitioner before giving a medical recommendation for the purposes of the application;

    (b) in the case of an emergency application, the period of 24 hours beginning at the time when the patient was examined by the practitioner giving the medical recommendation which is referred to in section 4(3) above, or at the time when the application is made, whichever is the earlier.

MHA, section 137 – Provisions as to custody, conveyance and detention

(1) Any person required or authorised by or by virtue of this Act to be conveyed to any place or to be kept in custody or detained in a place of safety or at any place to which he is taken under section 42(6) above shall, while being so conveyed, detained or kept, as the case may be, be deemed to be in legal custody.

(2) A constable or any other person required or authorised by or by virtue of this Act to take any person into custody, or to convey or detain any person shall, for the purposes of taking him into custody or conveying or detaining him, have all the powers, authorities, protection and privileges which a constable has within the area for which he acts as constable.

(3) In this section 'convey' includes any other expression denoting removal from one place to another.

Personal safety

Managing risk and assessing the health, wellbeing and safety of service users and others is a fundamental part of the AMHP role. In parallel with this, AMHPs must also be able to assess and manage any risks posed to themselves as AMHPs and to other members of the assessing team. Risk can occur within the assessment process itself but also as a result of stress caused by the challenges of the AMHP role and the unavailability of appropriate resources within the UK, and it is well known that stress can affect the concentration and perceptive skills of those who are assessing. The Health Care and Professions Council (HCPC) and Social Care Wales criteria for AMHP education focus on autonomous practice and make explicit reference to the management of risk. While risk is more frequently considered in respect of either the service user or the wider community, AMHPs must equally consider the risks posed to themselves and others during the assessment process, and how a lack of resources, both actual and emotional, may increase risk and diminish independence.

ESSENTIAL KNOWLEDGE: AMHP CRITERIA (STANDARDS RELEVANT TO EDUCATION AND TRAINING)

Autonomous practice

2.1 Be able to exercise appropriate use of independence, authority and autonomy in the AMHP role.

2.2 Be able to recognise, assess and manage effectively the risks related to the AMHP role.

2.3 Be able to manage anxiety, risk and conflict and understand its impact on AMHP practice.

Schedule 2 of the Mental Health (Approved Mental Health Professionals) (Approval) (England) Regulations 2008; Schedule 2 of the Mental Health (Approval of Persons to be Approved Mental Health Professionals) (Wales) Regulations 2008

MHA assessments should, where possible, be conducted jointly between the AMHP and at least one of the medical practitioners involved in the assessment (DH, 2015a, para 16.47 [England]; Welsh Assembly Government, 2016, para 14.35 [Wales]). The Codes of Practice identify the need for all participants within the assessment to be alert to the possible need to provide support to one another during the assessment process if risks should occur (para 14.47 [England and Wales]). They also state that consideration should be given to the involvement of the police in accordance with local policies and procedures (para 14.47 [England]; para 14.37 [Wales]). This process of joint working and awareness of the wellbeing and safety of others involved with the assessment is effective in minimising the potential risks to personal safety during the assessment process. One aspect that should be given careful consideration is the stipulation by the Codes of Practice that the person should usually be given the opportunity of speaking to the AMHP alone unless the AMHP has reason to fear physical harm, when they should insist that another professional is present (para 14.54 [England]; para 14.45 [Wales]).

Once the assessment has been completed and a decision made to make an application for the admission of the person to hospital, the role of the medical assessors is formally concluded. As noted previously, the AMHP has a professional responsibility to ensure all necessary arrangements are made for the patient to be transported to hospital. In some circumstances, other members of the assessing team may remain with the AMHP and service user until conveyance occurs, but often the AMHP may be left alone at this point if no risks to their own personal safety have been identified during the assessment process. This may leave the AMHP in a vulnerable situation with a potentially distressed or hostile service user.

That AMHPs feel fear when undertaking the role is little explored in the literature. One study of Approved Social Workers (ASWs) in Northern Ireland reported more than a quarter of its participants as feeling afraid or at risk, based, the authors suggest, on being left alone on their own in community settings with the person being assessed (Davidson and Campbell, 2010). There has been some examination of the skills needed during assessments, and these include building rapport and keeping things calm (Bowers et al, 2003, p 965). Using findings from a recent study, researchers have explored the behaviour of doctors and AMHPs during MHA assessments. They suggest that AMHPs from all professional backgrounds are, in effect, abandoned when the doctor feels their role is over. In turn, AMHPs tend to justify this abandonment or, to play on words, 'roll over' (Vicary et al, 2019).

When managing situations where the AMHP is alone awaiting the conveyance of the person to hospital, it is important to remain vigilant to any increasing risks to self, the service user or others. In such circumstances the AMHP should consider securing additional support through either an urgent request for police support or for support from internal services such as crisis support teams. However, the majority of assessments do not require such an escalation of support in the assessment setting. If the assessment has taken place in the person's home, good practice would indicate that using the time with the person to prepare basic items to take to hospital with them will enable the person to regain some control. Personal belongings such as toiletries and clothing can assist greatly in the process of settling into an unfamiliar hospital environment. The AMHP can also discuss with the person whether there is anyone else they would like notified of their admission and plan the best means of securing their property and effects once transport to hospital has arrived.

The impact of undertaking an MHA assessment can lead to other impacts on the personal wellbeing of the AMHP as a result of stress or exposure to situations of high expressed emotions. The importance of effective supervision and debriefing cannot be understated here (see Chapter 11).

REFLECTIVE ACTIVITY

Considerations relating to personal wellbeing

–   What are your priorities and needs for supervision in respect of the AMHP role?
–   How can you ensure that your needs are being met?
–   What additional support and wellbeing services are you able to access both during and outside the working day?

Other considerations

Children in the household

If you are aware that there are children at the property, there may be a need to liaise with children and young people's services for background information and to make a referral, and for the children to be cared for. This could be for several reasons: first, a child in this situation may be a child in need for the purposes of section 17 of the Children Act 1989, and if there is no one with parental responsibility in the family home, services will need to consider the implications of this. Assessments at places where children or young people are located need careful planning, and, for example, you may need to think about the time of the assessment, liaison with their school and if there need to be arrangements made for their care and support.

Property and pets

The responsibility for the temporary protection of property, including pets, is clearly defined as a duty placed on the LA by section 47 of the Care Act 2014 and section 58 of the Social Services and Wellbeing (Wales) Act 2014. In situations where an emergency or unplanned admission into hospital or residential care occurs, and the owner, due to the nature of their admission, is unable to make their own arrangements for their property, including pets, the LA must make appropriate arrangements to provide temporary protection. This is not necessarily the AMHP's responsibility alone, but in practice they will often undertake this role on behalf of the authority.

Environmental health considerations

There may be occasions where an MHA referral for a community assessment highlights that the dwelling where the person is residing contains environmental health and safety risks to the person concerned as well as, possibly, to those in neighbouring dwellings. This is also clearly a consideration for the assessing team and anyone entering the property. What counts as an environmental concern is too broad to list here. However, this may well require you to consult with an environmental health officer for advice on measures the assessing team need to take protect their own health and safety, as well as informing your responsibilities in relation to securing the property.

Personal protective equipment

The possibility that an AMHP and the assessing team might need personal protective equipment (PPE) such as face masks, aprons and over-clothing has always existed, particularly during assessments involving environmental health issues. More recently the demands for reviewing whether PPE should be carried as standard have gained greater impetus due to concerns relating to COVID-19. This is not the first time that the need for PPE has come squarely into focus due to viral infection concerns: previously, 'swine flu' (H1B1) and SARS (Severe Acute Respiratory Syndrome) have involved a similar need for precautions to be taken. It might increasingly become necessary for AMHPs to use such equipment, and for its use to be a planned rather than a reactive approach. However, despite its essential adoption in some cases, the necessity to wear PPE can conflict with our usual practices of engaging in an open and meaningful way, potentially causing relationship building through the social perspective approach to become diminished.

In times of public health crisis, AMHP services may require prioritisation of resources as a result of staff shortages arising from sickness absence, and MHA assessments may need to consider factors such as the risk of the person becoming infected or infecting others, and the availability of alternative legal powers, such as public health ones, to intervene. It is likely that viral protection will feature in MHA risk assessments as standard in future, as has been the case with hepatitis and immunodeficiency viruses. This could mean in practice that AMHPs must be immunised if a vaccine is available, and must wear certain protective clothing. Lastly, AMHP services may also need to ensure that AMHPs are not moving on from one assessment to the next without taking proper precautionary measures to limit the risk of contamination.

AMHPs are often grappling with balancing Articles 5 and 8 of the ECHR. However, during a public health emergency, engaging with Article 2 of the ECHR (the right to life) may increasingly become an important consideration. For example, it may be that a person with a mental disorder needs to be detained in hospital for treatment but is also infectious and therefore a risk to other hospital patients. In such cases AMHPs and hospital managers will need to review the best way of ensuring the person can get the treatment (both psychiatric and physical) that they need, while also minimising the risks to others. This decision may be assisted by government and other official guidance.

Securing property

As an AMHP you need to be ready to draw on resources such as locksmiths who can repair, make good or secure damage to doors and windows to secure property. This may also involve securing open or abandoned vehicles and arranging for such vehicles to be recovered. All should be done with the aim of avoiding loss, so an AMHP should consider disposing of food in the dwelling and rinsing dirty dishes to avoid infestations occurring, turning the heating onto frost protection only and taking any other measures to place the dwelling in the position where little can go wrong while it is unoccupied and to ensure that the person will not incur unnecessary utility costs. There may be occasions when an onward referral is needed to the LA's environmental health team.

Care of pets

At some point within your AMHP training you will have been alerted to the challenges that can arise from all manner of pets, from the seemingly harmless hamster through to the trio of alpacas owned by the person! AMHPs working in rural communities may have to consider farm animals as well. Organising pet handlers, when detention is used, who can care for any animals that the assessed person ordinarily cares for will depend upon their capacity and cooperation and knowing someone who can look after pets. If the person has mental capacity to decide what care they want for their pets, their decision (if they make one) will stand. However, if you feel this decision falls short of maintaining the welfare of the animal(s) you may have to involve the RSPCA as well. The challenge is, however, that this may involve leaving the pets where they are and losing access to the property while you do so. If the person lacks the relevant capacity, then a decision can be made in their best interests by the AMHP to arrange for the care of pets. This does not have to be a paid arrangement but it needs to be sustainable, for example leaving the dog with a neighbour is acceptable if you are confident they can look after it well, and they know it is likely to be for more than just overnight. Otherwise the AMHP will need to be prepared with a list of local sources of care, such as boarding kennels and animal shelters, and knowledge as how to fund them. It is perhaps important to consider that, without the appropriate vaccination records, it is unlikely that a private boarding kennel will be able to accommodate the pet(s). Care for smaller or exotic animals may be harder to organise than you think, too. Although often pet shops or specialist exotic handlers may be able to help, this is not an option out of hours. It is not unknown for AMHPs to take pets back to offices or temporarily care for them at home. However, this depends on local policy. Once a suitable destination has been identified for the pet(s), the AMHP is left with the final task of catching them, which, as many AMHPs will attest, may sound easier than it turns out to be.

Charging

Local authorities are able to recover from any adult any reasonable expenses incurred in protecting the adult's property. Who pays for this will depend on a number of considerations, including the personal finances of the person involved and whether the need for protection of the property has arisen from the actions of others (such as the police forcing entry).

 ESSENTIAL KNOWLEDGE: PRACTICE GUIDANCE

Property checklist

Resources:
- Details of locksmiths and when they are available
- Knowing how the locksmiths will accept bookings, for example, by phone or email
- Process to obtain purchase numbers to give to locksmiths.

Decisions:
- Are doors and windows secured and locked?
- Where are the keys?
- Have you been alerted to any specific valuables that need removal from the property?
- Are electrical appliances turned off and heating controls adjusted?
- Are there any perishable foodstuffs that need removal during the expected admission period?
- Do any repairs need to be undertaken to secure the property in the case of forced entry?
- Are there any vehicles or outbuildings that need securing?

 ESSENTIAL KNOWLEDGE: PRACTICE GUIDANCE

Animal checklist

Resources:
- Details of local boarding kennels, including opening times, contact numbers and costs
- Contact details of local animal wardens and emergency shelters

- Do you have contact details (if in rural settings) for the National Farmers Union to enlist assistance for farm and smallholding animals?
- How will they accept payment if needed?
- For the pet(s) in question:
  - name of vet (if known)
  - vaccination cards (if available)
  - information on general health and wellbeing
  - information on any known behavioural issues
- As the AMHP, are you willing/able/sufficiently skilled to take household pets home?

Decisions:
- By whom and where are the pets going to be cared for?
- Does the person looking after them have appropriate numbers for key people within the local authority and mental health services?

Safeguarding

The MHA assessment may be seen as a response to safeguarding concerns as it involves responding to risk; however, safeguarding should be seen as much wider than what an MHA assessment outcome may resolve. It is possible that involvement as an AMHP may uncover other matters which will need to be followed up by a safeguarding team. Not everyone who is assessed under the MHA has had previous social care involvement, and therefore the person may need to be referred for safeguarding interventions that need to be put in place during and following their admission to hospital. The relevant duty on LAs to carry out safeguarding enquiries is contained in section 42 of the Care Act 2014 in England and in section 126 of the Social Services and Wellbeing (Wales) Act 2014. Safeguarding concerns may have presented themselves where an AMHP decides not inform or consult an NR, or through broader awareness of abuse in all its forms.

The AMHP should also be ready to involve the police following an assessment where an NR has not been contacted due to domestic abuse or awareness of abuse in any form, and also where the assessed person has made direct and credible threats to other people when being assessed. This applies irrespective of whether or not the outcome of the assessment is that the patient should be detained under the MHA. Specifically, under the English Code of Practice, 'The local safeguarding team should be made aware of any patient being supported in longer term segregation' (DH, 2015a, para 26.153).

Scrutinising detention papers

Despite the best attempts of the assessing doctors and the AMHP, errors on the doctors' recommendations or the AMHP's application may occur. The key issue is whether these are fundamental errors that cannot be rectified, or minor errors that can be. The '*de minimis*' principle informs us that trivial errors do not need to be rectified at all. Minor errors may be corrected only by the author of the form and no one else, and within the relevant timescales (see MHA, section 15, or MHA, section 8(4) for guardianship, and the MHA Reference Guide).

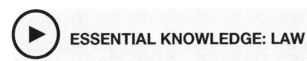 **ESSENTIAL KNOWLEDGE: LAW**

Errors on documents

Examples of minor errors capable of rectification are:

- leaving blank spaces on the form, which should have been completed, other than the space for signing it or for recording the doctor's reasons for believing the statutory criteria are satisfied;
- failure to delete one or more alternative clauses in places where only one can be correct;
- errors in the spelling of names, addresses or places;
- discrepancies in the spelling of a patient's name, in circumstances where there is no doubt the documents refer to the same person.

DH, 2015b, para 31.23

Examples of fundamental errors that are incapable of remedy and therefore invalidate the application are:

- a review of detention or CTO not taking place before it expires leading to an illegal deprivation of liberty (see also Code of Practice, paras 32.10 and 38.50);
- an application or medical recommendation which is unsigned; or
- an application signed by a person not qualified to complete it, ie an application not signed by an AMHP, a nearest relative, or a person authorised to exercise the nearest relative's functions; or
- a medical recommendation by a person without power to make such a recommendation, ie a medical recommendation from someone disqualified from making one by reason of [MHA] section 12, [MHA] section 12A or the Mental Health (Conflicts of Interest) (England) Regulations (SI 2008/1205).

DH, 2015b, para 31.19

Fundamental errors invalidate the application (DH, 2015b, para 31.20).

The following checklist gives guidance on how to avoid errors.

 ESSENTIAL KNOWLEDGE: PRACTICAL GUIDANCE

Checklist when scrutinising medical recommendation/s and application

Across forms check
- The person's name and address are identical on all documents.
- Doctors and the AMHP have signed and dated their forms.
- The date the person was seen is correct.

Medical recommendations check
- Doctors have indicated correctly whether they are section 12 approved and/or have previous acquaintance.
- The date of examination is complete and is no more than five days after the earlier medical examination.
- Doctors have indicated correctly why the detention is necessary, based on the risk categories – the person's own health or safety, or for the protection of others.
- Doctors have explained the rationale for making a medical recommendation, and identified the appropriate risks. If they have indicated a risk to others, they have explained what this is and why.
- (For MHA, section 3) Doctors have identified where 'appropriate treatment' is available from.

AMHP/NR application check
- The application is being made within 14 days of the last medical examination.
- The hospital or ward's address is written correctly so the ward will accept it.
- It is clear which LA you are acting behalf of, and which LA has approved you as an AMHP.
- The NR details/status are recorded correctly. If the NR is making the application they need to state their relationship to the person.
- You have indicated whether, for section 2, an NR has been informed or not and, for section 3, if the NR has been consulted or not, and if not, have given reasons why.
- If no doctors with previous acquaintance have been used, this has been explained.

It is advisable to carry with you a Form H3: sections 2, 3 and 4 – 'record of detention in hospital' – in case the ward does not have one, and also to take a copy of that form, once completed, as proof of admission.

If within the period of 14 days beginning with the day on which the person was admitted to hospital the forms are found to be incorrect or defective, they can be rectified by the person who signed them as long as the admitting hospital managers consent (MHA, section 15(1)). The effect is that the detention remains valid within the 14 days and thereafter as if the error has not been made. If a medical recommendation is found to be insufficient, the AMHP or NR may be contacted to arrange a fresh medical recommendation (MHA, section 15(2)).

Diplomats

If you become aware that a person who has been referred is a diplomat, you should seek legal advice. The Diplomatic Privileges Act 1964, section 2 and Schedule 1 prevent any diplomat or their dependant from being detained under any civil or criminal legislation, and that includes the mental health legislation, unless a waiver has been granted by the 'head of the mission of any State or any person for the time being performing his functions [which] shall be deemed to be a waiver by that State'. Therefore, if this arises seek additional legal advice, as the protection offered by section 139 of the MHA does not apply, and also call the Foreign and Commonwealth Office (Diplomatic Missions and International Organisations Unit) (see DH, 2015b, para 1.16).

Being recorded undertaking MHA assessments

With growing use and availability of smartphones and social media, there is a possibility that the person you are assessing or others in attendance at a community MHA assessment may attempt to record the assessment. Your role is to ensure the patient is interviewed in a suitable manner (see MHA, section 13(2)). In deciding how to proceed, you will need to consider and weigh up many different matters, such as the capacity of the person concerned to consent to the recording, the likely impact of recording the assessment, the views of the other assessors, the possibility of the interview not going ahead unless it is recorded, the purpose of the recording and the use that will be made of the recording. You will also need to consider legal provisions such as Article 8 of the ECHR (rights to private and family life) and section 129 of the MHA (the offence of obstruction).

Managing confidentiality

An AMHP needs to be clear as to the distinction between LA and hospital managers' responsibilities. One area of confusion can relate to upholding confidentiality. The MHA provides that the hospital managers must share certain information with the NR, except where the person requests otherwise (see MHA, section 132(4) and section 132A(4)). In many cases a person may have stated that they do not wish their NR, or anyone, to be given any information, or may place limitations on what information is shared by the hospital managers. Although section 132 is not binding on AMHPs, as it applies to hospital managers only, where a person has requested that information is not shared this can give an AMHPs a sense of how the person may react on contact. It may also mean that the reasons why the person has declined information to be shared may need to be stated in the social and health care records. In these circumstances, an understanding of why the person has taken this position is needed, although this will not necessarily preclude you from either informing the NR under section 11(3) of the MHA, or consulting with the NR under section 11(4) unless doing so would breach the person's Article 8 ECHR rights (see *TW v Enfield LBC* [2014] EWCA Civ 362). It is also worth remembering that although an NR may not be able to act as such for reasons of mental health and physical health, they are still the NR (until they are displaced).

Gaining direct information from the person being assessed about their relatives, and explaining the role of the NR can be invaluable in gaining clarity, and mitigating objection. This will also assist you in establishing who the NR appears to be more accurately. Sometimes ascertaining this may not be possible due to the distress being experienced by the person. However, the starting point should always be person–centred.

At this stage in the assessment process (before the assessment interview has occurred), you cannot inform the NR about any outcome of the MHA assessment; however, it is an opportunity to ask whether they would 'object' theoretically to an admission under section 3, and know this early on. The NR may be the person's attorney under a health and welfare Lasting Power of Attorney, but it will need to be carefully explained that the use of the MHA could trump this power.

At the time of writing, the NR role still lies within the MHA; however, suggested changes to the relevant legislation have been announced following the final report of the independent review of the MHA which, if introduced, will mean the NR is superseded by the role of 'Nominated Person' (DH, 2018). The new role would enable a person to choose their NR, if they have capacity to do so.

 Please see online resources for update

▶ KEY MESSAGES

- Undertaking MHA and risk work can be challenging and will stretch you intellectually and emotionally. Running through differing theoretical scenarios in reflective supervision sessions will enable you to prepare for such eventualities.

- As an AMHP, a broad but thorough understanding of the law will enable you to approach each scenario with confidence as to what can and cannot be legally undertaken.

- Safeguarding adults and children cannot be contained with the MHA process alone and needs to be undertaken jointly with relevant social care and law enforcement agencies.

KNOWLEDGE REVIEW

- The responsibility for the temporary protection of property including pets is clearly defined as a duty placed upon the LA by section 47 of the Care Act 2014 and section 58 of the Social Services and Wellbeing (Wales) Act 2014, and not that of the AMHP alone.

- Working effectively alongside your mental health NHS colleagues is an essential part of undertaking an MHA assessment, as the majority of care and support for those with a mental disorder arises from NHS resources, as it does similarly for inpatient care.

FURTHER READING

- McLaughlin, K. (2001) 'Fear, risk and mental health: observations on policy and practice', *Practice: Social Work in Action*, 3(3), pp 55–64.

- Spreadbury, K. and Hubbard, R. (2020) *Safeguarding practice handbook*, Bristol: Policy Press.

- Vicary, S., Young, A. and Hicks, S (2019) '"Role over" or roll over? Dirty work, shift, and Mental Health Act assessments', *British Journal of Social Work*, 49(8), pp 2187–206.

8

Applying the interface between the Mental Health Act and the Mental Capacity Act

Chapter aim

This chapter will enable you to meet the following AMHP key competence themes:

- Knowledge of legislation and policy

- Mental capacity legislation

- Mental health legislation

- Human rights

Schedule 2 of the Mental Health (Approved Mental Health Professionals) (Approval) (England) Regulations 2008 Key Competences 2(1)(a)(i) and (ii)

Schedule 2 of the Mental Health (Approval of Persons to be Approved Mental Health Professionals) (Wales) Regulations 2008 Key Competences 2.1(a)–(b)

As an AMHP engaging in mental health work with young people and adults, you will be using and interpreting the legislation contained within the MHA and the Mental Capacity Act (MCA) 2005, as well as the accompanying case law. When accepting a referral for an MHA assessment, the person being referred for assessment may be considered to lack capacity to make decisions regarding their care and treatment. In such cases, you will need to navigate the sometimes complex relationship between the two legal frameworks.

Introduction

In England and Wales, the non-consensual care and treatment of people with mental health problems is governed largely by two parallel legal schemes: the

119

MHA and the MCA 2005. In very broad terms, the MHA provides mainly for the detention and treatment of people in hospital for mental disorder on the basis of protection of the person and the public, and irrespective of mental capacity. The MCA 2005 applies only to those who lack the relevant decision-making capacity, covers (nearly) all decisions, and provides for deprivation of liberty based on the person's best interests. There is considerable overlap between the two regimes, and the relationship can be extremely complex. This chapter briefly sets out how the MCA 2005 enables care and treatment to be delivered. It then explores the three primary interfaces between the two Acts: inpatient care and treatment, deprivation of liberty in hospital, and community MHA powers.

Whereas the MHA has no age limit, the MCA 2005 applies to those aged 16 and over. The interface therefore only arises in relation to people aged 16 and over; consequently this chapter does not address the position of children aged below 16.

Care and treatment under the MCA 2005

Section 1(5) of the MCA 2005 requires that any action or decision for or on behalf of a person who lacks the requisite capacity must be done, or made, in his or her best interests. The notion of a person's 'best interests' is not defined in the MCA 2005. However, section 4 sets out a series of matters which must be, or must not be, considered when a decision-maker is making a determination. These matters include considering the person's past and present wishes and feelings (including written statements), the person's beliefs and values, and any other factors that the person would be likely to consider if they were able.

Section 5 of the MCA 2005 offers protection against civil and criminal liability for certain acts done in connection with the care or treatment of a person. In broad terms, a person providing care or treatment will not incur any liability that they would not have incurred if a person of full capacity had consented to the care or treatment, subject to certain conditions. These are that:

- the person is reasonably believed to lack the capacity to consent,
- consideration has been given to the principles of the MCA 2005, and
- the action taken is in the person's best interests.

In addition, section 6 provides that the use of restraint will not attract protection against liability unless the individual taking the action reasonably believes it is necessary to do so in order to prevent harm to the person; the act must also be a proportionate response to the likelihood of harm and the seriousness of that harm.

However, sections 5 and 6 cannot be relied on if the care regime amounts to a deprivation of liberty within the meaning of Article 5 of the European Convention on Human Rights (ECHR). This is an important distinction.

Inpatient care and treatment

The first interface between the two Acts arises when a person needs mental health care and assessment/treatment in hospital. The starting point should normally be whether care and treatment can be provided on the basis of consent. Section 131 of the MHA confirms that patients can be admitted 'informally', rather than under the formal detention powers of the MHA. The question of whether a person has capacity to consent to admission is likely to include consideration of their ability to understand the purpose of the admission, the proposed care and treatment, and the realistic alternatives to hospital admission.

ESSENTIAL KNOWLEDGE: VIEWS OF PERSONS WITH LIVED EXPERIENCE

Professionals should remember:

- that people can change their minds, particularly if they are stressed, tired or are experiencing or trying to escape from emotional or mental distress.

If the person has capacity to consent to their admission, the MCA 2005 is irrelevant. Where the person gives consent, they can be informally admitted and their ongoing care and treatment can be provided on the basis of consent. If they do not consent, the person cannot be admitted to hospital, unless decision–makers consider that use of the MHA is necessary.

If the person lacks capacity to consent to their admission, the MCA 2005 comes into play. In principle, a person who lacks the relevant capacity can be admitted to hospital informally provided it is in their best interests and the admission does not amount to a deprivation of liberty. The available options in cases of deprivation of liberty are discussed later in this chapter. But in the light of the Supreme Court decision in the case known as *Cheshire West* (summarised later in the chapter), which in effect widened significantly the meaning of deprivation of liberty, it is extremely doubtful that a person lacking capacity to consent could be admitted informally for mental health care and treatment without deprivation of liberty occurring.

Where the person is detained in hospital under the MHA, the main interface between the two Acts is contained in section 28 of the MCA 2005. This is reproduced in full below. The intended effect of section 28 is to place the two Acts within separate spheres when it comes to medical treatment for mental disorder.

ESSENTIAL KNOWLEDGE: LAW

Section 28 MCA – Mental Health Act matters

(1) Nothing in this Act authorises anyone—

    (a) to give a patient medical treatment for mental disorder, or

    (b) to consent to a patient's being given medical treatment for mental disorder,

    if, at the time when it is proposed to treat the patient, his treatment is regulated by Part 4 of the Mental Health Act.

(1A) Subsection (1) does not apply in relation to any form of treatment to which section 58A of that Act (electro-convulsive therapy, etc) applies if the patient comes within subsection (7) of that section (informal patient under 18 who cannot give consent).

(1B) Section 5 does not apply to an act to which section 64B of the Mental Health Act applies (treatment of community patients not recalled to hospital).

(2) 'Medical treatment', 'mental disorder' and 'patient' have the same meaning as in that Act.

Section 28 ensures that the MCA 2005 does not apply to any treatment for mental disorder that is being given in accordance with Part 4 of the MHA. It should be noted that the sole exception is electroconvulsive therapy under section 58A of the MHA ('informal patient under 18 who lacks capacity to consent'). Thus an incapacitated person aged 16 or 17 admitted informally could be given electroconvulsive therapy under the MCA 2005 if it was in their best interests.

This means that in respect of persons admitted under Part 4:

- the decision to provide medical treatment for mental disorder is not subject to a best interests determination;
- an attorney acting under a Lasting Power of Attorney or a deputy appointed by the Court of Protection cannot consent to or refuse treatment for mental disorder on the person's behalf; and
- an advance decision to refuse medical treatment for mental disorder is not binding on clinicians.

It is also important to remember Part 4 enables medical treatment for mental disorder to be given to persons detained under the MHA without their consent, whether or not they have capacity to give consent. It does not follow that because a person is subject to the MHA they lack capacity to make decisions, including care and treatment decisions. A study found that 15 per cent of detained individuals retained their capacity to make treatment decisions and concluded that lack of treatment-related decisional capacity is a 'common but by no means inevitable correlate of admission to a psychiatric in-patient unit' (Cairns et al, 2005, p 382).

Part 4 of the MHA regulates medical treatment for mental disorders. It does not regulate the treatment of physical conditions that are unrelated to mental disorders. Any person over 16 who requires treatment for a physical disorder and lacks capacity to consent to that treatment must be treated under the MCA 2005, even if they are subject to the powers of the MHA.

However, there is sometimes not a clear dividing line between treatment for mental disorder and treatment for physical disorder. For example, if a person experiences an acute confusional state due to a urinary tract infection, does medical treatment for mental disorder include the antibiotics needed to treat the infection? The leading case on the meaning of medical treatment for mental disorder is *B v Croydon Health Authority* [1995] Fam 133, [1995] 2 WLR 294, which is summarised below.

 **ESSENTIAL KNOWLEDGE: LAW**

Case law: B v Croydon Health Authority [1995] Fam 133, [1995] 2 WLR 294

This case concerned B, who had a psychopathic disorder and was detained under section 3 of the MHA. She was refusing to eat, as an act of self-harm, and her weight fell to dangerous levels. The question for the court was whether nasogastric feeding, without B's consent, would be lawful. The Court of Appeal held that medical treatment for mental disorder included a range of acts ancillary to the core treatment, including nursing and care 'concurrent with the core treatment or as a necessary prerequisite to such treatment' or to prevent the patient harming themselves or to alleviate the consequences of the disorder. Importantly, the court stressed that relieving the symptoms of the mental disorder is just as much part of the treatment as relieving its underlying cause. On the facts, it was held that nasogastric feeding constituted medical treatment for the mental disorder from which B was suffering and that, under the MHA, her consent was not required.

Section 145(1) of the MHA defines 'medical treatment' for the purposes of the Act as that which includes 'nursing, psychological intervention and specialist mental health habilitation, rehabilitation and care'. In 2007 the MHA was amended to include the statement that medical treatment for mental disorder means 'medical treatment the purpose of which is to alleviate, or prevent a worsening of, the disorder or one or more of its symptoms or manifestation' (MHA 1983, section 145(4), as inserted by the MHA 2007).

While Part 4 of the MHA applies to most categories of detained persons, it does not apply to those who are:

- subject to an emergency application under section 4;
- remanded to hospital for a report under section 35;
- detained in a place of safety in accordance with directions under section 37(4) or 45A(5) pending admission to hospital, on the basis of a hospital order or hospital and limitation directions;
- subject to a Community Treatment Order (CTO) and who have not been recalled to hospital;
- conditionally discharged;
- detained under the 'holding powers' in section 5; or
- detained in a place of safety under section 135 or 136.

Individuals who fall within these categories can be treated with their consent, or under the MCA 2005 if aged 16 and over.

Deprivation of liberty in hospital

The MCA 2005 does not authorise the deprivation of a person's liberty except in limited circumstances. These circumstances include if the deprivation of liberty is authorised by Schedule A1 to the MCA 2005 (known as the Deprivation of Liberty Safeguards, or DoLS). The other circumstances are under section 4B of the MCA or by order of the Court of Protection.

ESSENTIAL KNOWLEDGE: LAW

What is deprivation of liberty?

Article 5 of the ECHR guarantees the right to personal liberty and provides that no one should be deprived of their liberty in an arbitrary fashion. Article 5(1)(e) permits the lawful detention of, among others, 'persons of unsound mind' in accordance with a procedure prescribed by law. Article 5 also requires certain safeguards to be provided to persons deprived of liberty, including the right of access to speedy judicial proceedings to challenge the lawfulness of the detention.

In the context of a person of 'unsound mind', the European Court of Human Rights, in *Storck v Germany* [2005] ECHR 61603/00, confirmed that a deprivation of liberty has three elements:

(a) the objective element: confinement in a restricted space for a non-negligible period of time;

(b) the subjective element: the person has not validly consented to that confinement; and

(c) the detention being imputable to the state.

In a decision by majority, the Supreme Court in a case known as *Cheshire West* held that the objective element consisted of determining whether the person concerned was under continuous supervision and control, and not free to leave. Both conditions must be present in order to satisfy the objective element. This was referred to by Lady Hale as the 'acid test'. (See *P v Cheshire West and Chester Council and P and Q v Surrey County Council* [2014] UKSC 19, [2014] AC 896.)

In simple terms, the DoLS enable local authorities (and in Wales, Local Health Boards as well) to authorise the deprivation of liberty of an adult in a hospital or a care home, if that adult lacks capacity to consent to the arrangements. The DoLS were introduced by the government in response to the ruling by the European Court of Human Rights in *HL v The United Kingdom*. A summary of the case is provided below.

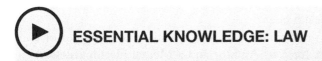

ESSENTIAL KNOWLEDGE: LAW

Case law: HL v The United Kingdom *[2005] 40 EHRR 32 (App No 45508/99)*

HL was a 48-year-old man who had suffered from autism since birth and had always lacked capacity to consent to medical treatment. From the age of 13, he lived in a psychiatric institution (Bournewood Hospital). In 1994 he was discharged, after a period of over 30 years of hospitalisation, to live with paid carers.

In 1997, following an incident of violent behaviour and self-harm at his day-care centre, HL was sedated and taken back to hospital. He was assessed by a psychiatrist as needing inpatient treatment and, because he appeared 'quite compliant' and had 'not attempted to run away', he was admitted informally. This was common practice at the time, and meant that he did not have access to the safeguards provided to formally detained patients (such as the right to apply to the mental health tribunal).

HL was fully compliant with his hospital treatment regime and always accepted his medication. However, hospital staff regularly sedated him. His carers were prevented from visiting him, in case he would want to go home with them, and clear instructions were given that he should be detained under the MHA if he tried to leave the hospital. His treatment regime was justified on the basis of the common law doctrine of necessity.

The carers brought legal proceedings against the hospital for unlawful detention, which went to the House of Lords and eventually to the European Court of Human Rights. It was held that HL had been deprived of his liberty for the purposes of Article 5 of the ECHR, and that the lack of any formalised admission procedure and inability to challenge the lawfulness of his deprivation of liberty amounted to breaches of Article 5(1) and (4).

The DoLS were introduced in order to remedy these breaches of Article 5 of the ECHR. They establish an administrative process for authorising a deprivation of liberty and access to a number of safeguards once an authorisation has been granted.

Summary of the DoLS

If it appears likely that at some point during the next 28 days a person is likely to need to be deprived of their liberty, the hospital or care home (referred to in the legislation as the 'managing authority') must apply to a local authority (the 'supervisory body') for a standard authorisation. In Wales, the supervisory body for hospitals is the local health board.

The supervisory body must conduct six assessments by a minimum of two assessors (including a Best Interests Assessor and a Mental Health Assessor) to see if the qualifying requirements are met. If they are met, the supervisory body must grant a standard authorisation. If any of the qualifying requirements are not met, then the supervisory body may not grant the authorisation (see MCA 2005, Sch A1, para 50). The six qualifying requirements are set out below.

 **ESSENTIAL KNOWLEDGE: LAW**

Qualifying requirements to authorise deprivation of liberty

The six qualifying requirements are:

- The person is an adult aged 18 or over (**the age requirement**).
- The person is suffering from a mental disorder within the meaning of the MHA ('any disorder or disability of the mind') (**the mental health requirement**).
- The person lacks capacity to decide whether or not they should be accommodated in the hospital or care home for the purpose of being given the relevant care or treatment (**the mental capacity requirement**).

- The deprivation of liberty is in the person's best interests, is necessary to prevent harm to them and is a proportionate response to the likelihood and seriousness of that harm (**the best interests requirement**).
- The person is 'eligible' for deprivation of liberty under the DoLS – in very broad terms this means that they are not detained under the MHA or 'within the scope' of the Mental Health Act and not objecting, or the authorisation would not be inconsistent with a community power of the MHA (**the eligibility requirement**).
- The authorisation would not conflict with a valid advance decision by the person to refuse any part of the treatment to be provided, or a valid decision by an attorney with a Lasting Power of Attorney or a deputy appointed by the Court of Protection about where the person should be cared for or treated (**the no refusals requirement**).

MCA 2005, Sch A1, paras 12–18

The Best Interests Assessor may recommend that particular conditions be attached to the authorisation, and the supervisory body must have regard to these recommendations when deciding what conditions to impose on managing authorities (MCA 2005, Sch A1, para 53).

If what may be a deprivation of liberty is already occurring, or will occur imminently, the managing authority can grant itself an 'urgent authorisation' for seven days, pending the supervisory body's consideration of its application for a standard authorisation. An urgent authorisation can be extended once, by the supervisory body, up to a maximum of 14 days (MCA 2005, Sch A1, paras 67–69 and 76).

The following safeguards must be provided to those subject to a standard authorisation:

- A 'relevant person's representative' (often a relative or friend of the person) must be appointed by the supervisory body to keep in touch with the person and to represent and support them.
- An independent mental capacity advocate must be instructed by the supervisory body where (in general terms) the person would otherwise be unable to exercise their rights. Advocates are given a number of specific functions, such as assisting the person to exercise the right to apply to court (MCA 2005, ss 39A to 39D).
- There is a duty on the supervisory body to carry out a review, for instance if circumstances have changed, and a power to do so at any other time.
- The person (and anyone else on their behalf) can make an application to the Court of Protection to challenge the authorisation (MCA 2005, Sch A1, Part 8).
- The Care Quality Commission is required to monitor and report on the use of the DoLS in England. In Wales, the monitoring and reporting role is carried out by the Care and Social Services Inspectorate Wales and Healthcare Inspectorate Wales (MCA 2005, Sch A1, para 162).

A DoLS authorisation does not in itself authorise care or treatment, only the deprivation of liberty that results from the implementation of the care regime. The person's care and treatment should be provided in accordance with section 5 of the MCA 2005.

The DoLS apply to hospitals (including psychiatric hospitals) and care homes in England and Wales; they do not extend to other settings, such as supported living, shared lives accommodation, and family and other domestic settings. A deprivation of liberty outside a hospital or a care home can be authorised by an order of the Court of Protection under section 16(2)(a) of the MCA 2005.

The DoLS/Mental Health Act interface

In order to be placed on a standard authorisation the person must meet the eligibility requirement (discussed earlier). This requires the assessor to consider the interface between the MHA and the DoLS, which is set out in Schedule 1A to the MCA 2005. However, Schedule 1A is drafted in highly complicated and confusing terms, as acknowledged by Mr Justice Mostyn:

> In order to make the necessary declaration of deprivation of liberty, I have to navigate my way – I am mixing metaphors, for which I make no apology – through a thicket of legislative drafting which seems to be designed to confuse and which is characterised by extreme opacity … [T]he legislative scheme and language here is a veritable smorgasbord of double negatives and subordinate clauses, requiring a navigational exercise from provision to provision, which is an arduous task even for someone who administers justice in this field on a regular basis. (*An NHS Trust v A* [2015] EWCOP 71, [2016] Fam 223 at [8], referring to Sch 1A to the MCA, dealing with the interface between the DoLS and the MHA)

Schedule 1A sets out that a person is ineligible for the DoLS in five specific 'cases' (which are labelled as Cases A to E). These five cases are summarised below.

▶ ESSENTIAL KNOWLEDGE: LAW

Persons ineligible for DoLS authorisation

Case A: detained persons – the person is detained in hospital under the MHA, or another similar enactment.

Case B: persons on leave of absence or conditional discharge – where they are subject to a requirement with which the DoLS authorisation would be inconsistent, or where the DoLS authorisation would be for medical treatment for mental disorder in hospital.

Case C: persons subject to a Community Treatment Order – where they are subject to a requirement with which the DoLS authorisation would be inconsistent, or where the DoLS authorisation would be for medical treatment for mental disorder in hospital.

Case D: persons subject to Guardianship – where they are subject to a requirement with which the DoLS authorisation would be inconsistent, or where the DoLS authorisation would be for medical treatment for mental disorder in hospital.

Case E: persons 'within the scope' of the MHA and objecting to the proposed psychiatric treatment.

Case A is relatively straightforward. A person is ineligible for the DoLS if subject to the 'hospital treatment regime' and detained under the MHA. A person is subject to the hospital treatment regime if subject to a 'hospital treatment obligation' under the relevant enactment (sections 2, 4, 3, 35, 36, 37, 38, 44, 45A, 47, 48 or 51 of the MHA) or any other enactment which has the same effect (for example, the Criminal Procedure (Insanity) Act 1964) (see MCA 2005, Sch 1A, para 8).

A person cannot be simultaneously deprived of liberty both under the MHA and under the MCA 2005, whether as a result of an urgent or standard DoLS authorisation or a court order made under section 16 (section 16A prevents a court order in such circumstances). Even if the person requires medical treatment for a physical disorder unconnected to their mental disorder, they will still be ineligible for deprivation of liberty under the MCA 2005, although such treatment could be provided in circumstances which do not amount to a deprivation of liberty. The case of *A NHS Trust v Dr A* [2013] EWCOP 2442 (summarised in the following box) illustrates the legislative gap that can arise, albeit in an extremely small number of cases.

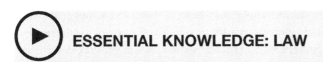 **ESSENTIAL KNOWLEDGE: LAW**

Case law: A NHS Trust v Dr A *[2013] EWCOP 2442*

An Iranian doctor, Dr A, went on hunger strike to recover his passport which had been confiscated by the UK Border Agency following his failed claims for asylum. He was diagnosed with delusional disorder. Dr A was actively resisting nasogastric feeding, and was detained under section 3 of the MHA.

The Court of Protection concluded that he lacked capacity to make decisions as to his nutrition and hydration, and that an order permitting forcible feeding by artificial nutrition and hydration was in his best interests. However, there was no dispute that subjecting Dr A to forcible feeding amounted to a deprivation of liberty.

The clinicians treating Dr A felt strongly that artificial nutrition and hydration and ancillary treatment were, on the facts of the case, treatment for a physical disorder, starvation and dehydration, and not for the underlying mental disorder. This was accepted by the court. The treatment could therefore not be provided under the MHA. Dr A was also ineligible for the DoLs as he fell within 'Case A', and the terms of section 16A(1) of the MCA 2005 meant that the Court of Protection had no jurisdiction. Instead, the court, under the inherent jurisdiction of the High Court (see Chapter 9), made a declaration authorising the forcible feeding of Dr A, an incapacitated adult, that included the provision for the deprivation of his liberty.

In a postscript to the judgment, it was noted that Dr A received artificial nutrition and hydration under restraint, as well as anti-psychotic medication. His mental state improved and he was discharged from MHA and made a capacitous decision to return to Iran.

Cases B to D are discussed later in this chapter.

It is the final category (Case E) that has caused professionals and the courts most difficulties.

First, the DoLS assessor must decide if the person is 'within the scope' of the MHA. This depends on whether the person could be detained under sections 2 or 3 of that Act. The assessor should not consider what a reasonable doctor would decide, or whether the person would inevitably be admitted (*GJ v The Foundation Trust* [2009] EWHC 2972 (Fam), [2010] Fam 70 at [80]).

The DoLS assessor must then determine whether the proposed DoLS authorisation would authorise the person to be a 'mental health patient'. This is defined as a person accommodated in a hospital for the purpose of being given medical treatment for a mental disorder. In *GJ v The Foundation Trust*, Mr Justice Charles held that assessors should apply the 'but for' test. Put simply, this test provides that if 'but for' their *physical* treatment needs the person would not be detained, they are eligible under DoLS. This test would also, in general, determine whether the person was within the scope of the MHA (*GJ v The Foundation Trust*, at [87] to [90]).

Secondly, the assessor is required to establish whether the person objects to being 'a mental health patient', or to some, or all, of the proposed mental health treatment. If so, they are ineligible for the DoLS (MCA, Sch 1A, para 5(4)). Some objections are verbal and persistent. But other cases are not so clear-cut. In deciding whether a person objects, consideration must be given to all the circumstances including their behaviour, wishes, views, beliefs, feelings and values, including those expressed in the past to the extent that they remain relevant (MCA, Sch 1A, paras 5(6)–(7)). The reasonableness of the objection is not the issue (DH, 2015, para 14.20).

The assessor must also determine whether any attorney or deputy has made a valid decision to consent to each matter to which the person objects. If they have not, the person will be ineligible for the DoLS.

If the person is within the scope of the MHA and does not object (and so does not fall within Case E), there may be a choice between detention under the MHA or the DoLS. In such cases, Mr Justice Charles in *AM v South London and Maudsley NHS Foundation Trust* held that decision-makers should consider which is the least restrictive way of achieving the proposed assessment or treatment, by adopting a 'fact-sensitive approach' and having regard to all relevant circumstances. It was accepted that it will generally, but not always, be more appropriate to rely on the DoLS in such circumstances (*AM v South London and Maudsley NHS Foundation Trust* [2013] UKUT 365 (AAC), [2014] MHLR 181).

MHA community powers

Cases B to D in Sch 1A to the MCA relate to individuals who are subject to a 'community power' of the MHA (such as guardianship or a Community Treatment Order [CTO]) and in addition need to be deprived of their liberty. In *MM v Secretary of State for Justice* [2018] UKSC 60 and *Welsh Ministers v PJ* [2018] UKSC 66, the Supreme Court confirmed that the MHA does not permit the mental health tribunal or the Secretary of State to order a conditional discharge of a restricted person subject to conditions which amount to a deprivation of liberty, or a responsible clinician to impose conditions in a CTO which have the effect of depriving a person of liberty. Therefore, where a person needs to be deprived of their liberty for the purposes of their care or treatment, separate legal authority is required. In cases where the person lacks the relevant capacity, the DoLS may provide an option. Schedule 1A provides that the DoLS can be used in respect of persons in the community under the MHA as long as this would not be inconsistent with a requirement contained in the relevant community power of the MHA. So, for instance, a person who is subject to a CTO under the MHA can, in general, be the subject of a standard authorisation under the DoLS, but not if (for example) that authorisation envisages them living in one care home when it is a condition of their CTO that they live in a different care home (as was set out in the letter from the Department of Health incorporated into the judgment in *DN v Northumberland Tyne & Wear NHS Foundation Trust* [2011] UKUT 327 (AAC)).

One of the consequences of this interface is that the mental health tribunal has no jurisdiction over a DoLS authorisation and, conversely, the Court of Protection has no jurisdiction over the MHA. This means that no one tribunal or court has authority to make decisions in relation to matters that are – in practice – usually entirely intertwined.

Deprivation of Liberty Safeguards: the future

Although they were intended to be 'an important safeguard against arbitrary detention', since their introduction the DoLS have been subject to widespread criticism from practitioners, academics and the judiciary alike. Many point to their complex and bureaucratic nature (see, for example, *C v Blackburn with Darwen BC* [2011] EWHC 3321 (COP) at [24] by Jackson J). A House of Lords Select Committee on the MCA 2005 found that the DoLS were 'frequently not used when they should be, leaving individuals without the safeguards Parliament intended' and care providers 'vulnerable to legal challenge'. The Committee concluded that 'the legislation is not fit for purpose' and proposed its replacement (see House of Lords Select Committee on the Mental Capacity Act: Report of Session 2013–14: Mental Capacity Act: Post-legislative Scrutiny, (2014) HL 139, para 32).

This was swiftly followed by the decision of the Supreme Court in the *Cheshire West* case (see earlier) which gave a significantly wider interpretation of deprivation of liberty than had been previously applied. This resulted in a considerable increase in DoLS referrals to local authorities and demands on the public purse, as well as consequential delays in DoLS assessments and reviews taking place, and an increasing backlog.

As a result of the House of Lords Select Committee report and the decision in *Cheshire West*, the government asked the Law Commission to undertake a review of the DoLS. Following a three-year review – which included a public consultation – a final report was published in 2017. The report recommended that the DoLS must be replaced as a matter of 'pressing urgency' and set out a replacement scheme (see Law Commission, 2017).

In July 2018 the government introduced the Mental Capacity (Amendment) Bill, to replace the DoLS with a new scheme based largely on the Law Commission's recommendations. The new scheme (called the Liberty Protection Safeguards) is intended to establish a proportionate and less bureaucratic means of authorising deprivation of liberty, and is summarised in the Essential knowledge box below. The Bill was passed by Parliament and received Royal Assent on 16 May 2019, becoming the Mental Capacity (Amendment) Act 2019. At the time of writing, the implementation date for the Liberty Protection Safeguards has not been confirmed.

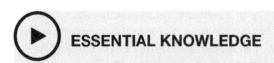

ESSENTIAL KNOWLEDGE

The Liberty Protection Safeguards (LPS)

Under the LPS, a responsible body (which in most cases will be either a hospital trust, a clinical commissioning group, a local health board or a local authority) will be able to authorise arrangements for care or treatment giving rise to a deprivation of a person's liberty. Unlike the DoLS, it does not matter where the care or treatment will be carried out: arrangements can be authorised, for example, in hospitals, care homes, supported living arrangements and domestic/family settings. Authorisations can be given for more than one set of arrangements, and can travel with the person as they move between different settings.

Before arrangements can be authorised, three assessments must be carried out: a capacity assessment, a medical assessment of whether the person has a mental disorder, and an assessment of whether the proposed arrangements are necessary and proportionate. Full consultation must also be carried out. Before an authorisation can be given, someone not involved in the day-to-day care or providing treatment to the person must carry out a pre-authorisation review. In cases where the individual objects to the proposed arrangements, that review must be undertaken by an Approved Mental Capacity Professional, who must meet with the person and determine whether the authorisation conditions are met.

Once an authorisation has been given, the person must be provided with a number of safeguards, including regular reviews, and the right to challenge the authorisation before the Court of Protection. There is also a duty on the responsible body to appoint an 'appropriate person' (such as a relative or friend of the person) or an independent mental capacity advocate to represent and support the person.

Broadly speaking, the LPS could not be used to authorise 'mental health arrangements' (which is where the person is detained under the Mental Health Act or is objecting to their admission or treatment in hospital for mental disorder). In the community a person could be subject to an authorisation under the LPS and subject to Mental Health Act requirements, so long as the authorisation does not conflict with those requirements.

 Please see online resources for update

Conclusion

The interface between the MHA and the MCA 2005 can be extremely challenging. The appropriate legal regime for an informal admission will be determined by a careful assessment of the person's capacity. If the person is detained in hospital under the MHA, the clear dividing line in law between mental treatment for mental disorder and physical disorder may not be straightforward in practice. When it comes to authorising a deprivation of liberty, decision-makers may face a choice between the MHA and the DoLS and will need to decide which is the less restrictive option based on the individual circumstances of the case. Those subject to the community powers of the MHA may be subject to both Acts. Of course, the need for an interface will always arise as long as there are two Acts governing the non-consensual care and treatment of people with mental health problems. This would not be the case if 'fusion law' were introduced. This describes a single legislative scheme governing the non-consensual care or treatment of people suffering from physical and/or mental disorders, whereby such care or treatment may only be given if the person lacks the capacity to consent. The Mental Capacity (Northern Ireland) Act 2016 introduced the first ever example of fusion law anywhere in the world, although at the time of writing it has not been implemented. Fusion law may represent the future direction for mental health law reform in England and Wales.

▶ KEY MESSAGES

- A lawful deprivation of liberty must comply with ECHR Article 5 and in particular must be in accordance with a 'procedure prescribed by law'. Both the MHA and DoLS provide such procedures; which procedure is appropriate relies on the application of the law and policy covered above.

- The MHA has no lower age limit, but the MCA 2005 is engaged when a person is 16 years or over, and DoLS is only relevant to those aged 18 years and over.

- The MHA is mainly for the detention of people in hospital for mental health assessment or treatment, on the basis of protection of the person and the public. The MCA 2005 applies only to those who lack the relevant decision-making capacity, covers (nearly) all decisions, and provides for deprivation of liberty based on the person's best interests.

KNOWLEDGE REVIEW

- The interface between the MHA and the MCA 2005 can be straightforward, but sometimes it can be extremely complex.

- The MCA 2005 does not authorise deprivation of liberty except under the DoLS, a Court of Protection order or section 4B.

- The DoLS have been widely criticised for failing to protect people's human rights and deal with the increased numbers of people considered to have been deprived of liberty following the *Cheshire West* judgment.

- Under the Mental Capacity (Amendment) Act 2019, the new Liberty Protection Safeguards scheme, which will replace the DoLS, will come into force on 1 October 2020.

 ## FURTHER READING

- 39 Essex Chambers (2019) Mental Capacity Guidance Note: Deprivation of Liberty in the Hospital Setting, available at www.39essex.com/mental-capacity-guidance-note-deprivation-liberty-hospital-setting/.

- Hubbard, R. and Stone, K. (2018) *The Best Interest Assessors practice handbook*, Bristol: Policy Press.

- Law Commission (2017) *Mental Capacity and Deprivation of Liberty*, Law Com No 372, London: HMSO, chapter 13. Available online at www.lawcom.gov.uk/app/uploads/2017/03/lc372_mental_capacity.pdf.

- DH (2018) *Modernising the Mental Health Act: Increasing choice, reducing compulsion: Final report of the independent review of the Mental Health Act 1983*, December, available online at https://assets.publishing.service.gov.uk/government/uploads/system/uploads/attachment_data/file/778897/Modernising_the_Mental_Health_Act_-_increasing_choice__reducing_compulsion.pdf.

9

The AMHP and community provisions

Chapter aim

This chapter will enable you to meet the following AMHP key competence themes:

- Application of AMHP values

- Application of knowledge relating to the legal and policy framework

- Application of knowledge of mental disorder

- Application of skills for working in partnership

- Application of skills for making and communicating informed decisions

Schedule 2 of the Mental Health (Approved Mental Health Professionals) (Approval) (England) Regulations 2008
Key Competences 1(a)–(d), 2(1)(a)–(e), 3(a)–(d), 4(a)–(k), 5(a)–(i)

Schedule 2 of the Mental Health (Approval of Persons to be Approved Mental Health Professionals) (Wales) Regulations 2008
Key Competences 1.1–1.7, 2.1–2.5, 3.1–3.5, 4.1–4.11, 5.1–5.6

In this chapter we will explore the occasions where AMHPs engage community provisions, under the MHA, other than through MHA assessments, and under other legislation. Inpatient treatment, care and support will, for the vast majority of people, only be a temporary phase in their life. Notwithstanding that, for some, detention under the MHA may recur again in their lives. To this end, some people need a legal framework around them to enable them to remain in the community. To this end, the MHA permits a person's freedom to be restricted to enable community living, but these restrictions must fall short of depriving that person of their liberty. This position has been crystallised by two important cases, *MM v Secretary of State for Justice* [2018] UKSC 60 and *Welsh Ministers v PJ* [2018] UKSC 66, which will be discussed later.

Introduction

The Guiding Principles of the MHA express that 'where it is possible to treat a patient safely and lawfully without detaining them under the [MHA], the patient should not be detained', and that the person's reasonably ascertainable past and present views, wishes and feelings should be considered (DH, 2015a, paras 1.2 and 1.8). To this end, enabling people to successfully reintegrate and live, or remain, in the community is the ambition, so as to promote recovery and uphold people's rights. Indeed, section 13(2) of the MHA requires that AMHPs, before they make an application, must be satisfied that detention in hospital is in all the circumstances of the case the *most appropriate way* of providing the care and treatment that the person needs. Therefore, the discussion of community options (including discharge) should begin as soon as possible either after a person is detained in hospital or when a referral is made for an MHA assessment. In the following sections of this chapter we will be discussing the differing community options that are available under the MHA.

Section 115 powers of entry and inspection, and section 135(1) removal powers

AMHPs have a unique power of entry and inspection, which can be found with section 115 of the MHA, which is a provision that gives an AMHP a mandate to avoid trespass when this power is needed to review a person's care. Section 115 provides a power for an AMHP to enter and inspect any premises (other than a hospital) in which a person with a mental disorder is living, if there is reasonable cause to suspect that the person is not receiving proper care. It has limitations, as it will not withstand a rebuttable by an owner refusing access, and it does not enable the person living there to be removed from the property. It also does not include properties which are classified as a hospital. Nonetheless, it does give an emphasis that AMHPs (as was the case with ASWs) should be involved in community engagement other than just through MHA assessments.

In addition, section 135(1) of the MHA allows a person to be removed from their home to a place of safety where it is believed that they have been or are being 'ill-treated, neglected or kept otherwise than under proper control'. This power can be granted by a magistrates' court, on application from an AMHP. It is often assumed that this power can be used only as a precursor to an assessment under the MHA, but it can also be used for the purposes of making alternative arrangements for care and support, for example informal hospital admission, or follow-up support from community mental health services. However, the utility of section 135(1) will often be limited because removal to a place of safety is only permitted for up to 24 hours, during which time it may be unlikely that adequate safeguarding arrangements can be put in place.

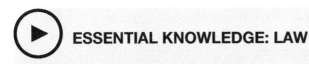

ESSENTIAL KNOWLEDGE: LAW

Section 115 – Powers of entry and inspection

(1) An approved mental health professional may at all reasonable times enter and inspect any premises (other than a hospital) in which a mentally disordered patient is living, if he has reasonable cause to believe that the patient is not under proper care.

(2) The power under subsection (1) above shall be exercisable only after the professional has produced, if asked to do so, some duly authenticated document showing that he is an approved mental health professional.

Section 7 guardianship

According to the Codes of Practice, the purpose of guardianship is to 'enable people to receive care outside hospital where it cannot be provided without the use of compulsory powers' (DH, 2015a, para 30.1 [England]; Welsh Assembly Government, 2016, para 6.2 [Wales]). Unlike the other 'community powers' of the MHA, the use of guardianship does depend on the person being detained under the MHA. It therefore could provide AMHPs with an alternative option to hospital admission, as well as being a possible vehicle to support the discharge of a person from detention under the MHA. Moreover, guardianship is 'social care-led and is primarily focused on patients with welfare needs' (DH, 2015a, para 31.3 [England]; Welsh Assembly Government, 2016, para 30.11 [Wales]).

Guardianship enables someone to be appointed (the guardian) to closely supervise a person in the community and ensure that their care and treatment is delivered through a more formal legal framework.

ESSENTIAL KNOWLEDGE: LAW

The Codes of Practice suggests that guardianship is most likely to be appropriate where:

England
- the person is thought likely to respond well to the authority and attention of a guardian, and so be more willing to comply with necessary treatment and care for their mental disorder; or

- there is a particular need for someone to have authority to decide where the patient should live or to insist that doctors, AMHPs or other people be given access to the patient.

DH, 2015a, para 30.9

Wales
- it appears necessary to use the guardian's power to require a patient to live in a particular place;
- there is a need to have explicit authority for the person to be returned to the place they are to live (for example, a care home);
- it is thought to be important that decisions about where the person is to live are placed in the hands of a single person or authority over a continuing period – for example where there have been disputes about where the person should live;
- the person is thought likely to respond well to the authority and attention of a guardian, and so be more willing to comply with necessary treatment and care (whether they are able to consent to it, or it is being provided for them under the MCA 2005).

Welsh Assembly Government, 2016, para 6.6

A guardianship application must be based on written recommendations by two doctors and be completed by an AMHP (or by the NR). It must include the name of the guardian – normally the local social services authority.

A guardianship application may be made if the person is aged 16 or over on the grounds that:

(a) he is suffering from mental disorder of a nature or degree which warrants his reception into guardianship …; and
(b) it is necessary in the interests of the welfare of the patient or for the protection of other persons that the patient should be so received. (MHA, section 7(2))

Section 8 of the MHA provides that the guardian has powers to require the person to live at a specified place, attend at specified places and times for medical treatment, occupation, education or training, and provide access at their home to a doctor or AMHP. Section 18 provides that a guardian can take the person to the specified place, using force if necessary. The person can also be returned to the specified place if they leave without having obtained permission, again by force if necessary. However, guardianship does not give any authority to deprive a person of their liberty (see Chapter 8), and nor does it provide the legal authority to give medical treatment in the absence of consent.

Guardianship lasts for up to six months and can be renewed for a further period of six months and then for yearly periods. A person subject to guardianship has the right to apply to the mental health tribunal (a collective term for the Mental Health Review Tribunal (MHRT) in Wales and the English First-tier Tribunal (Mental Health)). Guardianship can be discharged by the responsible clinician, the mental health tribunal, the local authority (LA) or the Nearest Relative (NR). Guardianship also terminates if the person is detained under section 3 of the MHA.

The figures show that guardianship is rarely used in practice and it continues to decline in England (statistics for Wales were not available). New cases totalled 105 in 2017–18 and 140 in 2016–17, compared to 430 in 2007–08. As at 31 March 2018, 300 people in England were subject to a Guardianship Order, 25 per cent fewer than at the same point the previous year. Of the 152 local authorities in England, only 59 reported new cases in 2017–18 and 59 in 2016–17, while 90 had cases remaining open at the end of 2017–18 (NHS Digital, Guardianship under the Mental Health Act 1983, England, 2016–17 and 2017–18, National Statistic).

In addition to section 7 guardianship, section 37 of the MHA empowers the Crown Court or magistrates' court to place certain categories of offenders under the guardianship of a local social services authority, or of such other person approved by social services. The effect of a Guardianship Order is to give the guardian similar powers to those provided for under the civil power in section 7 of the MHA.

Section 17 leave

Under section 17 of the MHA, a responsible clinician can grant leave of absence to a detained person. The main exception to this is restricted patients who may be granted leave by the responsible clinician but only with the Secretary of State's approval (see later).

Leave of absence allows a person to be temporarily absent from hospital where further inpatient treatment is still thought to be necessary. This can be:

- for a specified period or occasions (for example, leave might be granted to visit family or attend an appointment) or
- it could be longer term or even for an indefinite period (for example, to see how the patient copes with life outside hospital).

The Code of Practice advises that leave should normally be of a short duration and not normally for more than seven days. When considering longer periods of leave, the Code advises that that responsible clinician should consider the use of a Community Treatment Order (CTO) instead (DH, 2015a, para 27.11 [England]; Welsh Assembly Government, 2016, para 31.14 [Wales]).

Leave of absence may be granted subject to such conditions as considered necessary. This might, for example, include a requirement to attend a medical centre to receive treatment or to reside at a particular place. Leave can be revoked at any time if the responsible clinician considers it necessary in the interests of the person's health or safety or for the protection of other people.

A person who is on leave continues to be liable to be detained, and therefore subject to the consent to treatment provisions of the MHA. The Code of Practice advises that, should it be necessary to treat the patient without their consent, then consideration should be given to recalling them to hospital, although this is not a legal requirement (DH, 2015a, para 27.25 [England]; Welsh Assembly Government, 2016, para 17.40 [Wales]).

Section 17A Community Treatment Orders

The purpose of a CTO under section 17A is 'to allow suitable patients to be safely treated in the community rather than under detention in hospital, and to provide a way to help prevent relapse and any harm – to the patient or to others – that this might cause' (DH, 2015a, para 29.5 [England]; Welsh Assembly Government, 2016, para 30.3 [Wales]). The responsible clinician is responsible for making a CTO but only with the agreement of an AMHP, who must state in writing that they agree that the relevant criteria have been met (see below) and that it is appropriate to make the order (MHA, section 17A(4)).

To be eligible to be considered for a CTO, the person must be detained for treatment under section 3, or be a person unrestricted under Part 3 of the MHA. Persons detained under section 2, for example, are not eligible to be considered for a CTO. The relevant criteria under section 17A(5) which must be met are that:

- the person is suffering from a mental disorder of a nature or degree which makes it appropriate for them to receive medical treatment;
- it is necessary for their health or safety, or for the protection of other persons, that they should receive such treatment;
- subject to their being liable to be recalled as mentioned below, such treatment can be provided without their continuing to be detained in a hospital;
- it is necessary for their health or safety, or for the protection of other persons, that they should be liable to be recalled to hospital for medical treatment; and
- appropriate medical treatment is available for the person.

The CTO must specify conditions to which the person is to be subject while the order remains in force. These conditions, which must have been agreed by the responsible clinician and an AMHP, may include that the person:

- resides at a particular place;
- makes themselves available at particular times and at particular places for medical treatment;
- receives medical treatment in accordance with the clinical supervisor's direction;
- makes themselves available for examination – in particular, for the purposes of renewal of the CTO and a Second Opinion Approved Doctor (SOAD) certificate;
- abstains from specified conduct.

In all cases, conditions must be included to make sure the patient makes themselves available for medical examination, when needed for consideration of extension of the CTO, and, if necessary, to allow a SOAD to provide a Part 4A certificate authorising treatment.

In respect of the conditions agreed with the AMHP, these are not in themselves enforceable but, if a person fails to comply with any such condition, this may be taken into account when deciding whether or not to recall them to hospital. A person cannot be recalled unless the criteria for recall in section 17E of the MHA are met:

- the person needs to receive treatment in hospital for their mental disorder; and
- there would be a risk of harm to the health or safety of the person or to other persons if the person were not recalled.

The responsible clinician may also recall a person if they fail to comply with any condition that they make themselves available for examination – in particular, for the purposes of renewal of the CTO and a certificate under Part 4A of the MHA. The responsible clinician has the power to vary or suspend conditions; there is no requirement to obtain an AMHP's agreement before doing so.

CTOs, which were introduced in 2009 by virtue of the Mental Health Act 2007, have proved controversial. The independent review of the MHA 1983 (DH, 2018) found:

- 'Black or Black British' people are over eight times more likely to be given a CTO than white people compared to their representation in the general population.
- According to randomised studies, if success is measured by reducing the numbers of people being readmitted to hospital, the evidence that CTOs have achieved their goal is very limited.
- Academic literature currently does not give much support to the theory that CTOs reduce readmission.
- Many service users and carers identify that changing CTOs would be the one thing they would do when reforming the MHA, and qualitative evidence-gathering suggests that CTOs are often experienced as coercive and restrictive by people who are subject to them.

The review therefore recommended a number of reforms to limit the use of CTOs, including making the criteria more restrictive. It was further explained (DH, 2018, pp 132–4) that:

> The package of reforms we have identified is intended to at least halve the use of CTOs, and make sure they are only used when they are the least restrictive option. However, if within five years

of implementation, these reforms do not reduce the use of CTOs, or increase their effectiveness, then we recommend that CTOs are reviewed again with a view to removing them all together.

Section 37/41 conditional discharge

Conditional discharge can be an option in the case of mentally disordered offenders who are given a hospital order under section 37 of the MHA, together with a restriction order under section 41 of the MHA. A hospital order together with a restriction order can be imposed by the Crown Court if this necessary to protect the public from serious harm (MHA, section 41(1)). One of the principal effects of a restriction order is that the person cannot be discharged from hospital except by the Secretary of State or a mental health tribunal. Discharge can either be absolutely or conditional (sections 42(2) and 73 of the MHA).

A conditional discharge will mean that the person remains subject to recall as well as to certain conditions. Conditions can be imposed by the mental health tribunal or the Secretary of State, and the Secretary of State can vary the conditions at any time (MHA, section 73(4)(b)). The MHA says nothing about what the conditions may be. In practice the conditions will generally include: a requirement for the patient to maintain contact with their mental health care team; and to accept supervision from a social supervisor (such as a social worker) and psychiatrist. The conditions will also commonly include requirements that the person should live at a certain place, for example accommodation that can provide a particular level of supervision or support, or should stay away from a certain place, for example the place where the crime which led to their detention in hospital was committed.

Regular reports are submitted to the Ministry of Justice detailing the person's progress, current presentation and any concerns. The Secretary of State may recall a person at any time under sections 42(3) and 73(4)(a) of the MHA. This should occur 'where it is necessary to protect the public from the actual or potential risk posed by that patient and that the risk is linked to the patient's mental disorder' (DH, 2015a, para 22.82 [England]; Welsh Assembly Government, 2016, para 28.28 [Wales]).

Notional section 37

The term 'notional hospital orders' does not appear in the MHA. It refers to a situation where a transferred person ceases to be subject to a restriction direction because their sentence has expired. In such cases, if the person continues to need further treatment, they can remain as a 'detained patient' as if subject to section 37. Decisions on granting leave and discharge can be taken by the responsible clinician. The person can also apply to the mental health tribunal and hospital managers for discharge. Paragraph 22.77 of the Code of Practice in England (DH, 2015a) explains:

When a transferred offender becomes unrestricted, there is still a period when, if released, they will be subject to licence conditions and management by the National Probation Service. Hospitals should remain in contact with the offender manager and victim liaison officer therefore until the end of sentence.

Deprivation of liberty and the MHA community powers

In the cases of *MM v Secretary of State for Justice* [2018] UKSC 60 and *Welsh Ministers v PJ* [2018] UKSC 66, the Supreme Court held that the MHA does not permit the mental health tribunal or the Secretary of State to order a conditional discharge of a restricted patient subject to conditions which amount to a deprivation of liberty, or a responsible clinician to impose conditions in a CTO which have the effect of depriving a person of their liberty. The ability to use the MCA 2005 to deprive a person who is subject to the MHA of liberty is considered in Chapter 8.

Section 117 aftercare

Section 117 of the MHA imposes a duty on health and social services to provide aftercare services to patients who have been detained under sections 3, 37, 45A, 47 or 48 and then cease to be detained.

Section 117(6) of the MHA 1983 defines aftercare services as services which are intended:

> [to meet] a need arising from or related to the person's mental disorder and [to reduce] the risk of deterioration of the person's mental condition (and, accordingly, reducing the risk of the person requiring admission to a hospital again for treatment for mental disorder).

The MHA Codes of Practice confirm that health and social services:

> should interpret the definition of after-care services broadly. For example, after-care can encompass healthcare, social care and employment services, supported accommodation and services to meet the person's wider social, cultural and spiritual needs. (DH, 2015a, para 33.4 [England]; Welsh Assembly Government, 2016, para 33.5 [Wales])

The courts have held that section 117 imposes a strong duty on local social services and health authorities to arrange aftercare services, which is owed to, and enforceable by, individuals. Once it has been decided that a patient needs specific services under section 117, there is a duty on the authorities to provide the service in question irrespective of resource considerations (*R v Ealing District Health Authority ex p Fox* [1993] 1 WLR 373).

The courts have also held that it is unlawful to make charges for services provided under section 117 (*R v Manchester CC ex p Stennett* [2002] UKHL 34). It should be stressed that the section 117 duty only applies to section 117 aftercare. It does not apply to patients who do not fall under section 117 – for example, patients detained under section 2 of the MHA.

The duty to provide aftercare services continues until both social and health care services are satisfied that the patient no longer needs them. In the case of a patient on a CTO, aftercare must be provided for the entire duration of the CTO, but this does not mean that the patient's need for aftercare will necessarily cease as soon as they are no longer on a CTO (DH, 2015a, para 33.6 [England]; Welsh Assembly Government, 2016, para 31.16).

The Care Programme Approach

The Care Programme Approach (CPA) was established in 1991 through a joint health and social services circular, *The Care Programme Approach for People with a Mental Illness, referred to Specialist Psychiatric Services* (DH, 1990). It is the system that is used to organise the care and treatment of many people with mental health problems in the community by secondary mental health services, such as community mental health teams and assertive outreach services. The relevant guidance is currently *Refocusing the Care Programme Approach* (DH, 2008). The guidance explains that the CPA applies mainly to those with complex needs and who require multi-agency support (DH, 2008, pp 13–14). The CPA applies irrespective of section 117 entitlement, but nevertheless will apply to many section 117 service users.

In broad terms, there are four distinct aspects to support provided under the CPA:

- arrangements for assessing the health and social care needs of people accepted by the specialist mental health services;
- the formation of a care plan which addresses the identified health and social care needs;
- the appointment of a care coordinator to keep in close touch with the person and monitor care; and
- regular review and, if need be, agreed changes to the care plan.

The CPA does not apply in Wales. In 2012 it was superseded by Part 2 of the Mental Health (Wales) Measure 2010. In general terms, this places duties on Local Health Boards and LAs in Wales to work together and provides for individual care and treatment plans, the appointment of care coordinators, and all focus on the recovery model of care and treatment.

Social and health care legislation

To some extent, the MHA will interface with the legislation which enables social and health care services to be delivered. AMHPs will need, in particular, to be aware which services are, or might be, available to support the person in the community before making a decision as to whether detention in hospital is necessary in all the circumstances of the case. While government policy frequently emphasises the need to integrate services, as a matter of law, health and social care provision is separate. The following provides a brief summary of the legal frameworks.

LAs' responsibilities for the provision of adult social care are governed in England by the Care Act 2014, and in Wales by the Social Services and Well-being (Wales) Act 2014. Social care services are not defined by this legislation, and local authorities are given broad discretion to provide a range of care and support. LAs in England and Wales are given a number of general duties towards the local community. These include, for example, a duty to take steps to prevent, reduce or delay needs for care and support for all local people, and to establish an information service for people in their area. In addition, there are duties towards individual adults, including duties to assess, to meet the needs for care and support which meet the eligibility criteria, and to prepare a care and support plan. Similar duties are owed to carers. LAs are also required to make safeguarding enquiries in cases of actual or suspected abuse or neglect.

LAs are required to arrange for an independent advocate to be available to represent and support the adult or carer, if they would otherwise experience substantial difficulty in understanding, retaining, using, or weighing information, or communicating the individual's views, wishes, or feelings. The duty to arrange an advocate does not apply if the local authority is satisfied there is an 'appropriate person' (who is not a professional or paid carer) to represent and support the adult (see sections 67(5) and 68(4) of the Care Act 2014).

LAs have powers to charge for services, subject to a means test. Only those with capital below a certain level qualify for financial help, which is based on a sliding scale. Many people who use social care will pay all the costs. This is known as being a 'self-funder'. It is estimated that self-funders account for 40 per cent of all care home placements. However, the duty to assess and to undertake safeguarding enquiries apply, regardless of the level of the adult's financial resources.

Social care provision for children is governed primarily by Part 3 of the Children Act 1989 and Parts 4 and 6 of the Social Services and Well-being (Wales) Act 2014. For example, section 17 of the Children Act 1989 provides for the assessment and support of children who are 'in need' (in accordance with the definition found in that section) including disabled children and their parents in England. Local authorities have a duty to provide accommodation for certain children in need, under section 20. Many of the other functions under Part 3 arise as a result of a child being a 'looked after child'. In addition to the 1989 Act, section 2 of the Chronically Sick and Disabled Persons Act 1970 places local authorities under a duty to provide certain welfare services to individual disabled children, and the Children and Families Act 2014 includes a right for those with special educational needs to an Education, Health and Care Plan up until the age of 25.

The National Health Service (NHS) is governed in England by the National Health Service Act 2006 and in Wales by the National Health Service (Wales) Act 2006. In England, health care is commissioned from providers by local clinical commissioning groups under the supervision of the National Health Service Commissioning Board. Providers may include private providers and NHS trusts and NHS foundation trusts providing, as the case may be, primary, secondary and tertiary care in acute hospitals, ambulance services and mental health services. In Wales, local health boards are responsible for planning, securing and delivering services in their areas.

The legislation places a number of general duties on NHS bodies to provide a range of services. In broad terms, the Secretary of State and Welsh Ministers are required to promote a comprehensive health service designed to secure improvement in the physical and mental health of the people of England and Wales, and in the prevention, diagnosis and treatment of illness. The Secretary of State and Welsh Ministers must arrange for the provision of a number of services to such extent that they consider necessary to meet all reasonable requirements, such as hospital accommodation, nursing services, and services and facilities for the prevention of illness.

NHS continuing health care is a package of care that is arranged and funded solely by the NHS for individuals who are not in hospital and have been assessed as having a 'primary health need'. NHS continuing health care is available to those based in their own home or in a care home. NHS continuing health care is free of charge, unlike social care services.

The inherent jurisdiction of the High Court

In some mental health and mental capacity cases, the High Court can exercise its inherent jurisdiction. The inherent jurisdiction exists to remedy lacunae left by the common law or statute. The court's powers, when exercising the inherent jurisdiction, are wide and can include declaratory relief and the use of injunctions. Prior to the commencement of the MCA 2005, the courts developed this jurisdiction primarily in relation to those who lacked capacity to make decisions. But, following the MCA 2005, the inherent jurisdiction has also been, and continues to be, used in cases of adults who have capacity but who are 'vulnerable'.

In *Re SA* [2005] EWHC 2942 (Fam), Mr Justice Munby (as he was then) described a 'vulnerable adult' for the purposes of the inherent jurisdiction as a person who is not necessarily lacking mental capacity but is reasonably believed to be:

• under constraint;
• subject to coercion or undue influence; or

- for some other reason 'deprived of the capacity to make the relevant decision, or disabled from making a free choice, or incapacitated or disabled from giving or expressing a real and genuine consent'.

He went on to say (at para 82):

> In the context of the inherent jurisdiction I would treat as a vulnerable adult someone who, whether or not mentally incapacitated, and whether or not suffering from any mental illness, or mental disorder, is or may be unable to take care of him or herself, or unable to protect him or herself against significant harm or exploitation, or who is deaf, blind or dumb, or who is substantially handicapped by illness, injury or congenial deformity. This, I emphasise, is not and is not intended to be a definition. It is descriptive, not definitive; indicative rather than prescriptive.

This particular case involved an 18-year-old woman suffering from a range of disabilities, for example she was deaf, unable to communicate orally and visually impaired. The local authority assessment was that she functioned at the intellectual level of a 13- or 14-year-old, with a reading age of about 7 or 8. The issue before the court was whether it had jurisdiction to protect her from an unsuitable arranged marriage. She had capacity to make this decision but was described as being 'naïve' and 'immature'. On the facts of the case, the court made an order requiring that she be properly informed, in a manner she could understand, about any specific marriage before entering into it, and made a number of injunctions to put this into effect.

The Court of Appeal has since confirmed that the High Court's inherent jurisdiction was been displaced by the MCA 2005, and it continues to exist for vulnerable adults whose ability to make decisions for themselves has been compromised by matters other than those covered by the MCA. This particular case, *DL v A Local Authority* [2012] EWCA Civ 253, concerned an elderly couple – both of whom had capacity to make decisions about their living arrangements – who lived with their son. The LA had become concerned that the son was inflicting physical and mental abuse upon his parents, for example by restricting their access to friends and family, and trying to coerce his mother into residential care. The LA sought an injunction to prevent him from continuing with this behaviour, which was granted. The Court of Appeal upheld the injunction. In doing so, it explained that the purpose of this jurisdiction is 'in part aimed at enhancing or liberating the autonomy of the vulnerable adult whose autonomy has been compromised for one of the reasons outlined in *Re SA*'.

In many cases the inherent jurisdiction is used to prevent a vulnerable adult being placed in a situation whereby they are unable to exercise a free choice. However, it has also been used for wider purposes, such as interim measures while proper enquiries are made and the order simply protects the adult concerned.

For example, the case of *Hertfordshire County Council v AB* [2018] EWHC 3103 (Fam) involved a 28-year-old man (AB) with mild learning disabilities and a history of convictions for sexual offences. He had been conditionally discharged under the MHA into arrangements that amounted to a deprivation of liberty. AB had capacity to consent to these arrangements, and did so. The judge accepted that conditional discharge could not authorise a deprivation of liberty and that, since AB had capacity, the MCA 2005 was not relevant. The judge therefore used the inherent jurisdiction to authorise the deprivation of liberty.

The case of *An NHS Trust v Dr A* [2013] EWHC 2442 (COP) (see Chapter 8) also provides an example of a wider use of the inherent jurisdiction; in that case, to authorise a deprivation of liberty for the purposes of force-feeding in circumstances where a psychiatric patient fell outside the MHA and MCA 2005.

▶ KEY MESSAGES

- The MHA contains numerous community provisions which AMHPs engage other than through MHA assessments, and under other legislation. For the vast majority of people, inpatient treatment, care and support will only be a temporary phase in their life.

- The MHA will interface with the legislation which enables social and health care services to be delivered. AMHPs will need in particular to be aware which services are, or might be, available to support the person in the community before making a decision as to whether detention in hospital is necessary in all the circumstances of the case.

KNOWLEDGE REVIEW

- AMHPs have a unique power of entry and inspection, which can be found within section 115 of the MHA.

- The courts have held that it is unlawful to make charges for services provided under section 117 of the MHA.

- *The Care Programme Approach* (DH, 1990) is the system that is used in England to organise the care and treatment of many people with mental health problems in the community by secondary mental health services.

- The inherent jurisdiction exists to remedy lacunae left by the common law or statute. In some cases it can be used to authorise deprivation of liberty.

📖 FURTHER READING

- Burns, T., Rugkåsa, J., Molodynski, A., Dawson, J., Yeeles, K., Vazquez-Montes, M., Voysey, M., Sinclair, J. and Priebe, S. (2013) 'Community treatment orders for patients with psychosis (OCTET): a randomised controlled trial', *The Lancet*, 381(9878), pp 1627–33.

- Qurashi, I. (2008) 'Sections 37/41 Mental Health Act 1983: a study of judges' practice and assessment of risk to the public', *Medicine, Science, and the Law*, 48(1), pp 57–63.

- Shaw, J., Hatfield, B. and Evans, S. (2000) 'Guardianship under the Mental Health Act 1983', *Psychiatric Bulletin*, 24(2), pp 51–2.

Part 3
AMHP theory

10

Upholding rights and anti-oppressive practice

Chapter aim

This chapter will enable you to meet the following AMHP key competence themes:

- Application of values to the AMHP role

- Challenging and redressing discrimination and inequality

- Respect for diversity

- Respect for individuals' qualities, abilities and identity

- Challenging oppressive practice

- Promoting the rights, dignity and self-determination of patients consistent with their own needs and wishes

Schedule 2 of the Mental Health (Approved Mental Health Professionals) (Approval) (England) Regulations 2008
Key Competences 1(a)–(d), 2(1)(a)(i) and (ii), (c), (e)(i), (ii), 4(b), (k), 5(h)

Schedule 2 of the Mental Health (Approval of Persons to be Approved Mental Health Professionals) (Wales) Regulations 2008
Key Competences 1.2–1.7, 2.1, 4.2, 4.11

In this chapter we will be exploring the importance of upholding a person's rights as they interface with the mental health system and with ourselves as professionals. AMHPs are powerful professionals who can, when needed and in the right circumstances, deprive a person of their liberty. Therefore, we need to ensure that, as AMHPs, we are reflective and understand the frameworks that we must work within, and that we have a safeguarding function as well. This means upholding the rights of those who use mental health services to not be discriminated against and to be protected from unequal and equitable approaches. Discrimination within mental health services can manifest itself in many ways, as it can in every walk of life, through direct and indirect means, intentionally and unintentionally. One example is the disproportionate number of black people who are detained under the MHA, which was one of the reasons for the independent review of the MHA being undertaken.

Introduction

As an AMHP you need to be familiar with the variety of legislation, policy, guidance and regulation that exists to ensure that people have rights and that the vulnerable are protected. Anti-oppressive and anti-discriminatory practice draws on differing footings; these include:

- the MHA and Codes of Practice
- the Equality Act 2010
- the Public Sector Equality Duty (under the Equality Act 2010)
- the European Convention of Human Rights (ECHR)
- the UN Convention on the Rights of Persons with Disabilities (CRPD)
- the Charter of Fundamental Rights of the European Union
- anti-discriminatory practice (ADP)
- anti-oppressive practice (AOP)
- Professional Statutory and Regulatory Bodies (PSRBs)
- professional bodies' ethics.

ESSENTIAL KNOWLEDGE: VIEWS OF PERSONS WITH LIVED EXPERIENCE

Professionals should remember that:

- a person is a unique individual, with a unique history;
- a person's mental health history should not discriminate or stigmatise their current situation, and the AMHP should lead the team on values, morals and ethics;
- an AMHP is there to rebalance the power difference between the person being assessed and the doctors;
- the AMHP should be advocating for the person in a holistic manner that is in the person's interests and that challenges the medical model or any recommendations that are put forward by the rest of the team that may not be helpful to the person;
- people who are experiencing mental health problems are not weak, ignorant or necessarily selfish. Many have extraordinary resilience borne out of having survived extreme circumstances.

Mental Health Act 1983 and Codes of Practice

As discussed earlier, the Codes of Practice are issued under section 118 of the MHA. The leading case on the legal status of the MHA Codes of Practice is *R (Munjaz) v Mersey Care NHS Trust* [2005] UKHL 58, [2006] 2 AC 148. In this case, Lord Bingham stated (at para 22):

> It is in my view plain that the Code does not have the binding effect which a statutory provision or a statutory instrument would have. It is what it purports to be, guidance and not instruction. But the matters relied on by Mr Munjaz show that the guidance should be given great weight. It is not instruction, but it is much more than mere advice which an addressee is free to follow or not as it chooses. It is guidance which any hospital should consider with great care, and from which it should depart only if it has cogent reasons for doing so. Where, which is not this case, the guidance addresses a matter covered by s.118(2), any departure would call for even stronger reasons. In reviewing any challenge to a departure from the Code, the court should scrutinise the reasons given by the hospital for departure with the intensity which the importance and sensitivity of the subject matter requires.

Lord Hope added (at para 69):

> The Court of Appeal said in para 76 of its judgment that the Code is something that those to whom it is addressed are expected to follow unless they have good reason for not doing so: see *R v Islington London Borough Council, ex p Rixon* (1996) 1 CCLR 119, per Sedley J at p 123. Like my noble and learned friend Lord Bingham of Cornhill I would go further. They must give cogent reasons if in any respect they decide not to follow it. These reasons must be spelled out clearly, logically and convincingly. I would emphatically reject any suggestion that they have a discretion to depart from the Code as they see fit. Parliament by enacting section 118(1) has made it clear that it expects that the persons to whom the Code is addressed will follow it, unless they can demonstrate that they have a cogent reason for not doing so. This expectation extends to the Code as a whole, from its statement of the guiding principles to all the detail that it gives with regard to admission and to treatment and care in hospital, except for those parts of it which specify forms of medical treatment requiring consent falling within section 118(2) where the treatment may not be given at all unless the conditions which it sets out are satisfied.

This case concerned Mr Munjaz, who had been detained under the MHA in a high security mental health hospital. He had been placed in seclusion for periods in excess of four days. The Code provided that hospitals should have clear guidelines on the use of seclusion, including the frequency of reviews of the need to continue the procedure. The mental health trust's policy included large parts of the Code which had been reproduced in the policy, but it departed from it in providing for less frequent medical reviews after day seven. In the circumstances, the policy of an NHS trust governing the seclusion of psychiatric patients detained at its high security mental hospital was lawful, even though it departed from the Code of Practice. The trust's explanation for departing from the Code included that it had been directed to the generality of mental hospitals and had not addressed the special problems of high security hospitals. Moreover, the Code had not recognised the special position of patients whom it was necessary to seclude for longer than a few days. In the case of *Munjaz*, the House of Lords held that sufficient reason had been demonstrated for departing from the Code.

European Convention on Human Rights (ECHR)

The ECHR is an international convention (or agreement between states) made after the Second World War, as a result of which the signatory parties are bound to protect certain core human rights and fundamental freedoms of their citizens. The ECHR was adopted by the Council of Europe in 1951 and came into force in 1953. The UK was one of the first signatories.

The European Court of Human Rights is an international court established by the ECHR which applies and protects the rights and guarantees set out in the ECHR. It hears applications alleging that a contracting state has breached one or more of the human rights set out in the ECHR. An application can be lodged by an individual, a group of individuals or one or more of the other contracting states, and, besides judgments, the Court can also issue advisory opinions. The Court is based in Strasbourg, France.

▶ ESSENTIAL KNOWLEDGE: LAW

Broad categories of human rights

- **Absolute rights** – cannot be interfered with in any circumstances. For example, Article 4 does not allow, in any circumstances, slavery or forced labour.

- **Limited rights** – interference is only permitted in certain circumstances as specified in the relevant Article of the ECHR. For example, the right to liberty under Article 5 may be limited if a person is of 'unsound mind'.

- **Qualified rights** – can be interfered with only in order to protect the rights of other people, or the public interest for specific reasons. For example, interference with the right to private and family life is allowed if the public body can show that its action is lawful, necessary and proportionate in order to, for instance, protect public safety, or health, or morals.

Prior to 2000, it was difficult in practice for individuals to obtain a judgment because they needed to exhaust all domestic legal remedies before taking a case to the European Court of Human Rights. This led to the introduction of the Human Rights Act 1998 (HRA). The HRA gives effect to the rights and freedoms guaranteed under the ECHR by bringing these rights into the sphere of domestic law.

There are 16 basic human rights in the HRA, all of which are taken from the ECHR. Some of the most important ones for mental health professionals include:

- **Article 2:** Right to life
- **Article 3:** Prohibition of torture and inhumane or degrading treatment
- **Article 5:** Right to liberty and security
- **Article 8:** Right to respect for private and family life
- **Article 14:** Prohibition of discrimination – this is not a free-standing right but requires the exercise of the other rights to be carried out in a non-discriminatory way.

Any court or tribunal determining a question which has arisen in connection with the ECHR must take into account any decision of the European Court of Human Rights (section 2 of the HRA). So far as it is possible to do so, all primary and subordinate legislation must be read and given effect in a way which is compatible with the ECHR (HRA, section 3). If a higher court determines that a provision of primary legislation is incompatible with the ECHR, it can make a 'declaration of incompatibility' (HRA, section 4). The government must then consider whether to amend the relevant provision. Section 10 of the HRA, a 'fast track' option of a remedial order to make the amendment, can be used to amend non-compliant legislation which has been declared incompatible. If a court determines that subordinate legislation is incompatible with the ECHR, it can strike it down unless the primary legislation prevents removal of incompatibility (HRA, section 4(4)(b)).

Section 6 of the HRA makes it unlawful for a public authority, such as an NHS trust or local authority, to act in a way that breaches a person's ECHR rights. It does not apply directly to private companies or citizens unless they are carrying out public functions. Section 6 should be read alongside section 73 of the Care Act 2014, which provides that a registered care provider is a public authority for the purposes of the HRA if it is providing care to a person in their home or in residential accommodation, and such care has been arranged or funded (in part or in whole) by a local authority.

If a public authority does breach a person's ECHR rights, a case can be brought by the victim in a UK court. The court may grant such relief or remedy, or make such order, within its powers as it considers just and appropriate (HRA, section 8).

ESSENTIAL KNOWLEDGE: LAW

Mental health professionals acting as 'public authorities'

A decision-maker performing functions under the MHA (for example, an AMHP or a doctor making a medical recommendation) is exercising 'functions of a public nature' and is therefore a public authority for the purposes of the HRA. This means that it is unlawful for the professional to act in a way that is incompatible with the ECHR.

In *TM v London Borough of Hackney* [2011] EWCA Civ 4, a local authority was liable to pay compensation to an individual who had been unlawfully admitted to hospital under section 3 of the MHA because the individual's brother (the nearest relative) had objected to the admission under section 11(4)(a), so the detention had been contrary both to the Act and to Article 5 of the ECHR. The AMHP had made the application even though the nearest relative disagreed (in the belief that he had changed his mind). The High Court described (at para 35), why the local authority, rather than the individual AMHP, was the defendant against whom the case was brought:

> She is a professional who must make her own decisions and cannot be dictated to or influenced by the wishes of the Council. She may well be regarded as a person who is a public body within the meaning of the HRA. But, as the [MHA] makes clear, as an AMHP she has to be treated as acting on behalf of the local social services authority. S.145 (1AC) provides:
>
> > References in this Act to an approved mental health professional shall be construed as references to an approved mental health professional acting on behalf of a local social services authority, unless the context otherwise requires.
>
> Thus the relevant Council is vicariously liable for any lack of care or bad faith on the part of an AMHP. It is to be noted that one of the social services functions of a local authority is the appointment of AMHPs: see Local Authority Social Services Act 1970 (as amended), s.1A and Schedule 1 referring to s.114 of the MHA, which enables a local social services authority to approve a person to act as an AMHP. The first defendant is correctly named as a defendant and is responsible in law for the AMHP's actions.

The ECHR and the HRA have had a substantial impact on the development of mental health law. The MHA has proved to be one of the most fruitful areas of challenge under the HRA and was the subject of the first remedial legislation to be introduced under the Act, namely the Mental Health Act 1983 (Remedial) Order 2001 (SI 2001/3712). Moreover, the ECHR has produced a significant body of case law in this field. The main focus of the case law has been on Articles 5 and 8.

Article 5 of the ECHR protects the individual against arbitrary deprivation of liberty (*Engel v Netherlands* (1979–80) 1 EHRR 647 (App No 5100/71) at [58]). According to the landmark legal decision, *Winterwerp v Netherlands* (1979–80) 2 EHRR 387 (App No 6301/73), any lawful procedure for the deprivation of a person on the basis of unsoundness of mind must satisfy three minimum conditions:

1. The person must be reliably shown by objective medical expertise to be of unsound mind, unless emergency detention is required. The time at which a person must be reliably established to be of unsound mind is that of the adoption of the measure depriving that person of their liberty as a result of that condition (*OH v Germany* (2012) EHRR 29 (App No 4646/08) at para 78). The term 'a person of unsound mind' does not lend itself to precise definition, since psychiatry is an evolving field, both medically and in social attitudes. However, it cannot be taken to permit the detention of someone simply because their views or behaviour deviate from established norms.
2. The person's mental disorder must be of a kind to warrant compulsory confinement. This can only be justified if other, less severe, measures have been considered and found to be insufficient to safeguard the person (*Witold Litwa v Poland* (2001) 33 EHRR 53 (App No 26629/95)). The deprivation of liberty must be shown to be necessary in the circumstances. It may be necessary not only where the person needs therapy, medication or other clinical treatment to cure or alleviate their condition, but also where the person needs control and supervision to prevent them, for example, causing harm to themselves or other persons (*Hutchinson Reid v UK* App No 50272/99 at para 52).
3. Since the validity of continued confinement depends on the persistence of the mental disorder warranting compulsory confinement, there must be in place a mechanism to ensure that the persistence of such disorder is kept under appropriate review by the detaining authority.

Article 5(4) provides the right to a speedy judicial decision concerning the lawfulness of detention and ordering its termination, if it proves unlawful. It entitles a detained person to bring proceedings for review by a court of the procedural and substantive conditions which are essential for the lawfulness of the deprivation of liberty (*Idalov v Russia* App No 5826/03 at para 161). The opportunity for legal review must be provided soon after the person is taken into detention and thereafter at reasonable intervals if necessary (*Molotchko v Ukraine* App No 12275/10 at para 148). Special procedural safeguards may also be called for, in order to protect the interests of persons who, on account of their mental health problems, are not fully capable of acting for themselves (*Winterwerp v Netherlands* (1979–80) 2 EHRR 387 (App No 6301/73) at para 60).

Any deprivation of liberty will also entail by its nature a limitation of Article 8 rights to private and family life. A person who is deprived of liberty continues to enjoy 'all the fundamental rights and freedoms guaranteed under the ECHR save for the right to liberty' and moreover, 'when a person's personal autonomy is already restricted, greater scrutiny [should] be given to measures which remove the little personal autonomy that is left' (*Munjaz v United Kingdom* [2012] ECHR 1704 (App No 2913/06) at paras 79–80).

Although Article 8 of the ECHR contains no explicit procedural safeguards, it has long been established that it contains implicit procedural requirements; these are aimed at giving a person a degree of involvement in decisions affecting their private and family life that is sufficient to protect their interests, the requisite degree of involvement being calibrated to the circumstances of the case, and the seriousness of the interference with the rights that the Article protects (see, for example, *Shtukaturov v Russia* [2012] EHRR 27 (App No 44009/05) at paras 88–89). The European Court of Human Rights has also emphasised the serious nature of the interference with a person's integrity that is inherent in the forced administration of medication and the consequent requirement that any such administration be based on a law which guarantees proper safeguards against arbitrariness (*X v Finland* App No 34806/04 at para 220).

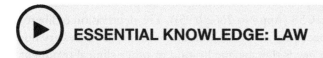

ESSENTIAL KNOWLEDGE: LAW

Case law: Glass v UK *[2004] ECHR 61827/00*

A hospital authority's decision to administer diamorphine to a severely mentally and physically disabled child against his mother's wishes, and to place a 'do not resuscitate' notice in his notes without her knowledge, was held to have interfered with their rights to private and family life under Article 8. The European Court of Human Rights noted that the actions taken by the hospital staff were intended, as a matter of clinical judgement, to serve the child's interests, but the Court considered that it had not been explained to its satisfaction why the authority did not, at any stage, seek the intervention of the High Court. The Court therefore considered that the decision of the authority to override the parent's objection to the proposed treatment, in the absence of authorisation by a court, resulted in a breach of Article 8.

Case law: Rabone v Pennine Care NHS Foundation Trust *[2012] UKSC 2*

In 2005, Melanie Rabone had been admitted to a psychiatric hospital on an informal basis after having tied a lamp flex around her neck, and she was placed on 15-minute observations. She was subsequently granted two days' home leave, despite the concern of her mother, and tragically after leaving the ward she took her own life.

Her parents brought claims in negligence for Melanie's estate and as victims in their own right under the HRA, claiming that the trust owed Melanie a duty under Article 2 to protect her life and had failed in this duty by allowing her to go home. They were unsuccessful in the High Court and the Court of Appeal on the basis that such a duty was owed only to patients who are detained under the MHA 1983 and that the parents were not victims in their own right.

However, the Supreme Court held that, despite Melanie's status as a voluntary rather than a detained psychiatric patient, the trust did owe her a duty under Article 2 to take positive steps to protect her from the real and immediate risk of suicide. The trust had also failed in its duty by allowing her to go home and held that Mr and Mrs Rabone were victims in their own right, entitled to damages for their bereavement as a result. They were awarded £5,000 each in compensation.

Case law: MH v United Kingdom *[2013] ECHR 11577/06*

M, who had Down's Syndrome, was detained under section 2 of the MHA and could have applied to the Mental Health Review Tribunal for discharge within 14 days. She did not do so because she lacked legal capacity to instruct solicitors, and after that 14-day period expired, she had no further right to apply to the tribunal. The local authority applied to displace her nearest relative, which had the effect of automatically extending M's detention under section 29(4). M's solicitors requested the Secretary of State for Health to make a reference to the tribunal under section 67 for M's discharge; the tribunal convened that month, but refused to discharge M.

It was held that there had been a breach of Article 5(4) within the initial 28 days of detention because M had been unable to challenge her detention speedily, and that special safeguards were needed for detained people who lack legal capacity.

United Nations Convention on the Rights of Persons with Disabilities (CRPD)

The CRPD was ratified by the United Kingdom in 2009. The Convention's purpose is to protect the rights of people who have long-term physical, mental, intellectual, or sensory impairments. While not directly incorporated into domestic law, it is applied both by the European Court of Human Rights and domestic courts as an aid to interpretation of the ECHR.

The CRPD has been lauded as a new paradigm and as a revolution in human rights law for persons with disabilities (see, for example, Flynn and Arstein-Kerslake, 2014). Its stated purpose in Article 1 is:

> [to] promote, protect, and ensure the full and equal enjoyment of all human rights and fundamental freedoms by all persons with disabilities, and to promote respect for their inherent dignity.

The CRPD has a wide field of application and encompasses civil and political rights as well as economic, social and cultural ones. These rights are extensive and cover matters such as the right to life, access to justice, independent living, education, work and cultural life. Two Articles of the CRPD are particularly relevant for the purposes of mental health and capacity law: Article 12 and Article 14.

Article 12 of the CRPD sets out that persons with disabilities have the right to legal capacity on an equal basis with others. The Committee on the Rights of Persons with Disabilities (which is responsible for monitoring the implementation of the CRPD) has clearly stated that systems of substituted decision-making deny legal capacity and are incompatible with Article 12, and therefore must be replaced with systems of supported decision-making (OHCHR, 2014).

Supported decision-making is a process of providing support to people whose decision-making ability is impaired to enable them to make their own decisions, whereas substituted decision-making involves someone making decisions on behalf of someone else on the basis of some objective standard, such as best interests. If the Committee on the Rights of Persons with Disabilities is correct, then the MCA 2005 clearly falls short since it provides for a substituted decision-making regime, where decisions are made on behalf of the person in their best interests. The wishes and feelings of the person are just one factor to be considered alongside others, and are not attributed any 'a priori weight or importance' (*ITW v Z* [2009] EWHC 2525 (Fam), [2011] 1 WLR 344 at para 35).

Article 14 of the CRPD states that 'the existence of a disability shall in no case justify a deprivation of liberty'. According to the UN High Commissioner for Human Rights, this means that the legal grounds for a detention must be 'de-linked from the disability and neutrally defined so as to apply to all persons on an equal basis' (United Nations Human Rights Council, 2009). Insofar as this is correct, it is difficult to see that either the MHA or the MCA 2005 (or indeed all mental health and capacity law in the UK) is remotely compliant.

The CRPD challenges existing understandings and categorisations of disability rights. There is much in its terms to be enthusiastic about. Its full implications are still being grappled with by governments across the world. But it may be that, in the future, the MHA and the MCA 2005 will come under pressure from those who feel it should reflect more directly the provisions of the CRPD.

REFLECTIVE ACTIVITY

Implications of the CRPD

–   What can the CRPD tell us about how AMHPs should be responding to the needs of those who are disabled?
–   What does the CRPD tell us about whether we should be promoting supported or substitute decision-making?

Charter of Fundamental Rights of the European Union

The EU's principal sources of law are the Treaty on the Functioning of the European Union and the Treaty on European Union. These are the constitutional treaties for the EU and its predecessor organisations. They establish the EU's institutions, their powers and responsibilities, and their relationship with the Member States. They also set out the overall purpose of the EU and its fundamental policies. The Member States have agreed a number of amending treaties over the years, such as the Lisbon Treaty, which entered into force in 2009. In addition to the changes it made to the constitutional treaties themselves, the Lisbon Treaty made the EU's Charter of Fundamental Rights binding on EU institutions and Member States; Article 6 of the Treaty on European Union provides that the Charter has 'the same legal value' as the treaties.

The Charter applies to the EU Member States when they are 'implementing Union law'. This means that the Charter is binding on the Member States when they are acting within the scope of EU law. Where domestic law conflicts with a Charter right, domestic judges are under a duty to 'disapply' the national legislation in that particular case if it cannot be interpreted in a manner consistent with the Charter.

The Charter is organised into six titles: Dignity, Freedoms, Equality, Solidarity, Citizens' Rights, and Justice. Although many of the rights and freedoms in the Charter mirror those contained in the ECHR, a number of additional rights come from the case law of the Court of Justice of the European Union or relate to EU citizenship.

Examples of relevant rights within the Charter include:

- **Article 25 (rights of the elderly)**, which recognises the right of older people to lead a life of dignity and independence and to participate fully in social and cultural life; and
- **Article 26 (disability rights)**, which provides for specific measures to be put in place to ensure the 'independence, social and occupational integration and participation' of disabled people in community life.

In the UK, the European Union (Withdrawal Agreement) Act 2020 provides that the Charter of Fundamental Rights will not be retained once the transitional period has ended in December 2020.

Anti-oppressive practice and anti-discriminatory practice

Values, principles and beliefs influence AMHP practice as they are the bedrock for the professions that may become AMHPs. Each professional will draw to a different extent on the various paradigms of what mental health is and how it should be supported and managed. In this sense, each and every AMHP will bring their own professional and personal values to the role, but these need to be managed to ensure that oppression and discrimination do not occur. AOP and ADP are fundamental to social work practice and are embedded in professional and ethical codes. As social work remains the largest contributor to the AMHP workforce, and was also the legacy workforce from the days of the Approved Social Worker, AOP and ADP have remained embedded in the AMHP role. The AMHP competences found in the regulations also complement this, as they require AMHPs to challenge and redress discrimination where possible in all its forms. AMHPs need to be mindful of the numerous forms of bias that can penetrate their decision-making, whether this be wilful (Heffernan, 2011) or unconscious bias (Banaji, 2016). Thompson (2016) helps us to understand that discrimination can occur at numerous personal, cultural and structural levels (the PCS Model) and therefore we need to be ready to challenge and redress discrimination in the appropriate places (see Chapter 12).

 **ESSENTIAL KNOWLEDGE: LAW**

Codes of Practice

England

14.41 AMHPs who assess patients for possible detention under the Act have overall responsibility for coordinating the process of assessment. In doing so, they should be sensitive to the patient's age, sex, gender identity, social, cultural or ethnic background, religion or belief, and/ or sexual orientation [see Chapter 3 for more information]. They should also consider how any disability the patient has may affect the way the assessment needs to be carried out. (DH, 2015a)

Wales

14.31 Unless different arrangements have been agreed locally between the relevant authorities, AMHPs who assess patients for possible detention under the Act have overall responsibility for co-ordinating the process of assessment. In doing so, they should be sensitive to the patient's age, sex, gender identity, social, cultural or ethnic background, religion or belief, and/or sexual orientation.

14.32 They should also consider how any disability the patient has may affect the way the assessment needs to be carried out. AMHPs should seek the views of carers, family members and relevant others in determining the most appropriate way to conduct the Assessment. (Welsh Assembly Government, 2016)

REFLECTIVE ACTIVITY

Challenging structural discrimination, and reflective supervision

– How might you as an AMHP challenge discrimination that you believe is occurring at a structural level?
– What arrangements do you have in place for reflective supervision with a peer AMHP?

Professional Statutory and Regulatory Bodies

Professional regulators are statutory bodies whose primary purpose is to ensure public safety. This is not only achieved by a process of 'weeding out' and disciplining those who fall short of professional standards but also by ensuring high standards of practice and behaviour, thus reducing the need for disciplinary intervention. Professional regulation is one element of a much broader system of ensuring the wellbeing and safety of patients and service users. In broad terms, its focus is on the regulation of individual professionals rather than, for example, organisations and systems.

There are currently nine regulatory bodies responsible for regulating 32 professions in the UK – consisting of approximately 1.44 million professionals (Professional Standards Authority, 2013, p 4). This includes all the professional groups eligible to become AMHPs (social workers, nurses, occupational therapists and psychologists). The relevant regulators in this respect are the Health and Care Professions Council, the Nursing and Midwifery Council, Social Work England, Social Care Wales and the British Psychology Society. In addition, Social Work England approves and monitors AMHP training and education programmes in England, this function having recently been transferred from the Health and Care Professions Council. Social Care Wales performs the same function in Wales. Each regulator is governed by its own Act of Parliament or Order in Council. In order to undertake their statutory functions, the regulators are given powers to make rules and regulations which in most cases must be approved by Order of the Privy Council and laid in Parliament.

Each regulatory body has the same overarching functions, which are as follows:

- setting the standards of behaviour, competence and education that professionals must meet;
- dealing with concerns from patients, the public and others about professionals who are unfit to practise because of poor health, misconduct or poor performance;
- keeping registers of professionals who are fit to practise; and
- setting the standards for periodic re-registration for each profession.

Professionals wishing to use titles such as 'social worker' must be registered with the relevant regulator. It is a criminal offence for any person to use a protected title without being registered. In some cases, specific activities or tasks are reserved to registered professionals.

The general position is that the regulators' jurisdiction in respect of health professionals is UK-wide. The regulation of social care professionals falls within the legislative competence of each country. England, Scotland, Wales and Northern Ireland have now introduced separate arrangements for the regulation of social workers and other social care staff. The regulators are accountable to the UK Parliament and in some cases also to the devolved assemblies.

Professional bodies

Any professional who is eligible to be an AMHP by virtue of their professional background can also opt to join a professional body for the profession. For social work there is the British Association of Social Work (BASW) and for nursing there is the Royal College of Nursing (RCN). Each professional body will offer additional codes of practice and ethical considerations that need to be adhered to in order to remain a member. There is no professional body for AMHPs in their own right, therefore causing tensions when seeking support from such a body. There is also disagreement as to whether being an AMHP is a role, status or profession, possibly reflecting the diversity in the structures that exist in the AMHP workforce, where some serve on a rota while for others being an AMHP is their full-time occupation.

Care Quality Commission

The Lunacy Commission, established in 1845, was the first national body set up to oversee the conditions in which people have been detained for reasons of mental disorder. This was succeeded by the Board of Control, which took over the responsibility between 1913 and 1959. There was then no regulator until 1983, when the Mental Health Act Commission was set up to monitor key aspects of the operation of the MHA 1983 in England and Wales. As a result of the Health and Social Care Act 2008, the Care Quality Commission (CQC) took over as the body in England with responsibility for monitoring the operation of the MHA. The CQC visits and interviews people currently detained in hospital under the MHA, and can require actions from providers when it becomes aware of areas of concern or areas that could be improved. The CQC also has specific duties under the MHA, such as to provide a Second Opinion Appointed Doctor service, review MHA complaints and make proposals for changes to the Code of Practice. As well as monitoring the MHA, the CQC is responsible for regulating health and adult social care service providers in England, including hospitals, GP practices, dental services, care homes and home care agencies. The Health and Social Care Act 2008 and associated regulations provide for the registration requirements and standards of quality and care that all providers have to meet when they register with the CQC, and on an ongoing basis after that.

In a report entitled *Monitoring the Mental Health Act in 2017/18* (CQC, 2019), the CQC highlighted that it had identified evidence to suggest that there had been improvement in the provision of information about their rights given to persons at the point of admission in an appropriate format they could understand, with such provision increasing from 89% to 94%. Furthermore, it was reported that there was evidence to suggest that provision of information to Nearest Relatives also rose, from 83% to 85%. Although it is not clear or convincing as to how the CQC has established these comparative figures (for instance, were the conditions and locations of the data-gathering sites comparable between periods?), it can be interpreted that some persons are not receiving information about their rights in an accessible format, or at all, or not at the right time to enable them to retain it.

The data indicate a two-percentage point increase, from 83% (6,513 out of 7,853) to 85% (5,482 out of 6,464) in further attempts to explain rights, or to explain rights to Nearest Relatives. There has been a two-percentage point improvement in rates of discussions about rights and assessments of the person's levels of understanding, from 91% (7,474 out of 8,236) to 93% (6,784 out of 7,300). The Code suggests that providers should carry out an assessment of how well the information was understood by the recipient and carry out regular checks to ensure that information has been properly given to each person and understood by them.

Welsh regulators

In Wales, Care Inspectorate Wales is responsible for regulating social care provision, and Healthcare Inspectorate Wales regulates health care (including hospitals).

Applying this in practice

While you are practising as an AMHP you will find yourself in situations you could not have fully predicted, as AMHP practice is diverse, varied and challenging. Therefore, your understanding of the framework for working anti-oppressively and anti-discriminately needs to be embedded in your everyday practice to ensure that you are conscious of this when making decisions. This can be particularly challenging when you recognise that by making an application for detention against someone's will this is inherently oppressive.

▶ KEY MESSAGES

- Upholding patients', carers' and relatives' rights is everyone's business.

- People experiencing mental health difficulties are more likely to be oppressed and discriminated against.

- There is law, policy and guidance that AMHPs must follow in respect of upholding people's rights and challenging oppression and discrimination.

- AMHPs must understand the frameworks they must work within, and the need to uphold the rights of those who use mental health services to not be discriminated against and to be protected from unequal and inequitable approaches.

KNOWLEDGE REVIEW

- The MHA Code must be followed unless there are cogent reasons for not doing so.

- The ECHR and the HRA 1998 have had a substantial impact on the development of mental health law.

- The CRPD has been lauded as a new paradigm and as a revolution in human rights law for persons with disabilities.

- There are a range of different regulators that operate in the field of health and care.

⧉ FURTHER READING

- Bartlett, P. (2017) 'Stigma, human rights and the UN Convention on the Rights of Persons with Disabilities', in W. Gaebel, W. Rössler and N. Sartorius (eds) *The stigma of mental illness: End of the story?*, Cham: Springer, pp 209–23.

- Callard, F., Sartorius, N., Arboleda-Florez, J., Bartlett, P., Helmchen, H., Stuart, H., Taborda, J. and Thornicroft, G. (2012) *Mental illness, discrimination and the law: Fighting for social justice*, London: Wiley-Blackwell.

- Flynn, E. and Arstein-Kerslake, A. (2014) 'Legislating personhood: realising the right to support in exercising legal capacity', *International Journal of the Law in Context*, 10(1), pp 81–104.

- Laing, J. (2015) 'Perspectives on monitoring mental health legislation in England: a view from the front line', *Medical Law Review*, 23(3), pp 400–26.

- Series, L. and Nilsson, A. (2018) 'Article 12 CRPD Equal Recognition before the law', in I. Bantekas, M.A. Stein and D. Anastasiou (eds) *The UN Convention on the Rights of Persons with Disabilities: A commentary*, Oxford: Oxford University Press, pp 339–82.

11

Resilience as an AMHP

Chapter aim

This chapter will enable you to meet the following AMHP key competence themes:

- Ability to challenge where appropriate

- Awareness of the accountability of being an AMHP

- Critical thinking and evaluation

- Assessing and managing risk

- Providing reasoned and clear oral and written accounts of AMHP decision-making

Schedule 2 of the Mental Health (Approved Mental Health Professionals) (Approval) (England) Regulations 2008
Key Competences 1(a), 2(1)(d)–(e), 4(f)–(h), 5(d), (f)

Schedule 2 of the Mental Health (Approval of Persons to be Approved Mental Health Professionals) (Wales) Regulations 2008
Key Competences 1.2, 2.3–2.5, 4.6–4.8, 5.3, 5.5

In this chapter we will consider what is needed to survive as an AMHP, both in training and in practice. Of late, there has been increased focus on building and sustaining resilience of AMHPs as an important consideration when ensuring good practice and maintaining a sustainable workforce. First, we will focus on the practicalities and implications of an experienced member of staff returning to full-time study as an AMHP trainee, and managing feelings of being de-skilled and frustrated by returning to education. Moreover, going on a placement with an organisation they already work in can impact on practitioners' resilience. The chapter will also explore why it is valuable to become an AMHP, how it fits into continuing professional development (CPD), engagement with research and how to maintain learning in this specialist role.

All this is highly relevant as the AMHP role can be challenging, and therefore there is a need for AMHPs to reflect on how they maintain their resilience and self-esteem in diverse and complex situations, including conflict management and acknowledging the emotional labour of the role. Finally, there will be an emphasis on reflective practice as an AMHP and ensuring that practitioners know what sources of support are available.

Introduction

As an experienced health and social care professional, you will know how challenging your work can be and how much energy it takes to do your job well. Social work and work in other health and social care professions is stressful, but practitioners also report that their work is rewarding, has meaning and provides the opportunity to help improve service users' lives (Huxley et al, 2005a; Beddoe, 2011; Collins, 2017). This chapter aims to help you reflect on the transition to becoming an AMHP and the experience of undertaking the role. Resilience is a term and concept used often with reference to service users and professionals. Here, we will discuss resilience in relation to how you, as a practitioner working in an often demanding and pressured role, can find ways to look after your own welfare while continuing to practise as an AMHP.

What is resilience?

'Resilience' can feel like an overused word and, as a consequence, may lose meaning and therefore application in our work. Before we can look at what resilience means for an AMHP, we first need to consider the roots of the concept. Resilience, in the field of health and social care, was originally researched in relation to service users, and particularly children (Adamson et al, 2014). In this context, the characteristics of resilient children were identified from a mainly psychological perspective, and consideration given to how to develop resilience characteristics in others (Henry, 2002). This early research considered that resilience was perhaps a fixed personality trait related to the child. However, researchers developing systemic approaches to working with families began to consider that resilience could be a more interactive and variable concept developed through the life course (Rutter, 1999).

There is no one single definition of what it means to be resilient. Examples of a straightforward definition of resilience may suggest that it is 'an adaptive state and personality trait' (Collins, 2007, p 255) or that it denotes an individual's ability to 'bounce back' (Grant and Kinman, 2013, p 357). We are sure these views of resilience are not lost on you, but they focus on the capacity within individual professionals for resistance to the external factors that are impacting on them. Grant and Kinman (2014a) suggest that resilience can be viewed in two different ways:

1. Resilience is essentially a *reactive* quality that practitioners develop. Being resilient helps practitioners to react to, or cope with, the stressful circumstances

of their jobs. In the context of AMHP practice, a resilient practitioner might be able to cope repeatedly with the last-minute changes in plans for admission of a person liable to be detained in hospital. The resilient practitioner has developed a set of skills and attributes that means this type of event is not one that overwhelms their ability to cope or undertake the role.

2. Resilience can be thought of in more *proactive* terms in which it is a protective resource that practitioners can draw on to cope with future challenges. This view of resilience suggests that it is a quality or resource that practitioners can build up and then employ in taking on/coping with new challenges. In the context of AMHP practice an experienced practitioner may use their resilience resources to problem-solve a new or infrequent aspect of the role, for example assessing a younger teenager under the MHA.

The purpose of being resilient might appear self-evident – practitioners staying well and being able to continue in their roles – and this is the primary interpretation that student social workers attribute to the concept (Collins, 2017). Qualified practitioners, however, attach a further interpretation beyond their own welfare: resilience is necessary for the benefit of service users (Grant and Kinman, 2014a). As an AMHP it is essential that you develop and maintain a level of resilience that supports you to undertake MHA assessments in which the welfare of the person remains a central focus. Practitioners who remain resilient and motivated work for the benefit of the person and can contribute greatly to their welfare (McFadden et al, 2015).

Resilience: the person, the environment and the interaction

Masten (2001) persuasively suggests resilience is not the preserve of a limited number of astonishing individuals, rather that it is just 'ordinary magic'; keep this in mind when you read this chapter. Resilience is a common, adaptive response to life's challenges. Resilience remains, however, potentially quite a tricky concept to grasp, but one way to think more deeply about its role in AMHP practice is to consider where and how it might be developed.

Adamson et al (2014) provide a conceptualisation of resilience to consider the concept in terms of the self, the practice context and mediating factors. Grant and Kinman (2013) suggested a similar tripartite analysis, noting first studies that highlight personality or individual characteristics; secondly, studies that focus on the role of environment and outcomes; and thirdly studies which, like Adamson et al (2014), promote an interactionist approach to the person and the environment.

First, resilience can be considered in relation to the individual as 'attributes and characteristics regarding the self … their personal and professional histories, and sensitising experiences and their values and ethics' (Adamson et al, 2014, p 530). This perspective locates some of the responsibility for being resilient with you, the practitioner. It suggests resilience is either an individual characteristic or one that might also be taught during training and is then further acquired through the experiences of professional practice. Here, the meaning you bring to your work – why it is important to you – is vital in understanding your perception of your own resilience.

Grant and Kinman (2013) identified resilient individuals as people who have: enthusiasm, optimism and hope; self-awareness and emotional literacy; well-developed social skills and social confidence to develop effective relationships; and flexibility and adaptability that draws on a wide range of coping strategies. Other authors note the importance of similar positive personality attributes and their positive behavioural implications in terms of practitioners being able to solve problems and cope with adversity (Collins, 2007; Carson et al, 2011). Individuals have different skills, experiences and abilities so it is logical that there are some practitioners who are more resilient than others. There is a risk, of course, that an approach that locates resilience as mainly within the individual could be viewed as 'blame-making, leading to individual workers being stereotyped as "not coping"' (Frost, 2016, p 438) when they experience difficulties at work.

The second aspect of Grant and Kinman's (2013) analysis identifies the significance of the environment, both the work/organisational environment and the wider practice environment in which practice takes place. The evolving nature of working environments has an impact on practitioners' behaviour as employees and their ability to practise safely as professionals (Jeyasingham, 2014; Travis et al, 2016). Many of the pull factors – those which keep social workers in their roles – are related to the working environment (Bowyer and Roe, 2015). These include workload, pay and conditions, access to supervision and career development opportunities (Baginsky, 2013). To separate out the concept of resilience away from the impact of the environment that you work in as an AMHP diminishes its usefulness. As an experienced practitioner training to be an AMHP you will most likely be aware of organisational factors that can make your working life more, or less, straightforward. The practice environment can be enhanced by ensuring that practitioners have access to training that promotes reflective practice and have regular supervision, peer coaching and opportunities to develop mindfulness skills and access experiential learning (Grant and Kinman, 2014b).

Finally, the interaction between the practitioner and the practice environment is important to consider: 'The environment in which social workers practise constructs the scope for the expression of the self and the exercise of professional identity' (Adamson et al, 2014, p 533). Here, the conceptualisation of resilience suggests it is not solely the provision of a positive working environment but the worker's interaction with that environment which influences their resilience in the practice environment (that is, in direct work with service users). Adamson et al's (2014) research suggested that the mediating factors between the individual and the practice context contribute to defining the concept of resilience and the continuation of resilient professionals in practice. These mediating factors include: the role of work–life balance; opportunities for developmental learning; coping behaviours; use of supervision and peer support opportunities; a strong sense of professional identity; and a sound educational base.

ESSENTIAL KNOWLEDGE

Professional standards that focus on staying well as a practitioner

Social work, occupational therapy and psychology
You must make changes to how you practise, or stop practising, if your physical or mental health may affect your performance or judgement, or put others at risk for any other reason.

HCPC, 2016, standard 6.3

Nursing
Maintain the level of health you need to carry out your professional role.

NMC, 2018, standard 20.9

Emotional labour, stress and resilience

Our next focus will be on the impact of the MHA assessment itself. MHA assessments are undertaken within the 'environment' identified earlier, but the impact of the assessment that occurs within that environment needs due consideration as well. There is an emotional aspect to MHA work, where AMHPs can be exposed to the distress of others through their engagement with people who are distressed, and the reaction that elicits in us as caring professionals. Stress and burnout are often referred to by practitioners and managers as factors that diminish the wellbeing of staff and carers.

It is worth differentiating between the concepts of stress and resilience to help understand why resilience may be the most useful, and forward-looking, concept to help AMHPs undertake their duties. Resilience is not the passive obverse of stress or emotional burnout; it is an active concept that promotes a positive response to the practice challenges (Adamson et al, 2014).

Ravalier (2018) identified the main sources of workplace stress as: high workload; lack of management support and excessive expectations of managers; lack of adequate supervision; the negative culture towards social work from outside the profession; and, finally, poor physical workplace environment and pay/conditions. Collectively, the existence of these issues would seem sure to place the average person in a state of stress.

REFLECTIVE ACTIVITY

Sources of workplace stress

This discussion may make concerning reading; how many of the factors identified by Ravalier's study can you identify in your workplace?

An AMHP is required to coordinate MHA assessments with other MHA work, with only a few exceptions. As we have discussed in Chapters 6 and 7 there are many aspects of the work that require organisation and resourcing to be effective. On top of this, an AMHP may be required in the ordinary function of their role to undertake more than one MHA assessment, or conversely may not undertake the AMHP role frequently enough to feel confident. Therefore, although the AMHP role requires great skill, there is a balance to be struck about workload expectations.

Research indicates that practitioners find the practice environment inherently stressful (Johnson et al, 2005), especially regarding statutory child protection (McFadden et al, 2015) and statutory mental health practice (Evans et al, 2005). The exposure to stressful practice scenarios that need practitioners to have high levels of resilience to sustain them is hard to ameliorate in AMHP practice. Effective practice approaches and well-organised services can reduce some of the stressful aspects of face-to-face practice but only to a degree. Some of the features of healthy working environments that reduce stress – such as access to reflective supervision and good management support – have also been identified as contributing to the development of resilient practitioners (Collins, 2017).

Adamson et al (2014), adopting a similar theme, summarise well the discussion regarding the relationship between the notion of coping or not coping. Practitioners who have adaptive coping strategies, such as good problem-solving or networking skills, are more likely to cope well – that is, to be resilient in the face of adversity. Coping, of course, is not just about problem-solving but also relates to the management of difficult emotions in difficult circumstances.

Hochschild's (1983) concept of emotional labour conveys how practitioners must manage their feelings and emotions in response to the work they undertake. Practitioners, faced with often difficult and upsetting practice situations, have, to an extent, to set aside their own emotional response in order to undertake their job. In AMHP practice, the presence of emotional labour is arguably heightened because of the complex legal and multidisciplinary nature of the work that must continue in the midst of service users' mental health crises. In some more extreme circumstances it is also possible that AMHPs will experience a degree of vicarious trauma (Van Heugten, 2011) through the emotional engagement with the issues and circumstances affecting the service user.

How the different experiences and emotions you have are processed and filtered in a practice context – 'feeling rules' (Winter et al, 2018) – links to how resilience is first conceptualised. Adamson et al (2014) suggest good coping strategies, an ability to see the value in the process (rather than being solely focused on outcomes), high levels of emotional intelligence, the presence of hope, and perceived subjective wellbeing are all factors that support the development and maintenance of resilient practitioners. As discussed later in this chapter the roles of supervision and peer support have been identified as particularly important in fostering practitioner resilience (Beddoe et al, 2014). Adamson et al's (2014) emphasis on seeing the value in the process of a task, rather than only valuing a positive outcome, is especially important in AMHP practice. In some instances the outcome of an MHA assessment may not be satisfactory from the AMHP's perspective – perhaps there was a lack of alternative resources to prevent admission – but the process and manner in which the assessment and admission were conducted are valuable in their own right.

Resilience and training to be an AMHP

As an AMHP trainee moving towards qualified status you are, by definition, developing your skills, testing your abilities and undertaking a period of concerted professional development. This may be a long planned for, stepwise, development, or perhaps an unexpected opportunity that you have seized. Either way you will probably find some aspects of your AMHP programme very demanding. It is important to consider how, as an experienced health and social care professional, you adapt to the expectations of you as a trainee AMHP.

REFLECTIVE ACTIVITY

Demands of AMHP training

Spend some time thinking about the AMHP training that you are undertaking (or have undertaken). Try to answer the following three questions:

  –   What opportunities does your training give you to develop your knowledge and skills?
  –   How are the demands of your training different from the demands of your usual role?
  –   In what ways are you preparing yourself to be able to manage the demands of your training?

Training as an AMHP may feel de-skilling. You have been selected as an AMHP trainee due to your competency and grade as an eligible professional. It may well be the case that you have wanted to undertake this training for some time and the opportunity has now availed itself. Now you will be learning new skills, acquiring new knowledge, getting things wrong and being assessed. This can leave some competent social work and health care professionals wondering what on earth they have embarked on, especially when hearing seasoned AMHPs emphasising how they will become experts in mental health law. It may take time for these feelings to surface in a way that you can articulate. It is also important to take time to think about some of the issues that might arise from returning to study if you have not been in education for a while. Similarly, it may feel unsettling to undertake a placement in the organisation that you already work for, so there are a few things you may need to think about.

 ESSENTIAL KNOWLEDGE: PRACTICE GUIDANCE

Preparation for AMHP training

1. Establish your professional identity as an AMHP trainee or student. Consider changing your email signature, out-of-office notifications and voicemail to reflect you are no longer in your previous role.
2. Prepare for starting the course by negotiating with your manager how your existing work is going to be managed while you are seconded to AMHP training, including redirecting calls or emails from people who don't realise you are now training.
3. Engage in shadowing experiences of MHA assessments prior to starting the course, to ensure first that you recognise what AMHP work can and does consist of, as well as preparing yourself for working with people in a mental health crisis.
4. As an AMHP trainee, you are going to be engaging in mental health work during the day and then probably completing written academic work in the evenings. Therefore, think about how you are going to manage this in the short term, and get the balance right.

If you are reading this book during your AMHP training, then you are in a good position to begin considering how to manage your own health and work patterns to promote your resilience. Completing an approved educational programme of study is only the initial stage of becoming an AMHP. It evidences that you have met the minimum competence required of an AMHP by meeting the HCPC requirements. The next stage is the time between qualification, which makes you eligible to be approved as an AMHP, and the actual local authority approval meeting. Throughout this time it is advisable to continue to undertake MHA work to the degree that is feasible as an unapproved AMHP, and to think about what support needs you should make your approvers aware of following approval. We mention this as making good use of this time may assist your preparations for undertaking the AMHP role independently.

Resilience and undertaking the AMHP role

The role of an AMHP can be very demanding and, as a qualified AMHP undertaking – or a practitioner soon to qualify to undertake – important statutory functions, it is important that you develop strategies that support you in your work.

ESSENTIAL KNOWLEDGE

Experiential learning

Some of the pressure points of the AMHP role might include:

- the limited resources you have to undertake and complete assessments;
- difficulties in working effectively with colleagues from different services and agencies;
- the essential nature of a key outcome of the role – detaining someone against their will, removing their liberty – might conflict with some of your long-held beliefs and values;
- the often urgent, stressful nature of the AMHP role;
- supporting service users, families and carers at a time of crisis in their lives;
- witnessing people being restrained and struggling.

Therefore, AMHPs need to develop defensible ways to work when faced with these challenges (for further discussion of the impact, see Chapters 7 and 12).

REFLECTIVE ACTIVITY

Building resilience

If you are a practising AMHP, or are soon to qualify, try to answer the questions below to develop your own approaches to building your resilience.

- What patterns of work are sustainable for me as an AMHP? How many days on duty are expected of me and how many do I need to undertake to maintain my confidence?

- How do I gain support if I need it when faced with an unfamiliar scenario?
- In what ways can I develop networks to assist me if I need to access or utilise resources in my AMHP role?
- What strategies are best suited to me to sustain a healthy work–life balance?
- Which aspects of the AMHP role cause me stress or fear, and what do I need to put in place or arrange in order to manage these feelings effectively?

What makes a resilient practitioner?

When considering what makes a resilient professional, Grant and Kinman (2013) suggest that there are key elements that support resilience, namely: emotional literacy; reflective ability; appropriate empathy; and social competence. These elements are now going to be considered in turn.

Emotional literacy

Emotional literacy, a corollary to emotional intelligence, means being able to understand our own emotions as well as those of other people. Practitioners who are able to develop emotional intelligence and emotional literacy are likely to become more resilient to the demands of AMHP practice. Emotional intelligence includes being able to manage your own moods, control impulses and to not be overwhelmed by the emotions of situations to the point where you are no longer able to think clearly (Goleman, 2006). Practitioners with well-developed levels of emotional literacy are able to manage their own emotional reactions – and the reactions of others – in complex practice scenarios. Undertaking MHA assessments can be stressful and a practitioner's ability to 'read' the situation is very important.

Most obviously, it is important that you develop emotional literacy to be able to feel and understand the emotions of the people you are assessing. This will help you judge how to manage the different aspects of the assessment and, crucially, not to inadvertently escalate the risks through misreading the situation. Emotional literacy will also help you to understand the perspectives of the different colleagues you will be working with during the assessment process; for example, the exhausted carer who desperately needs a break but is very reluctant to see their relative formally detained to a psychiatric hospital; or the anxious care coordinator who feels they have been juggling the risks of trying to care for a person in the community but now wants someone else to make the difficult decision about admission to hospital. If you have developed emotional literacy you will be able to understand the perspectives of others and respond in ways that encourage constructive dialogue and action.

This skill and quality is not unique to AMHP practice – many health and social care scenarios will benefit from the intervention of an emotionally literate practitioner – but emotional literacy is key to building your own personal levels of resilience. If you are able to spend time understanding your own emotional reactions to aspects of AMHP practice, then you are more likely to respond in ways that are constructive and not be drained or fatigued by some of the stress points of the AMHP role.

REFLECTIVE ACTIVITY

Emotional literacy

Consider this scenario. You assess a young man in the community and make an application for admission to hospital under section 2 of the MHA. During conveyance the detained person has to be restrained by the ambulance staff, and on admission the person is given medication by injection, which he resists.

- What do you think your emotional reaction to this scenario might be?
- Can you identify ways in which being emotionally literate in this situation may support you to cope well with the outcome of your decision to detain the person?
- What risks are there for future assessments if you over-identify with the detained person's experience?

Reflective ability

An important opportunity to develop your own ability to reflect on practice is through the supervision process. Reflective supervision is an established aspect of good social work practice (Fook, 2004) and it is a significant contributor to developing practitioner resilience (Beddoe et al, 2014). You may be supervised as part of your routine casework but it is important to establish some dedicated time to consider your AMHP practice.

The function of supervision varies between agencies, and some may emphasise caseload management, but it is also an opportunity for reflective conversations that appear to promote the development of resilience (Collins, 2017). Beddoe et al (2014), in a review of 27 experienced social workers, concluded that supervision is an opportunity for workers to develop individual characteristics that help them cope with the complex and demanding nature of their work. As you develop your knowledge and skills in relation to AMHP practice, you will be developing your professional identity and skills in a new area of work. AMHP supervision is a time when you will refine your knowledge base, seek guidance about the practice decisions you have made and gain confidence in your developing professional practice. Supervision may also be undertaken in different ways, other than with managers, by making peer arrangements with colleagues. One of the unique aspects of the AMHP role is AMHPs' independence and personal accountability for their own decisions. Therefore, structures need to be put in place that enable an AMHP to be open without fear of being judged or disciplined.

Carson et al (2011) similarly emphasise the importance of practitioners creating meaning in their work through interaction with colleagues and those who use services. This might be very important to you in working as an AMHP. Echoing the classic work of Eraut (1994), the authors stress the importance of informal learning in the workplace through recursive and discursive processes. The AMHP role can be very difficult and, in depriving a person of their liberty, very powerful. How you understand your part in the process and develop your own understanding of the value and meaning you attribute to your work as an AMHP will contribute to your development. If you are secure in your understanding of why you are undertaking the mental role, the values, knowledge and skills you employ and the ethical perspective you hold, then you are more likely to become a resilient practitioner.

The role of collegial support in promoting resilience is emphasised (Beddoe et al, 2014) and access to collegial support and regular supervision are key reasons experienced practitioners stay in their jobs (Frost, 2016). From an organisational perspective, employers have a responsibility to contribute to a safe workplace environment by providing access to quality supervision (Grant and Kinman, 2013). Therefore, collectively these factors should assist an AMHP to function in a working environment that is supportive and nurturing.

Appropriate empathy

Empathy is a key quality and skill for health and social care practitioners. The ability to understand the perspective of others is vital to being able to form relationships with service users and to subsequently help support the provision of appropriate services. For a practitioner to develop empathy through understanding a service user's perspective, or to develop feelings of warmth or compassion towards service users, is usually positive.

While often a distinction is made between empathy and sympathy, the risks of being empathetic have not always been so readily acknowledged. However, in AMHP practice, there is a challenge to remain empathetic towards service users when their reactions to you, or the services and interventions you may represent to them, may be hostile or negative. Practitioners may feel empathy towards others but this emotional engagement with the person and their situation carries a risk of distress and discomfort too. Therefore, managing empathy is important in contributing to your ability to maintain your resilience in AMHP practice.

The concept of 'appropriate empathy' has been developed to acknowledge the limitations that practitioners may need to put on the reach and form of empathy that they develop and express in their practice. As an AMHP you will need to be able to acknowledge and try to understand service users' perspectives but also to have clear boundaries in terms of your emotional engagement, as otherwise you risk your own welfare and resilience. Resilient practitioners can demonstrate appropriate empathy; they are deeply moved but not overwhelmed by practice (Collins, 2007).

Use the prompts in the 'Resilience builder' to think about how to ensure you remain resilient for AMHP practice.

REFLECTIVE ACTIVITY

Resilience builder

Take some time to consider how you can develop your own resilience for AMHP practice. Using the four key components that Grant and Kinman (2013) identified, think about steps you can take to develop your own practice in a way that will support you to undertake, or continue to undertake, the AMHP role.

Emotional intelligence and literacy
- How might you develop your skills for understanding the role of the professional relationships that underpin MHA assessments?

Reflective ability
- Are there opportunities you could access to talk though your assessments?

Appropriate empathy
- How can you make opportunities to check out how your empathy for service users impacts on your assessments?

Social skills
- Are there areas of AMHP practice you find difficult, for example asserting your views with the medics or negotiating police support? How can you develop your skills in these areas?

▶ KEY MESSAGES

- Resilience is not a fixed trait but a characteristic and resource that practitioners can develop.

- It is important to develop effective ways of developing your own resilience not only to safeguard your own welfare but also to ensure that you are able to practise safely for the benefit of service users and carers.

- Good supervision – a place to discuss your AMHP practice – is a vital aspect of developing resilient practice, both as a trainee AMHP and when you are approved.

KNOWLEDGE REVIEW

- Working with emotions is a core aspect of AMHP work but sociological concepts applied to it are contested.

- Establishing identity as an AMHP underpins confident practice.

- Understanding and being able to practise appropriate empathy is a core AMHP skill.

FURTHER READING

- Grant, L. and Kinman, G. (2014) *Developing resilience for social work practice*, London: Palgrave.

- Greer, J. (2016) *Resilience and personal effectiveness for social workers*, London: Sage.

12

AMHP decision-making

Chapter aim

This chapter will enable you to meet the following AMHP key competence themes:

- Making decisions relating to risk

- Weighing up decisions

- Asserting social perspectives in decision-making

- Obtaining, analysing and sharing appropriate information to make decisions

- Demonstrating independent decision-making

Schedule 2 of the Mental Health (Approved Mental Health Professionals)
(Approval) (England) Regulations 2008
Key Competences 1(b)–(c), 2(d), 4(f), (h)–(k), 5(a)–(b), (d), (f), (h)

Schedule 2 of the Mental Health (Approval of Persons to be Approved
Mental Health Professionals) (Wales) Regulations 2008
Key Competences 1.2, 1.3, 2.5, 4.6–4.11, 5.1–5.3, 5.5

In this chapter we will consider the nature of the AMHP role in terms of its unique features and key responsibilities in relation to reaching a decision. AMHPs have to make significant decisions as part of their role, most obviously whether they apply for a person to be compulsorily admitted to hospital or not. However, AMHPs have to make a host of other practice decisions before and after the decision whether to detain under the MHA, including involvement of the Nearest Relative and family, the correct form of transport, whether to use 14 days to decide to detain or not, protection of property, and caring responsibilities, including pets, and these are discussed in Chapters 6 and 7. This chapter will support AMHPs to reflect on the factors that impact on their decision–making, introduce frameworks to support ethical decision–making and consider interprofessional working in the AMHP context. This chapter will also link to the discussions on risk and AMHPs' understanding their own risk thresholds, and the implications of this for practice.

Introduction

In AMHP practice you may find that some aspects of decision-making are more straightforward than others. Social care and health professionals make countless decisions in the work they undertake with people, their families and the support systems they engage with. Decision-making often appears fast and intuitive, powered by the professional's accumulated knowledge and practice experience. Decision-making in AMHP practice warrants specific consideration because the principal decision – whether to make a formal application for detention, and in doing so temporarily deprive a person of their liberty – is so serious. AMHPs need to be confident that they are able to articulate the reasoning behind the decisions they make, employ strategies to make appropriate decisions, and be aware of the factors that might influence their decision-making processes.

Key decisions in AMHP practice

AMHPs make a multitude of decisions, minute by minute, in the process of carrying out their duties. Although the most difficult decision you will make is probably whether to formally admit a person to hospital, many other decisions are important too. In terms of the MHA and its associated guidance and Codes of Practice, some of the key AMHP decisions are outlined below.

ESSENTIAL KNOWLEDGE: LAW

Key decisions and judgements made by AMHPs

- Consideration of a request for an MHA assessment (or any case where the local social services authority has reason to think that an admission to hospital or guardianship may be needed) and deciding whether to proceed with its organisation (MHA, section 13(1))

- Identification of appropriately qualified doctors to attend the assessment, noting the requirements for prior acquaintance and specialist experience in section 12(2), conflicts of interest (section 12(3)) and specialist expertise (DH, 2015a, para 14.39 [England]; Welsh Assembly Government, 2016, para 2.58 [Wales])

- Along with the other assessors, considering whether the police should be asked for assistance (DH, 2015a, paras 14.47–14.48 [England]; Welsh Assembly Government, 2016, para 2.7 [Wales])

- Deciding whether to apply for a warrant of entry to search for and remove people (under MHA, section 135(1), (2), together with DH, 2015a, paras 16.3–16.16 [England] or Welsh Assembly Government, 2016, para 2.55 [Wales])

- Judgement of what constitutes an interview in a suitable manner (section 13(2)) and identifying whether the person has any particular communication needs (DH, 2015a, para 14.42 [England]; Welsh Assembly Government, 2016, para 2.36 [Wales])

- Judgement that statutory criteria for detention have been met in terms of the presence of mental disorder and risk criteria (MHA, sections 2(2) and 3(2), together with DH, 2015a, chapter 14 [England] or Welsh Assembly Government, 2016, chapters 2–5 [Wales])

- Judgement that, in all the circumstances of the case, detention in hospital or admission into guardianship is required and deciding which section is appropriate (MHA, section 13(2), together with DH, 2015a, chapter 14 [England] or Welsh Assembly Government, 2016, chapters 9–13 [Wales])

- Correct identification of the Nearest Relative (NR) (MHA, sections 26–28) and informing the NR that application under section 2 has been or will be made (MHA, section 11(3)) or informing the NR before a section 3 application is made (MHA, section 11(4)(b))

- Judgement whether it is practicable or would involve unreasonable delay to contact an NR (MHA, section 11(4)(b))

- Decision about the appropriate means to convey the person to hospital (MHA, section 137, together with DH, 2015a, chapter 17 [England] or Welsh Assembly Government, 2016, chapter 9 [Wales])

The AMHP role therefore requires you to make a series of consecutive decisions – from the point of initial referral onwards – in order to carry out the functions of the role. It is important to consider how you will approach making those decisions so that you are able to practise in a safe and effective way.

Reflection, critical analysis and practice wisdom

Reflection

As an AMHP you will, by definition, be a social worker, psychiatric nurse, occupational therapist or clinical psychologist. You will have considerable experience in your profession and will have undertaken further specialist training to undertake the AMHP role. It is appropriate therefore that you should have a degree of confidence in your own abilities to undertake the role.

It is also important to reflect on how your accumulated professional knowledge and experience might influence your decision-making and how you might consciously use it to do so. There is an established literature concerned with the importance of critical reflection as a key tenet of professional practice

(Schön, 1983; Fook and Gardner, 2007; Rutter and Brown, 2015) and using the essential aspects of critical reflection will help you to make better decisions.

REFLECTIVE ACTIVITY

Developing reflection in practice

Consider the prominence of reflection in your professional practice and how you might need to develop this with a specific focus on your AMHP role.

- How do you incorporate reflection into your existing professional practice?
- When are you going to reflect on your AMHP practice (e.g. after each assessment)?
- What resources can you access to support you to reflect on your AMHP decision-making?

Reflecting on your practice will be key to learning about how you, as an individual practitioner, approach the decision-making aspect of your role.

Critical analysis

AMHPs need to use their critical analysis skills when scrutinising what they are told and the information that they have access to as part of the assessment; and should adopt the principle of not accepting information at face value. The ability to analyse in this way is key to effective decision-making, as you will be able to record and thus defend how you arrived at the decision. Practice wisdom will have a part to play, while experience and tacit knowledge development will enable you to recognise familiar referrals and weigh up risk. However, such skills are not easy to objectively quantify and therefore you will need to be able to articulate this. Also, there is a danger that over-recognising a referral will create rigid and not dynamic thinking, as there may be failure to see each individual referral on its merits.

One aspect of your critical analysis might be to consider how your decision-making, and the outcome of an assessment, follows the principles set out in the relevant Code of Practice (see Guiding Principles box in Chapter 1, on p 28).

Analysis is a core skill that involves examining information critically in order to try and make sense of it, evaluate it and place it in sequence for a particular purpose, in this instance the referral and assessment. In terms of decision-making, AMHPs need to be able to show that they have taken into account all available relevant information, ensuring that the conclusion reached can be explained, including what has informed the decision. On occasion, this means choosing between competing alternatives.

Practice wisdom

Practice wisdom, combined with other types of knowledge such as theoretical, procedural, empirical and personal knowledge, can be used to describe the composition of a professional's knowledge base (Hudson, 1997). Sometimes erroneously equated with common sense (Cheung, 2017), practice wisdom is knowledge derived from the enactment of professional values and ethics in specific contexts and locations. Those contexts often contain a high degree of uncertainty which is why professional judgement is so important. It is through reflection and deliberation on previous experiences that practice wisdom is accrued (Chu and Tsui, 2008).

AMHP practice is a very specific context for professional practice. Your AMHP training will have developed your procedural (legal) knowledge to frame and inform your decision-making but you will also have an opportunity to integrate and utilise your accumulated practice wisdom from your previous professional practice context too. AMHP practice requires a judgement to be made, taking into account a set of specific circumstances beyond straightforward procedures and techniques (Chu and Tsui, 2008). The law, guidance and procedures will influence how you make your decision but it is your professional judgement, partly informed by practice wisdom, that will determine the decisions made.

Having an awareness of the concept of practice wisdom will support you to have confidence in your AMHP decision-making.

REFLECTIVE ACTIVITY

Practice wisdom

Think back to your professional practice before you embarked on your AMHP training and consider some of your accumulated knowledge, skills and experiences.

- What knowledge of theories and methods might contribute to your decision-making in AMHP practice?
- What understandings of human experience have you gained from your previous experience of working with service users that might contribute to your decision-making skills?
- Relationships are central to professional practice; how can you use your ability to form relationships with service users, family members and carers to better inform your AMHP practice?

Undertaking an MHA assessment is quite a tightly prescribed piece of practice in terms of the form it will take and the number of probable outcomes. Your ability to integrate previously accumulated practice experience and wisdom into your decision-making as an AMHP will improve the sophistication and depth of your professional practice.

Sound decision-making in AMHP practice

How are you going to know if the decisions you make as an AMHP are the right ones? It is difficult to judge. If a person who is detained under MHA, section 2 makes a good recovery in hospital and resumes their daily life soon afterwards, perhaps your decision to detain was the right one. However, assessing the value of a decision by its outcome is problematic. The person may have recovered in any case with appropriate care and support in the community, but this is something you will never know. In the midst of an MHA assessment you need a framework that will support you to make appropriate decisions, not one that only helps you to assess the value of a decision in hindsight.

O'Sullivan (2011) suggests that an 'effective decision' can be distinguished from a 'sound decision', and his distinction is helpful in framing your work as an AMHP. Effective decision-making is concerned with outcomes; an important focus but not an exclusive one. Sound decision-making is concerned with the *process*: that is, it is a decision that has been made appropriately. It is to be hoped that a sound decision becomes an effective decision, but this will not necessarily be the case.

 ESSENTIAL KNOWLEDGE: PRACTICE GUIDANCE

Sound decision-making

O'Sullivan (2011) proposes that the processes involved in making a sound decision are:

- being critically aware of the practice context;
- involving service users and carers to the highest level;
- working collaboratively with others;
- using knowledge, thinking clearly and managing emotions;
- framing decision situations in a clear and accurate way;
- analysing options and basing choices on reasoned analysis; and
- making effective use of supervision.

Some of O'Sullivan's processes might be familiar from your previous professional practice context and, in relation to your AMHP practice, will be straightforward to utilise to support your decision-making. Other aspects of sound decision-making may have previously been less prominent in your professional practice but can now be employed to provide a framework (checklist) for your work. The following reflective activity encourages you to think through the different aspects of sound decision-making in relation to your AMHP practice.

REFLECTIVE ACTIVITY

Sound decision-making – making the connections to AMHP practice

Use the different components of sound decision-making to reflect on how you approach making decisions in your AMHP practice.

Being critically aware of the practice context
–   (For example) Are you part of a multidisciplinary team or separate AMHP service?

Involving service users and carers to the highest level
–   Are you confident the service user's views were heard and that you interviewed in a suitable manner?

Working collaboratively with others
–   Did you ensure your decision was taken after professionally robust conversations with the two assessing doctors?

Using knowledge, thinking clearly and managing emotions
–   What professional knowledge – wisdom – informed your decision?

Framing decision situations in a clear and accurate way
–   Were you clear why an assessment was required?

Analysing options and basing choices on reasoned analysis
–   Is your decision defensible and your reasoning clearly presented?

Making effective use of supervision
–   Do you regularly reflect upon and review your assessment decisions?

In this chapter, two aspects of sound decision-making are considered in more detail to help you undertake the AMHP role: framing decision situations and managing emotions.

Framing decision situations

It is important that you have a clear picture of the factors at play with regard to the decisions you are making as part of your AMHP practice. Research into the decision-making of child protection social workers by Saltiel (2016) concluded that professionals often make important decisions based on 'unreliable or incomplete information, poorly defined and fluid situations, pressures of time and heavy workloads – which favour quick, intuitive decision making. Workers talked frequently about building pictures and getting a snapshot' (Saltiel, 2016, p 2114). The work of AMHPs can easily be seen to have similar characteristics, and creating a decision frame – a mental (or visual or written) picture of the key information and elements at play – will help to guide you in your work.

Taking the example of receiving a referral that proceeds to an MHA assessment, you will need to decide what information is relevant to the unfolding scenario. There is a process of selecting, interpreting and organising information to form a mental picture of the situation.

How you decide what to include in framing the situation is interesting to consider. You will need to identify factors germane to the situation and in doing so you will set aside details which are unlikely to impact on your decision-making. Some of this selection will be conscious and debated, some will be unconscious and automatic.

Key information in a decision frame, suggested by O'Sullivan (2011), might include:

- outcome(s) that decision-makers want to achieve,
- options available to achieve the outcomes, and
- ways of improving the chances of achieving a good outcome.

Drawing on social judgement theories, O'Sullivan (2011) notes that in deciding what factors will contribute to the framing of a situation, professionals need to be aware of the distinction between objective facts and the social construction of information. In the context of an MHA assessment, an objective fact might be the age of the person being assessed. An aspect of that person's life – such as reports from neighbours that the person is 'odd' – might be part of a social construction of the view of people with mental health difficulties living in the community. An aspect of your role in creating a decision frame is to apply a critical interpretation of the information you are being presented with to determine its provenance and relevance.

As noted later, a number of potential biases in decision-making have been identified (Rutter and Brown, 2015). In addition to considering how to create a decision frame, you will need to be mindful of appropriately applying a strengths-based perspective to support service user involvement, being aware of the impact of your own personal beliefs on your interpretation of the situation and ensuring the centrality of an anti-oppressive approach to your work. Additionally, it is important to consider the rule of optimism in how you frame your decisions. The 'rule of optimism', first coined in social work by Dingwall et al (1983), has been used to explain why social workers may have had a more positive view of parents' ability to meet the needs of their children than actually proved to be case (Kettle and Jackson, 2017). In AMHP practice, an awareness of this rule can be used to inform our approach to decision-making. Without discounting the role of hope and people's abilities to respond to offers of support, it is important that AMHPs are realistic about the risks presented and the safe options available in the context of an MHA assessment.

Managing your emotions in decision-making

Undertaking MHA assessments can be stressful, and AMHPs report that they need to be able to contain their own anxiety while acknowledging how that anxiety may be influencing their actions.

Emotional intelligence (Goleman, 2006) is a useful concept to consider in relation to decision-making. As discussed in Chapter 11, this approach emphasises our ability to recognise and manage our own emotions while also acknowledging and managing the emotions of others. A person's emotional intelligence can be developed and a professional can become emotionally competent. In relation to AMHP practice, you need to develop an awareness of how your emotions may affect your decision-making and so ensure that a particular emotion, such as anxiety or fear, does not exert an inappropriate influence. This is not to diminish the role of emotions in contributing to the decision-making process – you may feel anxious about a person's safety for very legitimate reasons – but rather to ensure that emotions are properly considered. Equally, you need to have an awareness of the potential impact of the emotions of other people on you. For example, the exhaustion and hopelessness that a carer of an older adult with dementia may feel might translate into your feeling pressure to apply for formal detention in hospital before other less restrictive options have been considered.

REFLECTIVE ACTIVITY

Case study: Jessica

You are on duty as an AMHP and a referral is made for a person named **Jessica** who has an established medical diagnosis of emotionally unstable personality disorder. The police have detained her under section 136 of the MHA and taken her to the health-based place of safety at the local psychiatric hospital after a member of the public alerted police that Jessica was threatening to jump from a high-rise car park. This is the third referral in one month for Jessica, and each time the scenario is substantially the same. Jessica has been threatening suicide for the last month since her close friend ended her life through suicide, but her behaviour is escalating and becoming more reckless. Staff who know her say that she should be assessed quickly so she does not remain at the place of safety for long; her family, on the other hand, are very concerned and feel she should be admitted.

Questions
- What are your initial thoughts about this referral? And how does this influence your next steps?
- What are your initial thoughts as to whether Jessica may need hospital admission?
- What steps may you have to take to ensure that bias does influence your views?
- What types of bias may be influencing your views?

Decision-making bias

As well as considering the impact of emotions on AMHP decision-making it is important to highlight other influences, and specifically biases that might influence practice.

AMHP decision-making, like all professional decision-making, involves having an awareness of the conscious or unconscious factors that may impact on your thought processes. Rutter and Brown (2015, p 7) suggest six areas of bias that are applicable to AMHP practice:

- *Anchoring effect:* where a professional might rely too much on one piece of 'anchoring' information to inform their decision. An AMHP might be unduly influenced by the views of an assertive NR who is certain that without admission the person will experience a further relapse in their mental health condition.
- *Bandwagon effect:* where a professional might not prioritise their own judgement but too readily go along with the views of others. This is a very risky bias for an AMHP. Central to the construction of the legal powers to detain people is the fact that the AMHP is required to exercise their independent professional judgement.
- *Confirmation bias:* this is the tendency of decision-makers to seek out and interpret information to support their own initial view. A key role for an AMHP is assessing referral information and deciding whether or not to undertake an MHA assessment. In gathering and assessing referral

information, you will begin to form your opinions about the situation, the need for an assessment and probable outcome. It is important that you are not unintentionally influenced in your decision-making by your initial impressions of the referral information.

- *Hindsight bias:* here, professionals overestimate the predictability of an adverse outcome in light of a previous experience. The pressure to mitigate risks and ensure the safety of service users might mean an AMHP will be influenced by the post hoc assessment of previous untoward incidents. If previous decisions *not to detain* are later considered to have been wrong, and to be decisions that led to an adverse incident, it might be tempting to become too risk averse.
- *Pseudo-certainty effect:* this can occur when a decision-maker views the outcome of a decision as certain when, in fact, they have little evidence for this judgement and the outcome is inherently uncertain. You will need to be mindful that you do not approach assessments with a predetermined view about the likelihood, or not, of detention being the outcome. Service users' histories should inform, but not determine, how AMHPs make their decisions.
- *Outcome bias:* here, a decision is made with undue emphasis on the outcome rather than the quality of the decision-making at the time the decision was made. With the relative certainty and safety that detention in hospital can bring to a difficult MHA assessment, AMHPs must be mindful that their decision-making is not unduly influenced by a focus solely on admission as an outcome.

As you undertake your AMHP duties, keeping an awareness of the potential for these biases to be influencing your decision-making is very important.

Decision-making, risk assessment and hope

Chapter 7 considers in detail the importance of risk assessment in AMHP practice. This section will consider the relationship between risk assessment and decision-making, with reference to the importance of maintaining hope and promoting recovery.

In undertaking MHA assessments you will often find your ability to make decisions that promote risk-taking compromised by organisational and resource demands. These demands may often reduce the space for proactive, empowering engagement with service users and their carers (Campbell, 2010, p 332). How can you, in your AMHP role, make decisions that properly take into account risk assessments without overshadowing the role of recovery approaches to mental health care?

The recovery approach to mental health care has developed in the UK since the 1990s, and one of its key tenets is the role of *hope* rather than the presence of *hopelessness* that has historically dominated risk assessment tools (Heller, 2015). Its advocates hope that people's mental health can improve and that each episode of being unwell is unique; any relapse might arise from differing reasons. Therefore, the key message for professionals is that pre-judgement or generalisation does not lead to person-centred care. Recovery-focused approaches mean recognising the importance of relationships and positive risk-taking, and practice that is de-stigmatising and which recognises and works to overcome feelings of shame and low self-esteem (Pilgrim, 2013).

AMHPs undertake assessments in difficult situations where it is appropriate to pay careful attention to the serious risks that may be present in terms of harm to self and harm to others. In relation to formal admission under MHA, sections 2 and 3, the legislation requires applicants to consider the health and safety of the person and the protection of other people. Nevertheless, you are also required to take into account all the circumstances of the situation and consider the possibility of alternatives to admission (MHA, section 13).

Therefore, perhaps an appropriate emphasis for your risk assessments will be to consider *balancing* the risks that are present. Balancing risk factors is different from encouraging people – professionals and/or service users – to take positive risks; the latter suggests taking risks that might ultimately lead to a negative experience, such as the breakdown of an independent living arrangement, while the former suggests making decisions that acknowledge that all options have risks to all parties. The purpose of the risk assessment is to make a judgement about how to balance the different nature of those risks. One commentator suggests that managing such uncertainty and developing practice wisdom is an inherent part of decision-making for AMHPs and that moving towards this expert practice underpins confident AMHP practice (Hemmington, 2014).

Influences on outcomes

Decision-making in AMHP practice, and especially the decision whether to detain, may be influenced by factors other than the presentation of the person being assessed. Quirk et al (2003) identified five 'non-clinical and extra legal' factors that impacted on the decision-making of Approved Social Workers (who previously held the AMHP role). This observational participant study took place over 20 years ago but its findings will resonate with AMHPs today. The first identified influence on decision-making was how services are organised; some models of service provision – such as community-based multidisciplinary teams – promoted considered responses to referrals and so reduced the chances of detention. Other service models – such as crisis teams – were found to lead to a firefighting approach to referrals that led to higher detention rates. It seems likely that a key issue here is not just service organisation but service capacity.

Secondly, limited resources were identified as a reason that professionals were unable to identify realistic alternatives to admission to hospital. Thirdly, the extent of team support of positive risk-taking by not detaining someone influenced social workers' decisions whether to detain or not. Fourthly, Quirk et al (2003) noted that local operational norms, for example the extent of post-assessment peer discussion, exerted an influence on practitioners' decision-making. A culture of debrief and discussion resulted in greater scrutiny of a worker's decisions in that they were required to justify their decisions. Finally, the conditions at the hospital to which persons could be admitted might determine the threshold for admission; workers were reluctant to detain people in hospitals that they thought were in a poor condition or did not provide a good standard of care.

Becoming an experienced AMHP and the impact on decision-making

Training and then practising as an AMHP is a part of a professional's development and, perhaps unsurprisingly, can lead to a re-evaluation of previously held beliefs and assumptions about the role. Buckland (2016), who interviewed practising social work AMHPs, found a change in attitude from a broadly anti-psychiatry perspective to one that valued the knowledge base of psychiatry. This development was not straightforward, and the complexities of how the medical categorisation of mental health problems within law relates to other concepts such as the social model of disability or the recovery approach were acknowledged.

Similarly, Buckland (2016) reported that some AMHPs experienced a change in perspective from focusing on civil liberties, for example the right to freedom and liberty, to acknowledging a stronger rights-based influence in their decision-making, for example people's rights to access treatment. A theme that was present for all the AMHPs interviewed was the importance of being human – the role of the head and the heart – in undertaking this difficult role.

It is important in your decision-making as an AMHP that you develop an awareness of your own perspective about the context and systems within which you undertake your duties. To critically reflect on the influences that impact on your decision-making enables you to articulate and justify to others how you undertake the role.

 ESSENTIAL KNOWLEDGE: PRACTICE GUIDANCE

SPIRAL Model

S – Decisions you make need to be **SOUND** rather than good or bad, as outcomes cannot be reliably predicted. A sound decision is demonstrated by adhering to a rational and reasoned process.

P – Your decisions must demonstrate a **PROPORTIONATE** application of the law in the management and mitigation of the presenting needs and risks associated with the person being assessed. You can show this by indicating how you have weighed up your actions.

I – Your **INDEPENDENCE** should be demonstrated through the discussions that you hold, and how you account for your decision-making in your recording.

R – Is what you have recorded **RELIABLE**? Could the contributory information you are founding your decisions on be verified if the need arises? This includes information such as the dates and times of any telephone calls and other information you have used to make your decision. Can you show how the information you have gained from key stakeholders, such as the assessed person and their relatives, carers and professionals, has influenced your decision? If so, you are thereby demonstrating that you have acted in good faith and with reasonable care.

A – Is your decision justifiable in **ALL** the circumstances of the case? It is important that a social perspective of mental health has informed your assessment and, where necessary, enabled you to challenge an overly medical perspective.

L – Have you applied what you have **LEARNT** through reflective supervision? Is your practice and decision-making within the scope and acceptability of your peer AMHPs?

Stone and Vicary, 2019

Conclusion

This chapter has explored AMHP decision–making. There are numerous decisions that AMHPs need to make, from accepting the referral through to whether to make an application for detention. Reflective and critical thinking are essential skills for an AMHP to have, alongside an ability to dig deeper and scrutinise what you see and hear. Whether you are a trainee or an experienced AMHP, ensuring that you have reflective supervision is key to analysing the decisions you have made and whether they were sound or not. Decision bias can come in various different forms; being aware of these conscious and unconscious biases will enable AMHP practice to be better informed.

▶ KEY MESSAGES

- AMHPs are required to make numerous decisions in the course of their work.

- Reflection on practice, critical analysis of decision-making and the role of practice wisdom are key to decision-making.

- The concept of 'sound decision-making' provides a framework for AMHPs to consider their decision-making, with an appropriate focus on the process rather than the outcome of decisions made.

KNOWLEDGE REVIEW

- Working with uncertainty is an accepted part of AMHP work.

- The possibility of bias is something that AMHPs need to be mindful of.

- Having confidence in decision-making is an important attribute.

FURTHER READING

- For further information on the sound decision-making approach, see: O'Sullivan, T. (2011) *Decision making in social work*, 2nd edn, Basingstoke: Palgrave Macmillan.

- Hemmington, J. (2014) 'Managing uncertainty and developing practice wisdom', in S. Matthews, P. O'Hare and J. Hemmington (eds) *Approved mental health practice: Essential themes for students and practitioners*, Basingstoke: Palgrave Macmillan.

- Taylor, C. and White, S. (2006) 'Knowledge and reasoning in social work: educating for humane judgement', *British Journal of Social Work*, 36(6), pp 937–54.

Closing remarks: looking forward

Since the Mental Health Act 1983 (MHA) was implemented in 1984, it has been amended on a regular basis; since 1990, there have been over 70 pieces of legislation that have made amendments to it, some substantive, others less so, but all with the intention of modernising the MHA legislation in England and Wales. We have witnessed, through the enactment of the Mental Capacity Act 2005, the amendments in the Mental Health Act 2007 and the anticipated amendments within the Mental Capacity (Amendment) Act 2019, that the original MHA 1983 has been insufficient to respond to all circumstances in which an impairment or disturbance in the functioning of a person's mind or brain is placing them (or others) at risk of harm. The result is that we still have a mosaic of mental health legislation. It is possible that in the future in England and Wales we may have a single piece of legislation covering all matters of mental health and mental capacity, or 'fusion law' as it is sometimes called, as we have seen introduced in Northern Ireland.

The independent review of the MHA, chaired by Sir Simon Wessely, made 154 recommendations in its report (DH, 2018), two of which have been confirmed for enactment. On 6 December 2018 the Westminster government announced:

> The government will introduce a new Mental Health Bill to transform mental health care, following the publication of the final report from the Independent Review of the Mental Health Act 1983. The government is accepting two of the review's recommendations to modernise the Mental Health Act.
>
> Those detained under the Act will be allowed to nominate a person of their choice to be involved in decisions about their care. Currently, they have no say on which relative is contacted. This can lead to distant or unknown relatives being called upon to make important decisions about their care when they are at their most vulnerable.
>
> People will also be able to express their preferences for care and treatment and have these listed in statutory 'advance choice' documents.
>
> (Department of Health and Social Care, 2018)

It is believed that the other recommendations may influence a change in the Codes of Practice for the MHA, but details remain unknown. The most obvious candidates for change may be the Guiding Principles as currently contained within the Codes of Practice. However, as there are distinctive Codes for England and for Wales it will be interesting to see how the Westminster government and Welsh Assembly Government respond and whether they will each give different weight to the various recommendations. No new Mental Health Bill has been presented to Parliament as yet. It is likely that there will be a White Paper and pre-legislative scrutiny before any legislation is introduced. As we stated at the beginning of the book, mental health legislation is in a constant state of change and amendment; the prospect that this might continue to be the case should not come as any surprise.

The AMHP role moving forward

The AMHP role and the MHA process exist because of primary legislation. Yet the law does provide for practice wisdom, experience and tacit knowledge. Undertaking the AMHP role is not straightforward; it can be fraught with complications. Nonetheless, it is a valuable role: one that seeks to balance safeguarding the interests of people who are being assessed in a very specific legal context with the wider needs of carers, nearest relatives, families, communities and professionals.

Whether you are an AMHP undertaking training, or a qualified AMHP, it is important to think about how you can develop and maintain your own resilience for practice (see Chapter 11). Reflective practice plays a key role in developing practitioners' abilities and has been identified in the development of resilience too (Grant and Kinman, 2014a). Linked to resilience is the centrality of supervision, which may be individual or group supervision, but it is essential that this occurs.

How AMHP services support practitioners varies, but the opportunity to discuss cases with a senior colleague, or in a peer supervision/coaching setting should prove helpful. During AMHP training experiential learning will be key to developing such resilience. AMHP approval courses have a substantial practice placement element, and it is here that you will be able to develop some good techniques in both the practical aspects of the role but also managing the emotional impact of it.

AMHP training and experience as a basis for progression to Approved or Responsible Clinician

One area that is underdeveloped is the number of eligible mental health professionals who go on to become Approved or Responsible Clinicians. Oates et al (2018) suggest that between 2007 and 2017 only 56 nurses, occupational therapists, psychologists or social workers had become Approved Clinicians. This is a lower uptake than for those becoming AMHPs from those same professional backgrounds (ADASS, 2018). For those with AMHP training, becoming an Approved or Responsible Clinician might be the next progressive step in developing their professional role. To date the numbers of Approved or Responsible Clinicians who are not doctors are small compared to the numbers of medical Approved or Responsible Clinicians undertaking the role currently. A small minority of Approved or Responsible Clinicians are nurses or psychologists, and they are to be found in only a couple of localised mental health trusts. The low uptake may be explained by challenges similar to those that nurses (Stone,

2019), occupational therapists and psychologists have faced in becoming AMHPs, namely structural barriers, low expectations and the dominance of an established professional group in the existing workforce. Nonetheless, the legislation is in place to enable these roles to exist for those from non-medical professions if there is the organisational and political will to enable the move to occur.

Changing roles in mental health services are not new; the roles of AMHP and Approved or Responsible Clinician, despite their low take-up by eligible professionals coming from outside the traditional professional background, are now relatively well known. However, other professionals are now being trained for roles such as associate physician, and they are coming into the mental health workforce to undertake previously held medical positions. Therefore, it is likely that we will see workforce development and functions undertaken by traditional mental health professionals being diversified.

When speaking to those who have lived experience, they have differing views on what changes are needed moving forward. This was the response from one person we asked.

PERSPECTIVE: PERSON WITH LIVED EXPERIENCE

I think that it would be helpful to all if there was a trained, lived experience 'expert by experience' on the assessing team, and also two social workers and one doctor rather than one social worker and two doctors.

For the overall assessment to be social model-led rather than medical model. Whatever the professional mix, there needs to be lived experience, and there needs to be at least one professional who actually knows the person. This is particularly important when the person is alone without family or friends.

COVID-19 pandemic: an example of how the MHA can be amended at a time of national crisis

Sometimes in cases of public emergency, primary legislation, including the MHA, needs to be modified to enable public services to deliver an effective response. The Coronavirus Act 2020, which received Royal Assent on 25 March 2020, provides a recent example of this. The Act was introduced in response to the COVID-19 outbreak and enables changes to legislation if the pressures of demand and workforce illness during the pandemic mean that public services are unable to carry out their duties. Most of the changes are contingent upon secondary legislation, such as regulations, in order to be brought into force. The changes would be temporary, lasting only for the duration of the emergency. Some of the key changes to the MHA provided for by the Act are summarised below.

Applications for detention

The Coronavirus Act provides that an application by an AMHP for detention under section 2 or section 3 of the MHA can be based on a recommendation by a single registered medical practitioner (rather than by two practitioners, as currently is the case). This single recommendation may be given by a registered medical practitioner who is section 12(2) approved or an approved clinician. There is no requirement to gain a doctor with 'previous acquaintance'. This would only apply if seeking a second recommendation was 'impractical or would involve undesirable delay'.

Holding powers

The Coronavirus Act provides that the report needed to trigger the 'holding powers' in section 5(2) need not be provided by the doctor or approved clinician in charge of the patient's treatment if this is 'impractical or would involve undesirable delay'. Instead, any doctor or approved clinician may provide the report. The Act also provides for an extension of the time limits for the use of the holding powers from 72 hours to 120 hours (in the case of section 5(2), where the decision is taken by a doctor or approved clinician) and from six hours to 12 hours (in the case of section 5(4), where the decision is taken by a registered mental health or learning disability nurse).

Mentally disordered offenders

The Coronavirus Act makes several modifications to Part 3 of the MHA. First, the power of the court to remand an accused person to hospital for a report or treatment would no longer be limited to 12 weeks.

Secondly, the courts would be able to rely on a single medical recommendation (rather than two recommendations, as currently is the case), if seeking a second recommendation would be 'impractical or would involve undesirable delay', when using the following powers:

- **section 36(1)** – power to remand accused person to hospital for treatment;
- **section 37(1)** – power to order detention in hospital, or guardianship, of convicted person;
- **section 38(1)** – power to order interim detention of convicted person in hospital pending final hospital order or other disposal;
- **section 45A(3)** – power to direct that a person sentenced to imprisonment be detained in hospital instead of prison;
- **section 51(5)** – power to order detention of a person in hospital in the absence of the person.

Thirdly, a transfer direction to hospital may be given under section 47(1) or 48(1) (removal of prisoners to hospital) on the basis of a single medical recommendation (rather than two recommendations, as currently is the case), if the Secretary of State is satisfied that seeking a second recommendation is 'impractical or would involve undesirable delay'.

Finally, there would be a relaxation of the time limits to convey accused or convicted persons to hospital to allow for transfers to take place 'as soon as possible' after the statutory time limit.

Medical treatment requiring consent or a second opinion

The Coronavirus Act provides that the certificate required under section 58 of the MHA, for medical treatment beyond three months, could be supplied by the approved clinician, rather than the Second Opinion Approved Doctor (SOAD), if arranging the SOAD would be 'impractical or would involve undesirable delay'. Also, the Act provides that only one professional would need to be consulted if consultation with two was 'impractical or would involve undesirable delay'.

Places of safety

The Coronavirus Act provides that period during which the police can detain a person in a place of safety under section 135 and section 136 of the MHA can be extended from 24 hours to 36 hours.

Reflections

The rationale behind these types of powers is to enable public services to continue operating during times of emergency and to ensure that people get the assistance they need. However, for the person themselves, this may be seen as reducing the safeguards that would normally be guaranteed under the MHA, such as the need for a second medical recommendation for detention and for a SOAD to approve the continued provision of treatment. The AMHP may need to explain to the person and their family why the normal procedures do not currently apply and seek to reassure them that their situation has still been considered very carefully.

PERSPECTIVE OF PERSON WITH LIVED EXPERIENCE

... it seems that under the current circumstances it would be acceptable. It is hard to imagine what it would be like just now to be severely distressed. Also, it must be particularly difficult due to staffing issues within a service that is 'thin on the ground' under regular circumstances.

Whatever the mental health workforce looks like in the future, consultation and the involvement of those with lived experience has to be at the heart of mental health services to ensure that those series are fit for purpose. AMHPs have offered and continue to offer leadership in mental health services and what better opportunity is there to demonstrate this further than through enabling and empowering those with lived experience to shape AMHP practice?

References

Adamson, C., Beddoe, L. and Davys, A. (2014) 'Building resilient practitioners: definitions and practitioner understandings', *British Journal of Social Work*, 44, pp 522–41.

ADASS (Association of Directors of Adult Social Services) (2018) *AMHPs, Mental Health Act Assessments and the Mental Health Social Care workforce*, available from: www.adass.org.uk/media/6428/nhsbn-and-adass-social-care-national-report.pdf.

APPG (All-Party Parliamentary Group) (2019) *Social Workers and a new Mental Health Act: Final Report*, House of Commons, London.

Banaji, M. (2016) *Blind spot*, Bantam: New York.

Bailey, D. and Liyanage, L. (2010) 'The role of the mental health social worker: political pawns in the reconfiguration of adult health and social care', *British Journal of Social Work*, 42, pp 1113–31.

Banks, S. (2001) *Ethics and values in social work*, Basingstoke: Palgrave.

Baginsky, M. (2013) *Retaining experienced social workers in children's services: The challenge facing local authorities in England*, London: Department for Education.

BASW (British Association of Social Workers) (2005) *Evidence to the Joint Committee on the Draft Mental Health Bill, Session 2004-2005*, Vol II, EV 577.

BASW (2018) *The Code of Ethics for Social Work*, available from: www.basw.co.uk/system/files/resources/Code%20of%20Ethics%20Aug18.pdf (accessed 16/02/20).

Beddoe, L. (2011) 'Health social work: professional identity and knowledge', *Qualitative Social Work*, 12(1), pp 24–40.

Beddoe, L., Davys, A.M. and Adamson, C. (2014) 'Never trust anybody who says "I don't need supervision": practitioners' beliefs about social worker resilience', *Practice*, 26(2), pp 113–30.

Blom-Cooper, L. (1996) *The case of Jason Mitchell: Report of the independent panel of inquiry*, London: Duckworth.

Bogg, D. (2011) National AMHP Leads data. Unpublished, AMHP Leads Network.

Bogg, D. (2014) 'Ethics and values', in S. Matthews, P. O'Hare and J. Hemmington (eds) *Approved mental health practice: Essential themes for students and practitioners*, Basingstoke: Palgrave Macmillan.

Bowyer, S. and Roe, A. (2015) *Social work recruitment and retention*, Totnes: Research in Practice.

Bressington, D.T., Wells, H. and Graham, M. (2011) 'A concept mapping exploration of social workers' and mental health nurses' understanding of the role of the Approved Mental Health Professional', *Nurse Education Today*, 31, pp 564–70.

British Psychological Society (2018) *Codes of ethics and conduct*, available from: www.bps.org.uk/sites/www.bps.org.uk/files/Policy/Policy%20-%20Files/BPS%20Code%20of%20Ethics%20and%20Conduct%20%28Updated%20July%202018%29.pdf (accessed 16/02/20).

Brown, R. (2002) 'The changing role of the Approved Social Worker', *Journal of Mental Health Law*, December, pp 392–9.

Buckland, R. (2016) 'The decision by Approved Mental Health Professionals to use compulsory powers under the Mental Health Act 1983: a Foucauldian discourse analysis', *British Journal of Social Work*, 46, pp 46–62.

Campbell, J. (2010) 'Deciding to detain: the use of compulsory mental health law by UK social workers', *British Journal of Social Work*, 40, pp 328–34.

Cairns, R., Maddock, C., David, A.S., Hayward, P., Richardson, G., Szmukler, G. and Hotopf, M. (2005) 'Prevalence and predictors of mental incapacity in psychiatric in-patients', *British Journal of Psychiatry*, 187, pp 379–85.

Care Services Improvement Partnership/National Institute for Mental Health in England (2007) *Workbook to support implementation of the Mental Health Act 1983 as amended by the Mental Health Act 2007*, London: NIMHE.

Carson, E., King, S. and Papatraianou, L.H. (2011) 'Resilience among social workers: the role of informal learning in the workplace', *Practice*, 23(5), pp 267–78.

Cheung, J.C.S. (2017) 'Practice wisdom in social work: an uncommon sense in the intersubjective encounter', *European Journal of Social Work*, 20(5), pp 619–29.

Chu, W.C.K. and Tsui, M. (2008) 'The nature of practice wisdom in social work revisited', *International Social Work*, 51(1), pp 47–54.

College of Occupational Therapists (2015) *Code of Ethics and Professional Conduct*, available from: www.rcot.co.uk/sites/default/files/CODE-OF-ETHICS-2015_0.pdf (accessed 16/02/20).

Collins, S. (2007) 'Social workers, resilience, positive emotions and optimism', *Practice*, 19(4), pp 255–69.

Collins, S. (2017) 'Social workers and resilience revisited', *Practice*, 29(2), pp 85–105.

CQC (Care Quality Commission) (2019) *Monitoring the Mental Health Act in 2017/18*, London: HMSO.

Davidson, G. and Campbell, J. (2010) 'An audit of assessment and reporting by Approved Social Workers (ASWs)', *British Journal of Social Work*, 40, pp 1609–72.

DH (Department of Health) (1990) *Caring for people: The Care Programme Approach for people with a mental illness, referred to specialist psychiatric services*, HC(90)23/LASSL(90)11, London: Department of Health.

DH (1999) *Review of the Mental Health Act 1983: Report of the Expert Committee* (chair: G. Richardson), London: Department of Health.

DH (2005) *Reform of the Mental Health Act: Summary of consultation responses*, London: Department of Health.

DH (2007) *New ways of working for everyone: A best practice implementation guide*, London: Department of Health.

DH (2008) *Refocusing the Care Programme Approach: Policy and Positive Practice Guidance*, London: Department of Health

DH (2015a) *Mental Health Act 1983: Code of Practice*, London: HMSO/Department of Health; accessed 19/01/18 at: www.gov.uk/government/publications/code-of-practice-mental-health-act-1983.

DH (2015b) *Reference Guide to the Mental Health Act 1983*, Norwich: TSO, available from: https://assets.publishing.service.gov.uk/government/uploads/system/uploads/attachment_data/file/417412/Reference_Guide.pdf.

DH (2018) *Modernising the Mental Health Act: Increasing choice, reducing compulsion: Final report of the Independent Review of the Mental Health Act 1983*, available from: https://assets.publishing.service.gov.uk/government/uploads/system/uploads/attachment_data/file/778897/Modernising_the_Mental_Health_Act_-_increasing_choice__reducing_compulsion.pdf (accessed 16/02/2020).

Department of Health and Social Care (2018) 'Government commits to reform the Mental Health Act', available from: www.gov.uk/government/news/government-commits-to-reform-the-mental-health-act (accessed 22/02/2020).

Department of Health and Social Care (2019) *National Workforce Plan for Approved Mental Health Professionals (AMHPs)*, London: Department of Health and Social Care, available from: https://www.gov.uk/government/publications/national-workforce-plan-for-approved-mental-health-professionals-amhps.

Dickens, J. (2013) *Social work, law and ethics*, Abingdon: Routledge.

Dingwall, R., Eekelhaar, J. and Murray, T. (1983) *The protection of children: State intervention and family life,* 2nd edn, London: Blackwell.

Eraut, M. (1994) *Developing professional knowledge and competence,* Abingdon: Routledge.

Evans, S., Huxley, P., Webber, M., Katona, C., Gately, C., Mears, A., Medina, A., Pajak, S. and Kendall, T. (2005) 'The impact of "statutory duties" on mental health social workers in the UK', *Health and Social Care in the Community*, 13(2), pp 145–54.

Fisher, M., Newton, C. and Sainsbury, E. (1984) *Mental health social work observed*, London: George, Allen & Unwin.

Flynn, E. and Arstein-Kerslake, A. (2014) 'Legislating personhood: realising the right to support in exercising legal capacity', *International Journal of the Law in Context*, 10(1), pp 81–104.

Fook, J. (2004) 'Critical reflection and organisational learning and change: a case study', in Gould, N. and Baldwin, M. (eds) *Social work, critical reflection and the learning organisation,* Aldershot: Ashgate Publishing.

Fook, J. and Gardner, F. (2007) *Practising critical reflection: A resource handbook*, Maidenhead: Open University Press.

Frost, L. (2016) 'Exploring the concepts of recognition and shame for social work', *Journal of Social Work Practice*, 30(4), pp 431-46, https://doi.org/10.1080/02650533.2015.1132689. Available from https://uwe-repository.worktribe.com/output/910062.

Goleman, D. (2006) *Emotional intelligence: Why it can matter more than IQ*, 10th edn, New York: Bantam Books.

Grant, L. and Kinman, G. (2013) '"Bouncing back?" Personal representations of resilience of student and experienced social workers', *Practice*, 25(5), pp 349–66.

Grant, L. and Kinman, G. (2014a) *Developing resilience for social work practice*, London: Palgrave.

Grant, L. and Kinman, G. (2014b) 'Emotional resilience in the helping professions and how it can be enhanced', *Health and Social Care Education*, 3(1), pp 23–34.

Hale, B. (2017) *Mental health law*, London, Sweet & Maxwell.

Hatfield, B. (2008) 'Powers to detain under mental health legislation in England and the role of the Approved Social Worker: an analysis of patterns and trends under the 1983 Mental Health Act in six local authorities', *British Journal of Social Work*, 38, pp 1553–71.

HCPC (Health and Care Professions Council) (2016) *Standards of Performance, Conduct and Ethics*, London: HCPC.

Heffernan, M. (2011) *Wilful blindness*, New York: Simon & Schuster.

Heller, N.R. (2015) 'Risk, hope and recovery: converging paradigms for mental health approaches with suicidal clients', *British Journal of Social Work*, 45, pp 1788–803.

Hemmington, J. (2014) 'Managing uncertainty and developing practice wisdom', in S. Matthews, P. O'Hare and J. Hemmington (eds) *Approved mental health practice: Essential themes for students and practitioners*, Basingstoke: Palgrave Macmillan.

Henry, D.L. (2002) 'Resilient children', *Social Work in Health Care*, 34(3–4), pp 283–98.

Hochschild, A.R. (1983) *The managed heart: Commercialization of human feeling*, Berkeley: University of California Press.

Hubbard, R. and Stone, K. (2018) *The Best Interests Assessor Practice Handbook*, Bristol: Policy Press.

Hudson, J. (1997) 'A model of professional knowledge for social work practice', *Australian Social Work*, 50(3), pp 35–44.

Hudson, J. and Webber, M. (2012) *The National AMHP Survey 2012 final report. Stress and the statutory role: Is there a difference between different professional groups?*, London: King's College.

Hurley, J. and Linsley. P. (2007) 'Expanding roles within mental health legislation: an opportunity for professional growth or a missed opportunity?', *Journal of Psychiatric and Mental Health Nursing*, 14, pp 535–41.

Huxley, P. and Kerfoot, M. (1994) 'A survey of Approved Social Work in England and Wales', *British Journal of Social Work*, 24(3), pp 311–24.

Huxley, P., Evans, S., Webber, M. and Gately, C. (2005a) 'Staff shortages in the mental health workforce: the case of the disappearing Approved Social Worker', *Health and Social Care in the Community*, 13(6), pp 504–13.

Huxley, P., Evans, S., Gately, C., Webber, M., Mears, A., Pajak, S., Kendall, T., Medina, J. and Katona, C. (2005b) 'Stress and pressures in mental health social work: the worker speaks', *British Journal of Social Work*, 35, pp 1063–79.

Jeyasingham, D. (2014) 'Open spaces, supple bodies? Considering the impact of agile working on social work office practices', *Child and Family Social Work*, 21(2), pp 209–17.

Johns, R. (2016) *Ethics and law for social workers*, London: Sage.

Johnson, S., Cooper, C., Cartwright, S., Donald, I., Taylor, P. and Millet, C. (2005) 'The experience of work-related stress across occupations', *Journal of Managerial Psychology*, 20(2), pp 178–87.

Jones, R. (2019) *Mental Health Act Manual*, London: Sweet & Maxwell.

Kettle, M. and Jackson, S. (2017) 'Revisiting the rule of optimism', *British Journal of Social Work*, 47, pp 1624–40.

Kinney, M. (2009) 'Being assessed under the 1983 Mental Health Act: Can it ever be ethical?', *Ethics and Social Welfare*, 3, pp 329–39.

Knott, G. and Bannigan, K. (2013) 'A critical review of the Approved Mental Health Professional role', *British Journal of Occupational Therapy*, 76(3), pp 118–26.

Laing, R.D. (1959) *The divided self*, London: Tavistock.

Law Commission (2017) *Mental Capacity and Deprivation of Liberty*, Law Com No 372, London: HMSO.

Leah, C. (2019) 'Approved Mental Health Professionals: a jack of all trades. Hybrid professional roles within a mental health occupation', *Qualitative Social Work*, https://doi.org/10.1177/1473325019873385.

McFadden, P., Campbell, A. and Taylor, B. (2015) 'Resilience and burnout in child protection social work: individual and organisational themes from a systematic literature review', *British Journal of Social Work*, 45, pp 1546–63.

McNicoll, A. (2016) 'Warning over "severe" AMHP shortages as hundreds leave', *Community Care*, 7 September.

Manktelow, R., Hughes, P., Britton, F., Campbell, J., Hamilton, B. and Wilson, J. (2002) 'The experience and practice of Approved Social Workers in Northern Ireland', *British Journal of Social Work*, 32, pp 443–61.

Masten, A.S. (2001) 'Ordinary magic: resilience processes in development', *American Psychologist*, 56(3), pp 22–38.

Matthews, S. (2014) 'Underpinning themes, theories and research', in S. Matthews, P. O'Hare and J. Hemmington (eds) *Approved mental health practice: Essential themes for students and practitioners*, Basingstoke: Palgrave Macmillan, pp 7–22.

Mechanic, D. (1959) *Mental health and social policy*, Englewood Cliffs, NJ: Prentice-Hall.

Morriss, L. (2015) 'AMHP work: dirty or prestigious? Dirty work designations and the Approved Mental Health Professional', *British Journal of Social Work*, 46(3), 703–18.

Murr, A. and Waterhouse, T. (2014) 'The impact of space and place', in S. Matthews, P. O'Hare and J. Hemmington (eds) *Approved mental health practice: Essential themes for students and practitioners*, Basingstoke: Palgrave Macmillan.

Myers, F. (1999) 'Social workers as mental health officers: different hats, different roles?', in M. Ulas and A. Connor (eds) *Mental health and social work*, London: Jessica Kingsley.

NMC (2018) *The Code: Professional standards of practice and behaviour for nurses, midwives and nursing associates*, available from: www.nmc.org.uk/globalassets/sitedocuments/nmc-publications/nmc-code.pdf (accessed 16/02/20).

Oates, J., Brandon, T., Burrell, C., Ebrahim, S., Taylor, J. and Veitch, P. (2018) 'Non-medical approved clinicians: results of a first national survey in England and Wales', *International Journal of Law and Psychiatry* 60, pp 51–6.

OHCHR (Office of the High Commissioner for Human Rights) (2014) *OHCHR Report*, available from: https://papuanewguinea.un.org/sites/default/files/2019-10/OHCHR%20Report%202014.pdf (accessed 12/04/20).

O'Sullivan, T. (2011) *Decision making in social work*, 2nd edn, Basingstoke: Palgrave Macmillan.

Payne, M. (2014) *Modern social work theory*, 4th edn, Basingstoke: Palgrave Macmillan.

Peay, J. (2003) *Decisions and dilemmas: Working with mental health law*, Oxford: Hart.

Percy Commission (1957) *Report on the Committee relating to mental illness and mental deficiency 1954–1957*, London: HMSO.

Pilgrim, D. (2013) *Recovery and mental health: A critical sociological account*, New York: Red Globe Press.

Professional Standards Authority (2013) *Annual Report and Accounts 2012–13*, London: TSO.

Quirk, A. (2008) *Obstacles to shared decision-making in psychiatric practice: Findings from three observational studies*, Brunel University, UK, doctoral thesis.

Quirk, A., Lelliott, P., Audini, B. and Buston, K. (2003) 'Non-clinical and extra-legal influences on decisions about compulsory admission to psychiatric hospital', *Journal of Mental Health*, 12(2), pp 119–30.

Ravalier, J.M. (2018) 'Psychosocial working conditions and stress in UK social workers', *British Journal of Social Work*, 49(2), pp 371–90, https://doi.org/10.1093/bjsw/bcy023.

Reith, M. (1998) *Community care tragedies: A practice guide to mental health inquiries*, Birmingham: Venture Press.

Roberts, C., Peay, J. and Eastman, N. (2002) 'Mental health professionals attitudes towards legal compulsion in England and Wales: report of a national survey', *International Journal of Forensic Mental Health*, 1(1), pp 69–80.

Rutter, M. (1999) 'Resilience concepts and findings: implications for family therapy', *Journal of Family Therapy* 21(2), pp 119–44.

Rutter, L. and Brown, K. (2015) *Critical thinking and professional judgement in social work*, 4th edn, London: Sage Publications.

Saltiel, D. (2016) 'Observing front line decision making in child protection', *British Journal of Social Work*, 46, pp 2104–19.

Scheff, T. (1963) 'The role of the mentally ill and the dynamics of mental disorder' in O. Grusky and M. Pollner (eds) (1981) *The sociology of mental illness: Basic studies*, New York: Holt, Rinehart & Winston.

Schön, D. (1983) *The reflective practitioner: How professionals think in action*, London: Maurice Temple Smith.

Sheppard, M. (1990) *Mental health: The role of the Approved Social Worker*, Sheffield: Joint Unit for Social Service Research.

Sheppard, M. (1993) 'Theory for approved social work: the use of the Compulsory Assessment Schedule', *British Journal of Social Work*, 23, pp 231–37.

Social Services Inspectorate (2001) *Detained: SSI inspections of compulsory mental health admissions*, CI (2001).1, London: Department of Health.

Stone, K. (2018) 'Nurse AMHPS: an exploratory study of their experiences', *The Journal of Mental Health Training, Education and Practice*, 14(2), pp 86–95.

Stone, K. (2019) 'Approved Mental Health Professionals and detention: an exploration of professional differences and similarities', *Practice*, 31(2), pp 83–96.

Stone, K. and Vicary, S. (2019) 'Decision making by approved mental health professionals, approved social workers, and mental health officers', *Professional Social Work*, 22 March.

Szasz, T. (1961) *The myth of mental illness*, London: Paladin.

Tew, J. (ed) (2005) *Social perspectives in mental health: Developing social models to understand and work with mental distress*, London: Jessica Kingsley.

Thompson, N. (2016) *Anti-discriminatory practice: Equality, diversity and social justice* (in Practical Social Work series), Basingstoke: Palgrave Macmillan

Travis, D.J., Lizano, E.L. and Morbarak, M.E. (2016) '"I'm so stressed!": a longitudinal model of stress, burnout and engagement among social workers in child welfare settings', *British Journal of Social Work*, 46(4), pp 1076–95.

United Nations Human Rights Council (2009) *Annual report of the United Nations High Commissioner for Human Rights and reports of the Office of the High Commissioner and the Secretary General: Thematic Study by the Office of the United Nations High Commissioner for Human Rights on enhancing awareness and understanding of the Convention on the Rights of Persons with Disabilities*. Available from: www2.ohchr.org/english/bodies/hrcouncil/docs/10session/A.HRC.10.48.pdf.

Van Heugten, K. (2011) *Social work under pressure: How to overcome stress, fatigue and burnout in the workplace*, London: Jessica Kingsley.

Vicary, S. (2017) An interpretative phenomenological analysis of the impact of professional background on role fulfilment: A study of approved mental health practice, University of Manchester.

Vicary, S., Young, A. and Hicks, S. (2019) '"Role over" or roll over? Dirty work, shift, and Mental Health Act Assessments', *British Journal of Social Work*, 49(8), pp 2187–206.

Walton, P. (2000) 'Reforming the Mental Health Act 1983: an Approved Social Worker perspective', *Journal of Social Welfare and Family Law*, 22(4), pp 401–14.

Watson, D. (2016) 'Becoming an Approved Mental Health Professional: an analysis of the factors that influence individuals to become Approved Mental Health Professionals', *Journal of Mental Health*, 25(4), pp 310–14.

Welsh Assembly Government (2010) *The Mental Health (Wales) Measure*, Cardiff: Welsh Assembly Government.

Welsh Assembly Government (2016) *The Mental Health Act 1983: Code of Practice for Wales*, available from: www.wales.nhs.uk/sites3/documents/816/Mental%20 Health%20Act%201983%20Code%20of%20Practice%20for%20Wales.pdf (accessed 16/02/20).

Wickersham, A., Nairi, S., Jones, R. and Lloyd-Evans, B. (2019) 'The Mental Health Act assessment process and risk factors for compulsory admission to psychiatric hospital: a mixed methods study', *British Journal of Social Work*, doi: 10.1093/bjsw/bcz037.

Winter, K., Morrison, F., Cree, V., Ruch, G., Hadfield, M. and Hallett, S. (2018) 'Emotional labour in social workers' encounters with children and their families', *British Journal of Social Work*, 49(1), pp 217–33.

Legislation and case law

Statutes
Care Act 2014
Care Standards Act 2000
Children Act 1989
Children Act 2004
Children and Families Act 2014
Chronically Sick and Disabled Persons Act 1970
Criminal Procedure (Insanity) Act 1964
Diplomatic Privileges Act 1964
Equality Act 2010
Family Law Reform Act 1969
Freedom of Information Act 2000
Health and Social Care Act 2008
Human Rights Act 1998
Local Authority Social Services Act 1970
Mental Capacity Act 2005
Mental Capacity (Amendment) Act 2019
Mental Capacity (Northern Ireland) Act 2016
Mental Health Act 1959
Mental Health Act 1983
Mental Health Act 2007
National Health Service Act 2006
National Health Service (Wales) Act 2006
Police and Crime Act 2017
Police and Criminal Evidence Act 1984
Regulation and Inspection of Social Care (Wales) Act 2016
Social Services and Well-being (Wales) Act 2014

European and international legislation
Charter of Fundamental Rights of the European Union
European Convention on Human Rights
Treaty on European Union
Treaty on the Functioning of the European Union
United Nations Convention on the Rights of the Child
United Nations Convention on the Rights of Persons with Disabilities

Statutory instruments (SIs)
Health Professions Order 2001
Mental Health Act 1983 (Remedial) Order 2001 (SI 2001/3712)

Mental Health (Approval of Persons to be Approved Mental Health Professionals) (Wales) Regulations 2008

Mental Health (Approved Mental Health Professionals) (Approval) (England) Regulations 2008

Mental Health (Care and Treatment) (Scotland) Act 2003 (Consequential Provisions) Order 2005

Mental Health (Conflicts of Interest) (England) Regulations 2008 (SI 2008/136)

Mental Health (Hospital) (England) Regulations 2008

Nurses and Midwifery Order 2001

Case law

AM v South London and Maudsley NHS Foundation 36 Trust [2013] UKUT 365 (AAC), [2014] MHLR 181

An NHS Trust v A [2015] EWCOP 71, [2016] Fam 223

An NHS Trust v Dr A [2013] EWCOP 2442

AR v Broglais Hospital [2001] EWHC Admin 793

B v Croydon Health Authority [1995] Fam 133, [1995] 2 WLR 294

Bolam v Frien Hospital Management Committee [1957] 1 WLR 583

Bolitho v City and Hackney Health Authority [1997] 4 All ER 771

C v Blackburn with 29 Darwen BC [2011] EWHC 3321 (COP)

DD v Durham County Council [2012] EWHC 1503 QB

DL v A Local Authority [2012] EWCA Civ 253

DN v Northumberland Tyne & Wear NHS Foundation Trust [2011] UKUT 327 (AAC)

Engel v Netherlands (1979–80) 1 EHRR 647 (App No 5100/71)

Gillick v West Norfolk and Wisbech Area Health Authority [1986] AC 112

GJ v The Foundation Trust [2009] EWHC 2972 (Fam), [2010] Fam 70

Glass v UK [2004] ECHR 61827/00

Hertfordshire County Council v AB [2018] EWHC 3103 (Fam)

HL v The United Kingdom [2005] 40 EHRR 42 (App No 4508/99)

Hutchinson Reid v UK App No 50272/99

Idalov v Russia App No 5826/03

ITW v Z [2009] EWHC 2525 (Fam), [2011] 1 WLR 344

MH v United Kingdom [2013] ECHR 11577/06

MM v Secretary of State for Justice [2018] UKSC 60

Molotchko v Ukraine App No 12275/10

Montgomery v Lanarkshire Health Board [2015] UKSC 11

OH v Germany (2012) EHRR 29 (App No 4646/08)

P v Cheshire West and Chester Council and P and Q v Surrey County Council [2014] UKSC 19, [2014] AC 896

Rabone v Pennine Care NHS Foundation Trust [2012] UKSC 2

Re SA [2005] EWHC 2942 (Fam)

R v Ealing District 3 Health Authority ex p Fox [1993] 1 WLR 373

R v Islington London 26 Borough Council, ex p Rixon (1996) 1 CCLR 119,

R v Manchester CC ex p Stennett [2002] UKHL 34

R (Munjaz) v Mersey Care NHS Trust [2005] UKHL 58; [2006] 2 AC 148

Shtukaturov v Russia [2012] EHRR 27 (App No 44009/05)

Storck v Germany [2005] ECHR 61603/00

TTM v Hackney LB [2010] EWHC 1349 (Admin)

TW v Enfield LBC [2014] EWCA Civ 362

Welsh Ministers v PJ [2018] UKSC 66

Winterwerp v Netherlands 6301/73 [1979] ECHR 4

Witold Litwa v Poland (2001) 33 EHRR 53 (App No 26629/95)

X v Finland App No 34806/04

Index

Printed and bound by CPI Group (UK) Ltd, Croydon, CR0 4YY

13/04/2025

14656602-0001